STUDY GUIDE

Verna C. Pangman
University of Manitoba

Karen P. Saenz
Houston Community College System

Lifespan Development

Third Canadian Edition

Helen Bee

Denise Boyd
Houston Community College System

Paul Johnson
Confederation College of Applied Arts and Technology

PEARSON

Toronto

ISBN 13: 978-0-205-60595-8
ISBN 10: 0-205-60595-8

Acquisitions Editor: Ky Pruesse
Developmental Editor: Joel Gladstone
Production Editor: Avivah Wargon
Production Coordinator: Avinash Chandra

1 2 3 4 5   12 11 10 09 08

Printed and bound in Canada

CONTENTS

LIST OF HELEN BEE'S STUDENT PROJECTS

PREFACE

This study guide provides user-friendly guidance to the Third Canadian Edition of Boyd, Bee, and Johnson's *Lifespan Development*. Although this edition retains the scope and emphasis of the earlier ones, it has been expanded to include additional and updated significant changes pertaining to the Canadian population. This study guide has been designed to help you focus your reading and study of the key elements of each chapter. The ultimate goals of this guide are to facilitate your learning of the text content and your application of the concepts of human development to your life as well as to your career. Finally, this guide is designed to assist you to think critically about relevant trends and controversial issues.

Each chapter begins with a brief overview and a set of learning goals. The objectives provide a glimpse of the chapter as a whole. The guided study questions include the learning objective for each section and specific questions—an increased number of which are Canadian-focused— on the material covered in the text. The critical reflection exercises provided will help you think of alternative ways to apply your knowledge to real-life situations. A new feature in this edition is the addition of case studies in alternate chapters. The questions related to the case will assist you to apply your knowledge to real-life situations. The chapter concludes with the answers to the practice questions and the fill-in-the-blank questions from the guided study section. Most chapters include one or more student projects that your instructor may choose as part of a written assignment or for extra credit.

Two additional sections will help you make the most of your psychology course. The first, "What to Know About Studying Psychology" (p. ix), offers suggestions to maximize your study time. The second, "A Model for Critical Thinking" (p. xi), provides additional insights that will help you apply the course material. A brief description of Bloom's Revised Taxonomy is provided to assist you in the learning process.

Lifespan Development provides explanations and resources for your personal, family, social, and work relationships. It offers insight into the joys and concerns of parenting practices for both parents and grandparents. It also addresses many common family, social, and work-related issues. The Third Canadian Edition serves to increase your knowledge of current research-related developments in the lifespan perspective, and enables you to gain an appreciation of the cross-cultural issues presented by the diversity of the Canadian population. Enjoy!

ACKNOWLEDGMENTS

I wish to express my sincere gratitude to my husband, Clare Pangman, PhD, who, through his endearing support, proofreading edits, and scholarly comments, has assisted me greatly during the process of arranging and editing the content for the *Lifespan Development* Study Guide, Third Canadian Edition. In addition, I would like to thank the Dean and Faculty of Nursing at the University of Manitoba for their unending support.

Verna C. Pangman MEd. M.N.
Faculty of Nursing, Helen Glass Centre for Nursing,
University of Manitoba, Winnipeg, Manitoba

Unending thanks go to my family—both immediate and extended—for providing me with the lifespan perspective. During the process of writing this study guide, two of my aunts celebrated their birthdays; one turned 90 and the other 92. My in-laws (in their late 80s) moved to live closer to my sister-in-law. My husband and I celebrated our 55th birthdays; our daughter got engaged to be married (we're planning a wedding!); and our son's wife will shortly give birth to our first grandchild. Among us, we've got the chapters covered! Special thanks must be given to Susan Archer for proofing and editing, and to my part-time secretary, Norma Marquez, for patiently making corrections to the text—again and again. Thank you!

Karen P. Saenz
Houston Community College System, Southeast College
Houston, Texas

CLASS PREPARATION AND STUDY GUIDELINES

Although the study of psychology is not particularly difficult, it presents considerable body of valuable material. Students are expected to keep up with all of the assigned reading. By conscientiously working through this guide, you will understand the material and be able to relate it to real human behaviour. The information presented below is designed to help you learn the subject by providing study insights that you can employ successfully in any university or college class that you take.

HOW MUCH TIME SHOULD I SPEND STUDYING PSYCHOLOGY?

To be successful in any college class, a good guideline for the amount of time you need to invest outside of class is two hours for each hour you spend in class. If you make this commitment, you should encounter no serious problems in completing all assignments and preparing comfortably for all classroom activities and tests. You should spend your time doing the following:

Read Ahead

The best starting place is the course schedule in your syllabus. It will specify both the material that needs to be covered, and the sequence deemed most appropriate by your instructor. You should always maintain a disciplined reading schedule so that you can stay current with assigned readings; falling behind in your reading can be disastrous. You should read ahead all the material that will be covered in the next class. This reading will acquaint you with the learning objectives that will be covered in class. With this knowledge, you will be prepared to ask questions and discuss relevant topics.

Read Effectively

Create a comfortable reading environment for yourself. Guard against distractions and interruptions. Be alert and attentive. Don't rush yourself. These "little things" will increase your comprehension of the subject. Use your study guide as a valuable guide for your reading. Keep a dictionary by your side to look up any unfamiliar words. From time to time, you may need to look back at a previous chapter to remind yourself of certain concepts. Remember, as in sports, music, dance, or other arts, learning takes time and effort; the more you put in to the learning process, the more you will get out of it.

SHOULD I ATTEND CLASS?

Studies indicate that students who attend their classes do better than students who do not. In class, you will not only hear important course-related information, but also announcements, due dates, and study suggestions. At the post-secondary level, you are largely responsible for your own learning. Your professor or instructor is a facilitator. Use class time to ask questions, seek clarification, and participate in discussions. The more involved you are in your own learning, the more fruitful the activity will be for you —and the more you will learn.

WHAT SHOULD I DO DURING CLASS TIME?

There are several things you can do to improve your chances of being successful in your class. You are in control of all of them, so do the following things to maximize the benefits of being in class.

Be on Time

The start of class is an important time. Be prepared to take notes, participate, or take a test. Tardiness is disruptive to your instructor and classmates.

Take Good Notes

Good note-taking keeps your mind focused on the subject being discussed. Effective attentiveness always leads to better comprehension. Note-taking provides you with documentation about what the instructor feels is the most relevant, important, difficult, or interesting information about a subject. You should couple your notes with related text material for a comprehensive understanding of the subject. Use your notes to prepare for assignments and tests. Make sure your notes are legible, thorough, and organized.

Participate in Class Discussions

Whenever you have the opportunity to participate, do so! Contribute what you have learned, but do it in a way that contributes to a positive learning environment for you and your classmates. Be involved in the learning process. Ask relevant questions. Offer insights. Give examples. Participation should be constructive and fun.

Get to Know Your Classmates

Together you and your classmates can do several things that enhance learning. Every time you explain a concept to someone else, you increase your understanding of the material. You can share ideas and information. By being an active listener, you can check each other to make sure you are learning the material. You can bounce ideas around. You can study together in advance of tests. If you miss a class, someone you know will share notes with you, or tell you about upcoming assignments or tests.

These suggestions are offered to assist you in making the most of your study of psychology, and indeed, of your college experience. You are exceptional because you chose to pursue higher learning. **Invest in yourself and you will succeed.**

A MODEL FOR CRITICAL THINKING

Several good resources exist on how to develop and practice your critical thinking skills. In all courses and in life experiences critical thinking can be applied to specific issues and problems. Randolph Smith (1995) suggests the following seven characteristics of critical thinkers:

1. Critical thinkers are flexible—they can tolerate ambiguity and uncertainty.
2. Critical thinkers identify inherent biases and assumptions.
3. Critical thinkers maintain an air of scepticism.
4. Critical thinkers separate facts from opinions.
5. Critical thinkers don't oversimplify.
6. Critical thinkers use logical inference processes.
7. Critical thinkers examine available evidence before drawing conclusions.

Thinking and critical thinking differ in at least three important ways:

- Thinking involves basic information processing; critical thinking involves understanding that information in such a way that the information is meaningful and usable.

- Thinking is often based on emotion and supposition; critical thinking sets emotions aside and addresses a problem from the position of facts.

- Thinking is based on the information that is known; critical thinking requires more than what is already known because it may reveal that not enough is known. Such an important realization then requires that more facts be gathered.

Most individuals take for granted their ability to think. The development of critical thinking ability therefore requires that the individual be taught to take a more controlled and systematic approach to his or her thinking.

Benjamin Bloom (1956) argued that critical thinking requires going beyond the simple recitation of facts that most testing situations require. Bloom described a progression of cognitive levels that individuals can be taught to use in their thinking (see next page). Bloom's taxonomy suggests that thinking and understanding are truly accomplished only when an individual processes information through six levels.

Bloom's Cognitive Objectives

Level	Skill	Description
1	Knowledge	Has specific, isolated, factual information
2	Comprehension	Understands those facts
3	Application	Can generalize those facts to current and/or other situations
4	Analysis	Can break the problem down, recognize connections between sub-parts, analyze whether each sub-part is meaningful, and discard those that are deemed meaningless
5	Synthesis	Can reassemble meaningful parts into a more meaningful whole
6	Evaluation	Can look at the end product and critically evaluate and use that information to begin a continuous reassessment

A specific example may demonstrate how our thinking becomes more complex as we progress through the cognitive levels of Bloom's theory.

A friend of yours states that someone you are about to meet is aggressive. When you ask your friend how she knows this, she reports that she saw him yell at someone in the hall for absolutely no reason. Your job as a critical thinker is to take this piece of information and determine what to do with it. In order to accomplish this, you must take the information that you know and process it through the cognitive levels of Bloom's theory.

1. **Knowledge:** At this level, you have the statement by your friend that the individual is aggressive. You may also have some information about your friend, including the following:
   - how accurate she has been about others in the past
   - whether "aggressive" is a label she uses a lot
   - whether it is unusual for her to categorize someone

2. **Comprehension:** At this level, you utilize the facts that you have available in order to try to understand the implications of your knowledge. In this case, the only concrete fact you have is that your friend has labelled the other person as "aggressive." From this, you determine what you understand "aggressive" to mean.

3. **Application:** At the application level, you apply relevant information to the current situation. In this case, your friend has suggested that the person you are about to meet is aggressive, and she is using his "yelling at someone" as evidence for that label.

4. **Analysis:** From the application of facts to the current situation, you break the information down into meaningful units. In this scenario a label of "aggressive" is being placed on someone because he yelled at someone else. A critical thinker would ask him or herself several questions in this situation, including the following:
   - Is there a definite connection between "yelling" and being "aggressive"?
   - Are there any other possible explanations for why the individual yelled at someone else?

- Does yelling at someone in one situation predict that the individual will behave "aggressively" in other situations?

To the extent that you cannot answer these questions affirmatively, you should discard any assumptions based upon them.

5. **Synthesis:** Now that you have discarded any meaningless information, you put the meaningful pieces back together to draw your conclusions. In this case, you cannot critically utilize any of the information that you have been given. Thus, the only usable information you have going into the situation is that you are about to meet someone.

6. **Evaluation:** Once you have discarded meaningless information (or information that is based on opinion rather than fact), you are better suited to approach the situation in an unbiased fashion. You can objectively evaluate the person that you are meeting, make unbiased observations about his behaviour, decide whether his behaviour is normal given the situation in which you are observing him, and reach your own conclusions about his relative degree of aggressiveness.

What are the implications in this case if you had not done critical thinking before you approached the situation and met this new person?

It is highly probable that you would have approached the individual assuming that he was going to be aggressive. A few simple questions and their answers can reveal the potential impact of not engaging in critical thinking:

Q: How do we act toward individuals whom we assume are going to be aggressive?
A: We behave coldly or even aggressively.

Q: How do others act toward us when we act coldly or aggressively toward them?
A: They tend to be aggressive or hostile.

Q: What do we, then, assume about that individual?
A: That he or she is aggressive.

In this cycle, the expectations we had about the person caused us to behave in ways that elicited, in return, behaviour from the other person that verified our original assumptions. It is just as likely, however, that he would not have behaved aggressively if we had not precipitated such behaviour through our own actions. The cycle that results from the bias introduced into our behaviour by our expectations is called a self-fulfilling prophecy. It is defined as a tendency for our expectations about others to be confirmed because we engage in behaviour that elicits from others the very behaviour that we expected. In the situation we've been discussing, therefore, a lack of critical thinking may cause an unpleasant encounter that is actually preventable.

Revised Bloom's Taxonomy

Published in 2001, the revision includes several seemingly minor yet actually quite significant changes. The changes occur in three broad categories: terminology, structure, and emphasis.

- **Terminology Changes**. Bloom's six major categories were changed from noun to verb forms. The lowest level of the original, knowledge was renamed and became remembering. Comprehension and synthesis were retitled to understanding and creating. The new terms are defined as:

  o **Remembering**: Retrieving, recognizing, and recalling important knowledge from long-term memory.

  o **Understanding**: Constructing meaning from oral, written, and graphic messages through: interpreting, exemplifying, classifying, summarizing, inferring, comparing, and explaining.

  o **Applying**: Using a procedure through executing, or implementing.

  o **Analyzing**: Separating material into its constituent parts, deciding how the parts relate to one another and to an overall structure or purpose through differentiating, organizing, and attributing.

  o **Evaluating**: Making decisions based on criteria and standards by checking and critiquing.

  o **Creating**: Putting elements together to develop a coherent or functional whole; reorganizing elements into a new pattern by generating, planning, or producing.

- **Structural Changes.** With the addition of products, the Revised Bloom's Taxonomy takes a two dimension form. One of the dimensions identifies "The Knowledge Dimension" (or the kind of knowledge to be learned), while the second identifies "The Cognitive Process Dimension" (or the process used to learn). For example, one of the knowledge dimensions is *factual knowledge*; the cognitive process under the *remembering* category is *list*. Another example under the knowledge dimension is *procedural knowledge*; the cognitive process under the *analyzing* category is *differentiate*. The entire taxonomy table can be viewed at **Error! Hyperlink reference not valid.**

- **Changes in Emphasis**. Emphasis is the third and final category of changes. The revised version of the taxonomy is intended for a much broader audience. Emphasis is placed upon its use as a "more authentic tool for curriculum planning, instructional delivery and assessment."

BASIC CONCEPTS AND METHODS

OVERVIEW OF CHAPTER

The goal of scientists who study human development is to produce observations and explanations that can be applied to as wide an age range of human beings and contexts as possible. To accomplish this goal, they study both change and stability. Additionally, they study cultural expectations, make predictions about development, and use scientific methods to test these predictions. Ultimately, scientists hope that their findings can be used to positively influence development in individuals.

The Scientific Study of Human Development

* The philosophical concepts of original sin, innate goodness, and the blank slate have influenced Western worldviews on human development.

* The concept of developmental stages comes, in part, from Darwin's evolutionary theory. G. Stanley Hall identified norms at which developmental milestones happen. Freud's studies of his patients' childhood memories led to his stage theory of personality. Watson believed that most changes in childhood are due to learning. Gesell focused on genetically programmed sequential patterns of change. Piaget described stages of cognitive development that became the foundation of modern cognitive-developmental psychology.

A Brief History of the Roots of Psychology in Canada

* In 1889, modern scientific psychology became known in Canada through the efforts of James M. Baldwin, who lectured in psychology and established a psycho-physical laboratory at the University of Toronto.

* William Blatz, regarded as "the founder and leader of child study in Canada," opened the St George's School for Child Study in Toronto, in 1925. Gradually, it became known as the Ontario Institute for Studies in Education (OISE). Blatz is known for his work with the Dionne quintuplets in 1935.

* The Canadian Psychological Association (CPA) was founded in 1939 as a result of collaborations among psychologists from Canadian universities. In 1969, Mary Wright became the first woman president of the CPA.

* During World War II, Canadian psychologists not only focused on psychological issues related to the war but were empowered to address child care problems in particular.

- Donald O. Hebb, an internationally renowned pioneer in experimental psychology at McGill University, was president first of the CPA in 1953 and second of the American Psychological Association in 1960. In 1981, the Developmental Section of the CPA was established. Its goal is to facilitate communication among developmental psychologists in terms of research, teaching, and practice.

Contemporary Developmental Psychology

- Important changes occur during every period of development across the lifespan, and these changes must be understood in the cultures and contexts in which they occur. Developmental psychology has become more interdisciplinary to enhance psychologists' understanding of human development.

- Paul Baltes was a leader in the development of a comprehensive theory of lifespan human development. One of his most important contributions was his emphasis on the positive aspects of advanced age.

- Scientists who study age-related changes use three broad categories called the domains of development. The physical domain studies changes to the body. Changes in intellectual skills are included in the cognitive domain. The social domain includes the study of relationships among individuals. The domain classification helps to organize and ease the discussions of human development.

- Historically, developmentalists have regarded nature and nurture as an either-or controversy. Modern developmentalists comprehend that developmental change is a product of both genetics and environmental factors. Currently, the interactionist model considers development to be a result of complex reciprocal interactions between multiple personal and environmental factors.

- A key issue in the study of human development is the continuity-discontinuity issue. The question is whether or not age-related change is a matter of amount of degree (continuity), or it involves changes in type or kind (discontinuity). Modern developmental psychologists study three types of age-related changes: universal (common to every individual), group-specific (shared by individuals who grow up together in a specific group), and individual (changes resulting from unique, unshared events).

- Currently, the characteristics and needs of older adults in Canada are influencing many disciplines, including developmental psychology.

Research Designs and Methods

- Developmental psychology uses the scientific method to achieve its goals: to describe, explain, predict, and influence human development from conception to death.

- There are three choices for studying age-related change: a cross-sectional design to study different groups of people of different ages; a longitudinal design to study the same people over a period of time; and a sequential design to combine cross-sectional and longitudinal designs in some fashion.

- Case studies are in-depth examinations of single individuals. The naturalistic observation method observes people in their normal environments. Correlational studies measure the relationship between variables. To test causal hypotheses, experimental designs in which subjects are assigned randomly to experimental or control groups are necessary.

- Cross-cultural research assists developmentalists to identify specific variables that explain cultural differences. Such research is important in Canada because it involves the comparison of groups of people from across the lifespan and from different ethnic groups or communities. In 1971, Canada was the first nation in the world to make multiculturalism an official policy. The *Canadian Multicultural Act* was passed in 1988.

- Ethical principles in human developmental research are published by professional organizations such as the Canadian Psychological Association and address the following: protection from harm, informed consent, confidentiality, knowledge of results, and protection from deception.

LEARNING GOALS

After completing Chapter 1, students should be able to:
1. Summarize how the science of developmental psychology came into being.
2. Examine the main points regarding the historical development of psychology in Canada.
3. Describe how modern psychologists differ from the early pioneers with respect to a variety of issues.
4. List and explain the research designs and methods used by developmentalists.

GUIDED STUDY QUESTIONS

THE SCIENTIFIC STUDY OF HUMAN DEVELOPMENT

Philosophical Roots (p. 3)

Objective 1.1: Explain each of the philosophies that are important to the study of human development.

1. Define the following terms:
   a. developmental psychology
   b. original sin
   c. innate goodness
   d. blank slate

2. Compare how the philosophies of original sin, innate goodness, and the blank slate explain development.

The Study of Human Development Becomes a Science (pp. 4–9)

Objective 1.2: List the theorists and theories that have influenced modern developmental psychology.

3. Define the following terms:
    a. baby biographies
    b. norms
    c. behaviourism
    d. maturation

4. State the major contributions to developmental psychology by each of the following theorists:
    a. Charles Darwin
    b. G. Stanley Hall
    c. Sigmund Freud
    d. John Watson
    e. Arnold Gesell
    f. Jean Piaget

The Real World: Toys: More Than Just Playthings (p. 5)

Objective 1.3: Describe how toys promote the four different types of development of a child.

5. What is the Canadian Toy Testing Council (CTTC)'s (2004) responsibility regarding toys?

6. State the importance of the label information on toy products.

Development in the Information Age: Child-Rearing Experts (p. 7)

Objective 1.4: Summarize the advice of child-rearing experts over the years.

7. What is one consequence of the mass dissemination of information?

8. Describe the views that each of the following experts holds on child rearing, and the impact of these views on parenting.

Theorists	*Views*	*Impact on Parenting*
Dr. Benjamin Spock		
Ann Douglas		

9. How valuable is the internet regarding information on child rearing for parents?

A Brief History of the Roots of Psychology in Canada (pp. 8–9)

Objective 1.5: List the historical developments of psychology in Canada.

10. State the important contributions to Canadian psychology made by each of the following psychologists:
    a. William Blatz
    b. Mary Salter Ainsworth
    c. Donald O. Hebb

11. What was the process involved in initiating the Canadian Psychological Association?

12. State the goal of the Developmental Section of the Canadian Psychological Association.

CONTEMPORARY DEVELOPMENTAL PSYCHOLOGY

The Lifespan Perspective (pp. 9–10)

Objective 1.6: Describe the importance of lifespan perspective.

13. Define lifespan perspective.

14. List two reasons why psychologists' views of adulthood have changed recently.

15. State the rationale why developmental psychology has become more interdisciplinary as interest in the entire lifespan has grown.

16. State Paul Baltes's contribution to the study of human development.

The Domains of Development (pp. 10–11)

Objective 1.7: List and describe the three domains of development.

17. Give brief descriptions of developmental changes in the following domains:
    a. physical
    b. cognitive
    c. social

18. State the usefulness of the domain classification in human development.

Nature and Nurture Interact in Development (p. 11)

Objective 1.8: Define the nature-nurture controversy, and describe the ways of looking at both types of influences.

19. Define the following terms:
    a. nature-nurture controversy
    b. interactionist model
    c. vulnerability
    d. resilience

20. Consider the importance of vulnerability and resilience (protective factors):

    a. How do vulnerability and resilience (protective factors) interact with a child's environment?
    b. What conditions produce the most negative outcomes for Canadian children?
    c. How can these negative conditions be overcome?

Continuity and Discontinuity in Development (pp. 11–13)

Objective 1.9: Describe the issue of continuity and discontinuity in development.

21. Differentiate between the two terms:
    a. quantitative change
    b. qualitative change

22. Define the following terms:
    a. universal changes
    b. social clock
    c. group-specific changes
    d. culture
    e. cohort
    f. individual differences
    g. on-time events
    h. off-time events

23. List two ways in which universal changes happen, and give an example of each.

24. How does culture affect group-specific changes?

25. Give examples of individual differences as age-related changes.

26. Differentiate among the following:
    a. critical period
    b. a sensitive period
    c. atypical development

27. Give examples of how off-time events can pose more difficulties for an individual than on-time events.

28. List several synonyms for atypical development. Give examples of atypical development.

RESEARCH DESIGNS AND METHODS

Relating Goals to Methods (pp. 14–15)

Objective 1.10: List and describe the four goals of developmental psychology.

29. Define the following terms:
    a. theories
    b. hypotheses

30. List and define the four goals of developmental psychology.

31. Why are theories important in studying developmental psychology?

Studying Age-Related Changes (pp. 15–18)

Objective 1.11: Describe the three types of age-related research, and state the advantages and disadvantages of each.

32. Define the following terms:
    a. cross-sectional design
    b. longitudinal design
    c. sequential design

33. Identify the advantages and disadvantages of each of the following designs.

Design	Advantages	Disadvantages
cross-sectional		
longitudinal		
sequential		

Identifying Relationships Between Variables (pp. 18–20)

Objective 1.12: Distinguish among the types of studies used to identify relationships between variables, and state the advantages and disadvantages of each.

34. Define the following terms:
    a. variable
    b. case study method
    c. naturalistic observation method
    d. observer bias
    e. inter-rater reliability
    f. correlational method
    g. causal relationships
    h. experimental method
    i. random assignment
    j. experimental group
    k. control group
    l. independent variable
    m. dependent variable
    n. quasi-experiment

35. State the advantages and disadvantages of each of the following research methods:

Method	Advantages	Disadvantages
case study		
correlational		
experimental		
naturalistic observation		

36. How do researchers prevent possible observer bias?

37. What does each of the following correlations indicate?
    a. +1.00
    b. -1.00
    c. 0.00

38. Give an example of a relationship (such as the example of temperature and air-conditioner use in the text) of each of the following:
    a. positive correlation
    b. negative correlation

39. Why is random assignment to groups essential to an experiment?

40. Suppose you want to see if children who watch violence on television are more aggressive than children who do not watch violent television. Identify the following parts of the experiment:
    a. independent variable
    b. dependent variable
    c. experimental group
    d. control group

41. Why are quasi-experiments used instead of fully controlled experiments?

Cross-Cultural Research (p. 20–21)

Objective 1.13: Describe cross-cultural designs.

42. Define ethnography.

43. Describe two ways in which investigators may conduct cross-cultural research.

44. What particular Canadian features make cross-cultural research important?

45. List two reasons why cross-cultural research is important to developmental psychology.

Research Ethics (p. 21)

Objective 1.14: Identify five areas of ethical concern in human developmental research.

46. Define research ethics.

47. Describe each of the following ethical standards:
    a. protection from harm
    b. informed consent
    c. confidentiality
    d. knowledge of results
    e. deception

CRITICAL REFLECTION EXERCISES

Critical Evaluation of Research

1. In your newspaper you read a story about a product called Melatonic. Melatonic is described as a derivative of a natural brain chemical and is touted to "make you feel better, help you sleep, and increase your sex drive." The article goes on to cite the research evidence supporting these claims. According to the article:

    • white mice that were given 500-mg doses slept 40% longer than mice that were not given the tonic; and

    • subjects who were given a free 30-day trial sample of the tonic reported "feeling invigorated, having fewer troubles falling asleep, and having sex once each week during the trial period."

Write down your answers to the following questions; and cite your rationale for each answer:
    a. What are the facts as they are presented?
    b. What are the implications if these facts are true?
    c. How have those facts been applied to the current research?
    d. When you analyze the information to determine what is verifiable, and discard what is meaningless, what facts are left?

e. What questions do you have about the information that would need to be answered to make the original information more meaningful? (For example, "Is a 500 mg dosage a lot for a white mouse?").

f. Now that you have only the meaningful pieces of information, what conclusions can you draw about the effects of Melatonic?

g. What kind of a study could you develop to test the claims made in the article about Melatonic? Make sure that your study includes methods for testing (rather than assuming) that the claims are accurate.

2. You are a teacher in an elementary school. One of your colleagues tells you that Rachel (a second grader) is a victim of child maltreatment. When you ask how she has reached this conclusion about Rachel, she states, "Rachel has all of the classic symptoms:

- she can't sit still,
- she is performing below her ability,
- she has trouble making friends,
- she has difficulty concentrating, and
- she only partially completes her assignments."

Write out answers to the following questions and cite the reasons you have for each of your answers.

a. What evidence is the teacher citing for her conclusion that Rachel is an abuse victim?

b. Can you verify that this evidence is accurate? How might you verify this?

c. What other information would you need to gather (or what other questions do you think would need to be answered) in order for you to determine if this teacher's conclusion is accurate?

d. Describe how this teacher's conclusion, if invalid, could actually lead to a self-fulfilling prophecy as outlined earlier in this chapter.

e. Based on the facts that you have, what conclusions can be drawn about Rachel?

f. What other alternative explanations can you think of (besides abuse) that might explain Rachel's behaviour?

g. How could you attempt to test your alternative explanations from the previous question?

PRACTICE QUESTIONS

1. The scientific study of age-related changes in behaviour, thinking, emotion, and personality is called _____.
   a. ageism
   b. maturation
   c. cohort effect
   d. developmental psychology

2. The philosophy that proposes that adults can mould children into whatever they want them to be is called _____.
   a. morality
   b. the blank slate
   c. original sin
   d. innate goodness

3. The term used to describe the average age at which milestones happen is _____.
   a. norms
   b. baby biographies
   c. case studies
   d. cohort effect

4. _____ defines development in terms of behaviour changes caused by environmental influences.
   a. Personality development
   b. Hysterical distress
   c. Behaviourism
   d. Maturation

5. Genetically programmed sequential patterns of change are called _____.
   a. growth
   b. maturation
   c. learning
   d. development

6. Modern cognitive-developmental psychology is based on the foundation of the stages discovered and the theory proposed by _____.
   a. G. Stanley Hall
   b. John Watson
   c. Sigmund Freud
   d. Jean Piaget

7. The goal of the Developmental Section of the Canadian Psychological Association is to facilitate communication among developmental psychologists in terms of
    _____.
    a. teaching and writing scholarly papers
    b. conducting research studies abroad
    c. teaching, research, and practice
    d. pursuing monetary funds for counselling practice

8. The perspective that maintains that important changes occur during every period of development and that these changes must be understood in the cultures and contexts in which they occur is the _____.
    a. cognitive-developmental perspective
    b. lifespan perspective
    c. psychosocial perspective
    d. central timing perspective

9. Age-related changes whether or not they are a matter of degree, or changes in type or kind are called _____.
    a. nature-nurture
    b. universal-specific
    c. continuity-discontinuity
    d. individual differences

10. Canadian studies have indicated that by far the most negative outcome for a child is the result of a _____.
    a. highly vulnerable child
    b. poor or unsupportive environment
    c. combination of high vulnerability and poor environment
    d. combination of low vulnerability and unsupportive environment

11. Thomas is forced to retire at age 70, even though he is physically and mentally healthy and does his job well. This is an example of _____.
    a. age norms
    b. ageism
    c. the social clock
    d. culture

12. The term used by social scientists to describe groups of individuals born within some fairly narrow band of years who share the same historical experiences at the same times in their lives is _____.
    a. "cohort"
    b. "age mates"
    c. "time banding"
    d. "the co-existence phenomena"

13. The idea that experiences occurring at the expected times for an individual's culture or cohort will pose fewer difficulties for an individual than experiences occurring at unexpected times is called _____.
    a. the critical period
    b. the historical period
    c. the sensitive period
    d. on-time and off-time events

14. Sets of statements that propose general principles to explain development are called _____.
    a. hypotheses
    b. independent variables
    c. theories
    d. critical periods

15. In the cross-sectional method, _____.
    a. the same group of subjects is repeatedly given the same test over a 20-year period
    b. surveys are administered to samples of people from around the country
    c. groups of subjects of different ages are observed
    d. the behaviours of subjects in a laboratory environment is compared with their behaviours in their natural setting

16. A study in which the intelligence test performance of the same group of children is assessed at different points in their lifetime is an example of which of the following designs?
    a. sequential
    b. longitudinal
    c. cross-sectional
    d. time-sampling

17. Which of the following is an advantage of a longitudinal study?
    a. The research is completed in a short period of time.
    b. The healthiest participants drop out.
    c. The better-educated participants drop out.
    d. It allows the researcher to compare performance by the same people at different ages.

18. Nicole studies parents and their children by watching them interact at the zoo. This is an example of the _____.
    a. naturalistic observation method
    b. case study method
    c. experimental method
    d. correlational method

19. As the temperature climbs, so does the number of air conditioners in use. This is an example of _____.
    a. a positive correlation
    b. a negative correlation
    c. no correlation
    d. a hypothesis

20. A quantitative study being used to test the effects of room change on test scores. The control group remains in the home room for their final test. Another group goes to another building for their test. The students' test scores are known as the _____.
    a. controlled variable
    b. independent variable
    c. dependent variable
    d. confounding variable

21. A group of researchers conduct an experiment in which the influence of an observer's presence on the subject's willingness to help is measured. The observer's presence is the _____.
    a. dependent variable
    b. independent variable
    c. controlled variable
    d. varied variable

22. Developmental psychologists cannot systematically manipulate many of the variables they are most interested in and often use _____.
    a. case studies
    b. ethnography
    c. quasi-experiments
    d. panel studies

23. The best explanation for the importance of cross-cultural research in Canada is that _____.
    a. more older females are available for research
    b. government offers grants for cultural research
    c. all ethnic groups will volunteer for a research study
    d. multiculturalism is an official policy

24. Which of the following ethical standards for research involves the right to a written summary of a study's results?
    a. knowledge of results
    b. deception
    c. informed consent
    d. confidentiality

25. Which one of the following statements is true regarding informed consent?
    a. Parents must sign for their children regardless of the child's age.
    b. Children older than seven must give their own consent.
    c. If the study is taking place at school, only the teachers are obligated to give their consent.
    d. After the consent is given the child cannot withdraw from the research study.

CASE STUDY

Lori's grandparents are both in their early 70s. They recently sold their ranch and would like to build a home in a new suburb close to a shopping centre. Lori is aware that this new suburb is populated with young families with many children. Although Lori knows her grandparents are avid golfers, entertain frequently, and love to be involved in community projects, she feels anxious about their wish to move to that location.

From your understanding of age norms, what is motivating Lori to feel anxious about her grandparents' move into this young community? Would you also feel anxious if they were your grandparents considering that particular move?

RESEARCH PROJECT

Student Project 1: A First Observation of a Child: An Example of a Narrative Report

There are several purposes in suggesting this project. First, if you have had relatively little contact with young children, you may need to spend some time simply observing a child to make other sections of the book more meaningful. Second, it is important for you to begin to get some sense of the difficulties involved in observing and studying children. Later projects involve other types of observation, but it is helpful to start with the least structured (but perhaps the most difficult) form, namely, a narrative report in which the observer attempts to write down everything a child does or says for about one hour.

Step 1: Locate a child between 18 months and 6 years of age; age 2, 3, or 4 would be best.

Step 2: Obtain permission from the child's parents for observation, using whatever form and procedure are specified by your instructor. When you speak to the parents, be sure to tell them that the purpose of your observation is for a course assignment, and that you will not be testing the child in any way but merely want to observe a normal child in his or her normal situation.

Step 3: Arrange a time when you can observe the child in his or her "natural habitat" for about one hour. If the child is in a nursery school, it is acceptable to observe him or her there as long as you get permission from the teachers. If not, the observation should be done in the home or in some situation familiar to the child. You must not babysit during the observation. You must be free to be in the background and cannot be responsible for the child during the observation.

Step 4: When the time for the observation arrives, place yourself in as unobtrusive a place as possible. Take a small stool with you if you can, so that you can move around as the child moves. If you are in the child's home, he or she will probably ask what you are doing. Say that you are doing something for school and that you will be writing things down for a while. Do not invite any kind of contact with the child; do not meet the child's eye; do not smile; and do not talk except when the child talks directly, in which case you should say that you are busy and will play a little later.

Step 5: For one hour, try to write down everything the child does. Write down the child's speech word-for-word. If the child is talking to someone else, write down the other person's replies, too, if you can. Describe the child's movements. Throughout, keep your description as free of evaluation and words of intent as you can. Do not write "Sarah went into the kitchen to get a cookie." You don't know why she went. What you saw was that she stopped what she had been doing, got up, and walked into the kitchen. There you see her getting a cookie. Describe the behaviour that way, rather than making assumptions about what is happening in the child's head. Avoid words like "tries," "angrily," "pleaded," "wanted," and the like. Describe only what you see and hear.

Step 6: When you have completed the observation, reread what you wrote and consider the following questions:

- Did you manage to keep all description of intent out of your record?

- Were you able to remain objective?

- Since you obviously could not write down everything that the child did, think about what you left out.

- Did you find that you paid more attention to some aspects of behaviour than others, such as listening to language rather than noting physical movements?

- What would such a bias do to the kind of information you could obtain from your narrative?

- Would it be possible for you or some other person doing the rating to obtain systematic information about the child from your record, such as a measure of the child's level of activity or a score reflecting the number of times the child asked for attention?

- What changes in this method of observation would you have to introduce to obtain other sorts of information?

- What do you think were the effects of your presence on the child?

RESEARCH PROJECT

Student Project 2: Naturalistic Observation of a Nursing Home Resident

Follow the same procedure as in Project 1, except instead of observing a young child, observe an elderly adult in a nursing home. Permission will be required from the nursing home, and from the individual to be observed, following whatever procedure your instructor specifies.

Arrange to spend at least an hour in the nursing home. Inquire about the daily schedule and choose a time when the residents are likely to be together in some kind of recreational activity, or at least when not isolated in their individual rooms. Place yourself as inconspicuously as possible by the side of the room, and observe your selected subject for one hour. As with the observation of the child, attempt to write down everything your subject does for that hour. When you are finished, ask yourself the same questions as in Project 1.

AT-HOME PROJECT

Student Project 1.3: Analysis of Research Presented in Popular Sources

Find at least eight separate mentions of research on children, adolescents, or adults in newspapers and magazines, and analyze each one. For each item, describe the research design that appears to have been used.

- Is that design appropriate for the question being asked?

- Are there any flaws you can detect?

- Does the report in the magazine or newspaper give you enough detail to decide whether the research was any good?

- What other information would you want to have to decide on the quality of the research?

Some sources you might try for suitable articles are as follows:

1. The *Globe and Mail* runs fairly regularly articles about health and scientific research. Also check your local newspapers. Many papers have excellent articles on health and development.

2. *Maclean's* magazine has feature articles and a section on health fairly regularly.

3. Most so-called women's magazines (*Chatelaine, Canadian Living, Today's Parent,* etc.) have columns on child-rearing or child development.

CHAPTER 1 ANSWER KEY

Practice Questions

1.d	6. d	11. d	16. b	21. b
2. b	7. c	12. a	17. d	22. a
3. a	8. b	13. d	18. a	23. c
4. c	9. c	14. c	19. a	24. a
5. b	10. c	15. c	20. c	25. b

Case Study

Chapter 1 (p. 12). Age norms can lead to ageism—a set of prejudicial or negative attitudes about older adults analogous to sexism or racism. In essence, Lori is anxious if her grandparents move into this community they won't fit in and will become isolated. Would you agree or disagree with Lori if those were your grandparents?

THEORIES OF DEVELOPMENT

OVERVIEW OF CHAPTER

Three "families" of theories have significantly influenced the study of human development. Current trends in research focus on other areas of study. The comparison of theories is based on three assumptions about theories and evaluated by criteria for usefulness.

Psychoanalytic Theories

- Freud's emphasis is on the importance of both conscious and unconscious processes. The personality is composed of the id, the ego, and the superego, which influence our motives. He proposed five psychosexual stages, and he believed that each of the first three stages potentially affects our development. His theory, although classical in nature, has been severely criticized.

- Erikson's theory states that social forces are more important than unconscious drives as motives for development. He proposed eight stages of personality development across the lifespan, each of which involves resolving a crisis.

- Psychoanalytic theories provide useful concepts, such as the unconscious, that contribute to our understanding of development. They are, however, difficult to test.

- Humanistic theories focus on the positive aspects of development while accepting the psychoanalytic assumption that behaviour is motivated by internal drives and emotions. They, too, are difficult to test empirically.

Learning Theories

- Classical conditioning involves learning through the association of unrelated stimuli so that we respond in a similar manner. It helps explain the acquisition of emotional responses such as fear.

- Operant conditioning involves learning based on the consequences of our actions. Reinforcement is said to occur when a behaviour is repeated because of the consequences that followed it. When a behaviour stops because of a consequence, punishment is said to have occurred.

- Learning theories assist developmentalists to understand how specific behaviours are acquired.

Cognitive Theories

- Piaget's focus is on the development of logical thinking across four stages in childhood and adolescence.

- Information-processing theory uses the computer as a model to explain intellectual processes such as memory and problem solving.

- Vogotsky's sociocultural theory emphasizes that complex forms of thinking have their origins in social interactions rather than in a child's private exploration.

- The social-cognitive variation of learning theory focuses on the cognitive elements of learning, such as modelling. Bandura focuses on reciprocal determinism as a process of human development, which is based upon three factors: personal, behavioural, and environmental. In regard to personal factors, the concept of self-efficacy is a belief in one's own ability to cause an intended event to occur.

- Research confirms the sequence of skills development that Piaget proposed, but critics have suggested recently that young children are more capable than Piaget believed. Most information-processing theorists favour a continuous rather than a stage model of cognitive development, because they believe that cognitive development takes place over time. Critics of the information-processing theory claim that human thinking is more complex than the working of a computer and that information-processing theory does not fully describe the ways in which memory works in the real world.

- Both Piaget and Vygotsky stressed the importance of active exploration for educational purposes. However, Vygotsky emphasized assisted discovery processes, which have to take place within the zone of proximal development of each child.

- Social-cognitive theory is intended to contribute to the understanding of age-related change. Generally speaking, critics of cognitive theories state that these theories ignore other important cognitive function of development such as emotions, imagination, and creativity.

Biological and Evolutionary Theories

- Biological processes play a critical role in human development. Across the lifespan, both genetic and epigenetic factors interact with environmental variables to shape the trajectory of an individual's health and wellness. The study of epigenetics will profoundly change the view of human development in the 21st century. Evolutionary theories claim that genetic and physiological processes that underlie human behaviour have changed slowly over time. This slow change has resulted from genetic mutation and natural selection.

- Gene sequences, contained in 23 pairs of chromosomes, make up the genetic codes for creating the proteins needed for the body to function.

- The unique genetic blueprint of each individual is called a genotype. The individual's observable characteristics are called the phenotype.

- The simplest genetic rule is the dominant-recessive pattern in which a single dominant gene strongly influences the phenotype. Individuals with either two dominant or two recessive genes are referred to as homozygous. Those with one dominant and one recessive gene are said to be heterozygous. Genes are transmitted from parents to children according to complex rules that include the dominant-recessive and polygenic pattern, and multifactorial inheritance.

- Researchers have found that epigenetic factors play a pivotal role in development across the lifespan. Epigenetics is the study of gene regulation patterns that alter gene function (phenotype) without changing gene structure (genotype). Findings from animal studies have provided some preliminary evidence regarding epigenetic changes that may occur in humans.

- Theories such as nativism, ethology, behaviour genetics, and sociobiology, are helping developmentalists better understand the role of physiological processes in development.

- Evolutionary psychology, an interdisciplinary approach to explaining human behaviour, focuses on the view that genetically inherited cognitive and social characteristics have evolved through natural selection to serve adaptive functions and promote survival. . Concepts about epigenetic inheritance are widening the view of evolutionary psychology.

- Evolutionary developmental psychology proposes the view that genetically inherited cognitive and social characteristics that promote survival and adaptation appear across the lifespan at various times.

- The prenate is able to use information about its current environment to adjust its physiology in anticipation that doing so will match future environmental conditions and optimize its chances to survive and reproduce in adulthood. This is known as the predictive-adaptive response. A mismatch between prenatal and postnatal environment can increase the risk of physical diseases and psychological disorders.

- Advances in human genomics will play a vital role in predicting and preventing disease in the 21st century.

- Critics claim that evolutionary theories underestimate the impact of the environment and place too much emphasis on heredity. Another concern is that these theories are difficult to prove.

Systems Theory

- Bronfenbrenner's bioecological systems theory explains development in terms of relationships among individuals and their environments, or contexts over time.

- Eclecticism is the use of multiple theoretical perspectives to explain and study human development.

- Bronfenbrenner's bioecological systems theory provides a way of conceptualizing development that captures the complexity of individual and contextual variables. However, this theory ignores physical environmental influences, ranging from pollutants to noise levels leaving the effects of these exposures on child development to further research. An eclectic approach urges developmentalists to devise more comprehensive theories from which to formulate hypotheses for further study.

LEARNING GOALS

After completing Chapter 2, students should be able to:
1. Summarize the key points of the following:
   a. psychoanalytic theories
   b. learning theories
   c. cognitive theories
   d. biological and evolutionary theories
   e. systems theory
2. Compare the theories listed above by using the assumptions about development.
3. State the contributions made by Canadian psychologists and researchers in the field of developmental psychology.

GUIDED STUDY QUESTIONS

PSYCHOANALYTIC THEORIES

Freud's Psychosexual Theory (pp. 26–28)

Objective 2.1: Describe Freud's theory of psychosexual development.

1. Define the following terms:
   a. psychoanalytic theory
   b. libido
   c. id
   d. ego
   e. superego
   f. defence mechanisms
   g. psychosexual stages

2. List the three parts of personality, and describe the function of each.

3. What would the three parts of the personality, according to Freud's theory, "say" to you about your desire for your favourite cheesecake? Choose one of the following for each of the examples listed: id, ego, superego.

   a. _____ "Don't even think about eating cheesecake. You know it has too much fat, too much sugar, and too much cholesterol. Besides, if you eat it all you'll get sick to your stomach. Forget it and go get a carrot stick!"

b. _____ "Go for it—and put whipped cream and a cherry on top! Just bring me the whole thing."

c. _____ "How about eating a small piece? If I eat some now, then I will have just a small salad for supper and I'll do extra exercises tomorrow."

4. According to Freud, what would happen to the tension in the personality without the defence mechanisms?

5. List, in order, Freud's five psychosexual stages.

6. What did Freud suggest might happen as a result of fixation?

Erikson's Psychosocial Theory (pp. 28–29)

Objective 2.2: Describe Erikson's theory and explain the focus of four of the eight stages.

7. Define psychosocial theory.

8. Erikson thought development resulted from the interaction between _____ and _____; thus, his theory refers to _____ rather than _____.

9. According to Erikson, how did a person develop a healthy personality?

10. List, in order, Erikson's eight psychosocial stages, and specify the appropriate age group for each.

11. Describe the parents' behaviour that might result in an infant learning trust.

12. Describe the parents' behaviour that might result in an infant learning mistrust.

13. What must an adolescent do to achieve identity?

14. Why did Erikson believe that identity must be established before intimacy?

15. List several ways a middle-aged adult could achieve generativity.

Evaluation of Psychoanalytic Theories (pp. 29–30)

Objective 2.3: Evaluate the psychoanalytic theory.

16. List five strengths of psychoanalytic theory.

17. What is the greatest weakness of psychoanalytic theory?

The Humanistic Alternative (pp. 30–32)

Objective 2.4: Summarize and evaluate the basic concepts of humanistic theories.

18. Define the following terms:
    a. self-actualization
    b. fully-functioning person

19. Distinguish between deficiency motives and being motives.

20. Explain Maslow's hierarchy of needs.

LEARNING THEORIES

Pavlov's Classical Conditioning (pp. 32–33)

Objective 2.5: Explain the process of classical conditioning.

21. Define the following terms:
    a. learning theories
    b. classical conditioning

22. How do learning theories differ from psychoanalytic theories?

23. Define the following terms:
    a. unconditioned (unlearned, natural) stimulus
    b. unconditioned (unlearned, natural) response
    c. conditioned (learned) stimulus
    d. conditioned (learned) response

24. In classical conditioning, the conditioned response is always very similar to the unconditioned response. Why?

25. A child learns to associate a teddy bear with a loud noise that scares him. Match the classical conditioning term to its appropriate action.

    a. ____fear (of teddy bear)   1. unconditioned (unlearned, natural) stimulus

    b. ____ fear (of loud noise)   2. unconditioned unlearned, natural) response

    c. ____ loud noise   3. conditioned (learned) stimulus

    d. ____ teddy bear   4. conditioned (learned) response

26. How is classical conditioning relevant to the study of development?

Skinner's Operant Conditioning (pp. 33–34)

Objective 2.6: Explain the process of operant conditioning.

27. Define the following terms:
    a. operant conditioning
    b. reinforcement
    c. punishment
    d. extinction
    e. shaping

28. How is operant conditioning different from classical conditioning?

29. You want your daughter to clean her room. Place one of the following three operant conditioning terms in the blank space beside the most accurate description of that operant conditioning term:

    positive reinforcement   negative reinforcement   punishment

    a. _____ If she cleans her room, she doesn't have to do the dishes.
    b. _____ If she cleans her room, she can go to the movies.
    c. _____ If she does not clean her room, she cannot watch TV.

30. Describe how you can use extinction to stop your son's whining.

31. Why does it take longer to learn a new behaviour under partial reinforcement conditions? Why is the behaviour, once it is established under partial reinforcement conditions, very resistant to extinction?

32. Your task is to teach a tiger to jump through a small flaming hoop. Arrange the following steps in shaping the behaviour in the correct order. (Write a number from 1 to 6 next to each step.)
    a. _____ Jump from one platform to another through a small hoop.
    b. _____ Sit on a platform.
    c. _____ Jump from one platform to another through a large hoop.
    d. _____ Jump from one platform to another through a large flaming hoop.
    e. _____ Jump from one platform to another through a small flaming hoop.
    f. _____ Jump from one platform to another.

The Real World/Parenting: Learning Principles in Real Life (p. 35)

Objective 2.7: Provide real-life examples of the principles of learning.

33. You're at the cereal aisle of the grocery store. At the same aisle is a mom with a preschool child in the shopping cart. The child wants an expensive sugary cereal and the mom says no. The child has a temper tantrum and everyone in the aisle turns to see

what happened. The mom gives in and puts the cereal in the basket, and the child stops screaming.
  a. Who received positive reinforcement? How?
  b. Who received negative reinforcement? How?
  c. How could extinction be used in this scenario?

Evaluation of Learning Theories (pp. 34–36)

Objective 2.8: Critique the learning theories.

34. Give an example of each of the following implications of the learning theories:
  a. Learning theories can explain both consistency and change in behaviour.
  b. Learning theories tend to be optimistic about the possibility of change.
  c. Learning theories give an accurate picture of the way behaviours are learned.

35. Why are traditional learning theories not considered to be developmental theories?

COGNITIVE THEORIES

Piaget's Cognitive-Developmental Theory (pp. 37–38)

Objective 2.9: Describe the basic concepts of Piaget's theory.

36. Define the following terms:
  a. cognitive theories
  b. scheme
  c. assimilation
  d. accommodation
  e. equilibrium

37. What is Piaget's central question?

38. List examples of the sensory and motor schemes with which we begin life.

39. Your present scheme for drive-in windows at fast-food restaurants includes the following:
  • order from a menu at the speaker box;
  • drive to the first window and pay;
  • drive to another window and pick up your food.

You stop at the drive-in window of a new fast-food restaurant and discover that the window to pay and pick up your food is on the passenger side of the car, not the driver's side. According to Piaget, what process is involved in changing the scheme, based on the new information?

40. List, in order, the four stages of Piaget's theory. Include the approximate ages associated with each.

41. Why is the acquisition of symbols crucial in a child's cognitive development from the sensorimotor stage to the preoperational stage?

Information-Processing Theory (pp. 38–40)

Objective 2.10: Explain the basic concepts of information-processing theory.

42. Define the following terms:
    a. information-processing theory
    b. encoding
    c. storage
    d. retrieval
    e. sensory memory
    f. short-term memory
    g. working memory
    h. long-term memory
    i. neo-Piagetian theory

43. Did you listen to music on the radio this morning while you were getting ready for school or work? If so, do you remember all the songs you heard? Probably not, even though you might have sung along with several of them. Which ones do you remember? Why don't we remember everything that enters our sensory memory?

44. According to the neo-Piagetian theories, how are Piaget's stages explained?

Vygotsky's Socio-Cultural Theory (p. 40)

Objective 2.11: Describe Vygotsky's socio-cultural theory.

45. Define the following terms:
    a. socio-cultural theory
    b. scaffolding
    c. zone of proximal development

46. List three things a parent must do to create an appropriate scaffold.

47. How does the role of the teacher differ in the Vygotskian classroom from the Piagetian classroom?

Bandura's Social-Cognitive Theory (pp. 40–41)

Objective 2.12: Give examples of observational learning, or modelling.

48. Define the following terms:
    a. observational learning, or modelling
    b. reciprocal determinism
    c. self-efficacy

49.   What is your understanding of the developmental process of reciprocal determinism? Give an example to illustrate your understanding.

50.   Give an example of a situation that a person with a strong sense of self-efficacy will most likely challenge.

Evaluation of Cognitive Theories (pp. 41–43)

Objective 2.13: Critique the cognitive theories.

51.   List three contributions of Piaget's theory.

52.   In what area has Piaget sometimes been considered incorrect?

53.   How has information-processing theory helped clarify some of the cognitive processes underlying Piaget's findings?

54.   What are the criticisms of information-processing theory?

55.   Compare and contrast the educational application of the theories of Piaget and Vygotsky.

56.   Explain how Bandura's learning theory is developmental in nature.

BIOLOGICAL AND EVOLUTIONARY THEORIES

Genetics (p. 44)

Objective 2.14: Describe the importance of genetics in human development.

57.   Where is deoxyribonucleic acid (DNA) located?

58.   Define the term "human genome."

59.   What are the essential functions of genes in the body?

Genotypes, Phenotypes, and Patterns of Inheritance (p. 44–47)

Objective 2.15: Describe the impact of genetics on inheritance.

60.   Differentiate between genotype and phenotype.

61.   The simplest set of genetic rules is the_____, in which a single dominant gene strongly influences the phenotype.

62.   Differentiate between homozygous and heterozygous.

63. Explain how a child's phenotype is influenced by the inheritance of a dominant gene. How does that differ from the inheritance of a recessive gene? Give examples.

64. Explain the impact of dominant versus recessive genes on the phenotype.

65. Define the following terms:
    a. polygenic inheritance
    b. multi-factorial inheritance
    c. mitochondrial inheritance

66. Give examples of polygenic traits in which the dominant-recessive pattern is at work.

67. How does multi-factorial inheritance differ from polygenic inheritance?

68. How does mitochondrial inheritance differ from other types of inheritance patterns?

Epigenetics (p. 48)

Objective 2.16: Examine the importance of epigenetics on development.

69. Define the following terms
    a. epigenome
    b. gene expression
    c. gene silencing
    d. epigenetics

70. Discuss a few animal research findings that indicate that epigenetic factors play a pivotal role in development across the lifespan.

71. Some preliminary evidence indicates that _____, linked to _____ alterations, may be inherited in humans.

Nativism, Ethology, Behaviour Genetics, and Sociobiology (pp. 48–49)

Objective 2.17: Compare the biological theories of development.

72. Define the following terms:
    a. nativism
    b. ethology
    c. behaviour genetics
    d. sociobiology

73. What is the main focus of sociobiology?

Evolutionary Psychology (pp. 49–50)

Objective 2.18: Describe the view of evolutionary psychology.

74. State the basic premise of evolutionary psychology according to Stephen Pinker.

75. Describe the premise put forth by the epigenetic theorists in regards to evolutionary psychology.

Evolutionary Developmental Psychology (p. 50)

Objective 2.19: Describe the view of evolutionary developmental psychology.

76. State a few suggestions given by theorists on evolutionary developmental psychology.

Evolutionary Prenatal Programming and Adult Health and Disease (p. 50)

Objective 2.20: Describe the influence of prenatal programming on later life development.

77. Explain briefly the predictive-adaptive responses by the fetus. What events occur if a mis- match results in the early (prenatal) and later (postnatal) environment?

78. What may be the consequences of epigenetic changes in the DNA made prenatally?

Evaluation of Evolutionary and Biological Theories (pp. 51–53)

Objective 2.21: Evaluate biological and evolutionary theories.

79. Discuss the relationship between epigenome and human health.

80. What concerns have been expressed about evolutionary and biological theories?

Research Report: Type 2 Diabetes Epidemic in a Remote Community (p. 52)

Objective 2.22: Identify each of the variables that interact between genetic and environmental factors in the occurrence of Type 2 diabetes in First Nations people.

81. State the health/social ramifications of Type 2 diabetes.

82. Describe preventative measures taken towards decreasing the severity of Type 2 diabetes.

SYSTEMS THEORY

Bronfenbrenner's Bioecological Systems Theory (pp. 48–50)

Objective 2.23: Describe Bronfenbrenner's bioecological theory.

83. Define the following terms:
     a. bioecological system theory
     b. contexts

    c.   macrosystem
    d.   exosystem
    e.   microsystem
    f.   mesosystem
    g.   individual context

84.   Give examples of each of the contexts in Bronfenbrenner's theory.

Eclecticism (p. 55)

Objective 2.24: Examine eclecticism as it relates to the study of human development.

85.   Define the term "eclecticism."

86.   State its importance to the study of behaviour in children.

Evaluation of System Theories (pp. 55–56)

Objective 2.25: Evaluate the systems theories.

87.   State a contribution of Bronfenbrenner's bioecological systems theory.

88.   State the limitation of this theory on child development.

89.   Identify the importance of developmentalists adopting an eclectic approach to study human   development.

CRITICAL REFLECTION EXERCISE

Match each theoretical perspective on the right to the statement that best describes it. (Some answers may be used more than once; not all answers are used.)

____ 1. Behaviour is associated with the consequences of our actions.

a. evolutionary psychology

____ 2. The most important internal drive is each individual's motivation to achieve his or her full potential.

b. psychoanalytic (Erikson)

____ 3. Genetically inherited cognitive and social characteristics have evolved through natural selection.

c. humanistic

____ 4. This theory explains the relationship between people and their environment, or contexts.

d. epigenetics

____ 5. Gene regulation patterns alter gene function (phenotype) without changing gene structure (genotype).

e. operant conditioning

____ 6. Complex forms of thinking have their origins in social interactions rather than in the child's private explorations.

f. Bandura's social-cognitive

___ 7. This theory proposes links between physiological processes and development.

___ 8. The goal of the theory is to explain how the mind manages information.

___ 9. The focus of the theory is on the development of logical thinking.

___ 10. Learning can occur by watching others.

g. Piaget's cognitive-developmental

h. information-processing

i. biological

j. Vygotsky's socio-cultural

k. Bronfenbrenner's bioecological

PRACTICE QUESTIONS

1. Which of the following parts of personality lies entirely in our unconscious?
   a. ego
   b. superego
   c. id
   d. Oedipus

2. Which term best describes Freud's theory of development?
   a. psychosocial stages
   b. ego development
   c. id integrity
   d. psychosexual stages

3. Erikson's theory differed from Freud's in that Erikson _____.
   a. emphasized instincts more heavily than Freud
   b. believed that our urges are primarily destructive
   c. believed that development continued throughout the lifespan
   d. is considered more pessimistic than Freud

4. Which of the following accurately summarizes Erikson's theory?
   a. A poor interpersonal relationship can cause individuals to fixate on problems.
   b. The superego is a more powerful force than the id and drives most behaviour.
   c. Without societal pressures to conform to, we would be overly destructive.
   d. Healthy development requires confronting and resolving crises throughout the lifespan.

5. Which of the following is a weakness of psychoanalytic theories?
   a. They are hard to test and measure.
   b. They provide helpful concepts, such as the unconscious, that are part of everyday language.
   c. They invented psychotherapy.
   d. They focus on the emotional quality of the child's earliest relationship with caregivers.

6. Which theories assume that individuals are motivated to achieve their full potential?
    a. cognitive
    b. humanistic
    c. learning
    d. psychosocial

7. According to Maslow's hierarchy of needs, when will we strive to fulfill higher order needs?
    a. at the same time that we strive to achieve the lower order needs
    b. only in the later years of our lives
    c. mainly during the middle adulthood years when health is best
    d. only when the lower order needs have already been met

8. Whenever the eye doctor puffs air in your eye, you blink. Now, before she puffs the air, she says "ready," puffs the air, and you blink. After doing this several times, you begin to blink as soon as she says "ready." In this example, what kind of learning has taken place?
    a. classical conditioning
    b. sensitization
    c. operant conditioning
    d. habituation

9. What is the unconditioned stimulus in the previous question?
    a. the blinking of the eye
    b. saying the word "ready"
    c. the puff of air
    d. the fear of the puff of air

10. You take aspirin for your headache. This is an example of which of the following?
    a. positive reinforcement
    b. negative reinforcement
    c. punishment
    d. extinction

11. Which of the following is an example of shaping?
    a. paying your son for mowing the lawn
    b. praising your son for his good grades
    c. reinforcing each step of your son's behaviour during toilet training
    d. withholding allowance from your son when he talks back

12. Which of the following is a limitation of learning theories?
    a. They give an accurate picture of the way in which many behaviours are learned.
    b. They are not really developmental theories.
    c. They tend to be optimistic about the possibility of changing behaviour.
    d. They can explain both consistency and change in behaviour.

13. Piaget felt that children develop cognitively by acquiring more complex schemes. How are schemes defined?
    a. the action of categorizing items into groups
    b. scientific theories about human development
    c. cognitive structures that provide a procedure to follow in a specific situation
    d. ideas we have about how to get what we want

14. You learn how to drive a car with an automatic transmission, and then you try to drive a car with standard transmission. The adjustment you make is an example of the process of
    a. equilibration
    b. assimilation
    c. accommodation
    d. hierarchical categorizing

15. Chris is in elementary school and has learned to solve problems logically. Which of Piaget's stages best describes her level of cognitive development?
    a. concrete operational
    b. sensorimotor
    c. preoperational
    d. formal operational

16. Which of the following is the goal of information-processing theory?
    a. to distinguish the relative impact of nature and nurture
    b. to trace the stages of how thinking develops
    c. to uncover the hidden meaning of dreams
    d. to explain how the mind manages information

17. In Vygotsky's theory, what does scaffolding mean?
    a. building new schemes
    b. developing a firm sense of self-identity
    c. acquiring new emotional experiences through direct experience
    d. modelling and structuring a child's learning experience

18. Bandura suggests that learning can take place without direct reinforcement. What is this type of learning called?
    a. positive reinforcement
    b. modelling
    c. instrumental conditioning
    d. classical conditioning

19. Which of the following is a limitation of Piaget's theory?
    a. He developed innovative methods of studying children's thinking.
    b. He was wrong about the ages at which children develop specific skills.
    c. His theory forced psychologists to think about child development in a new way.
    d. His findings have been replicated in virtually every culture and every cohort of children since the 1920s.

20. The unique genetic blueprint inherited from the parents that characterizes a specific individual is called a _____.
    a. phenotype
    b. chromosome
    c. gamete
    d. genotype

21. Which of these theories focuses on genetically determined survival behaviours that are assumed to have evolved through natural selection?
    a. ethology
    b. nativism
    c. psychoanalytic
    d. sociobiology

22. Community-wide preventative and health-educational programs designed towards the prevention and management of Type 2 diabetes in First Nations people should focus on each of the following *except*
    a. physical exercise.
    b. balanced diet.
    c. screening programs.
    d. religious practices.

23. According to Pinker, a leading advocate of evolutionary psychology, which of the following has been shaped by natural selection to serve adaptive functions to promote survival in an individual?
    a. mind
    b. spirit
    c. ego
    d. soul

24. Arrange the following contexts of Bronfenbrenner's bioecological theory in the proper order, from the largest circle to the smallest.
    a. macrosystem, exosystem, microsystem, biological context
    b. microsystem, biological context, macrosystem, exosystem
    c. biological context, exosystem, microsystem, macrosystem
    d. macrosystem, biological context, microsystem, exosystem

25. A developmentalist uses a multiple theoretical perspective to explain and study human development. This approach is called _____.
    a. evolutionary
    b. ecological
    c. epigenetic
    d. eclectic

CHAPTER 2 ANSWER KEY

Guided Study Questions

3.   a. superego   b. id   c. ego

8.   Erikson thought development resulted from the interaction between <u>internal drives</u> and <u>cultural demands</u>; thus, his theory refers to <u>psychosocial stages</u> rather than <u>psychosexual ones</u>.

25.   a. 4   b. 2   c. 1   d. 3

29.   a. negative reinforcement   b. positive reinforcement   c. punishment

32.   a. 4   b. 1   c. 3   d. 5   e. 6   f. 2

33.   a.   The child; he got the cereal he wanted.
       b.   The mom; the child's temper tantrum stopped.
       c.   Ignore the temper tantrum and go on to the next aisle.

61.   The simplest set of rules is the <u>dominant-recessive pattern</u>, in which a single dominant gene strongly influences the phenotypes.

71.   Some preliminary evidence indicates that <u>acquired epigenetic traits</u> linked to <u>chromosome structure</u> alterations may be inherited in humans.

81.   Incidence rate of Type 2 diabetes is escalating at alarming rates and is the leading cause of death in First Nations people. It leads to conditions such as heart disease, blindness, kidney failure, and gangrene

82.   Focus is on <u>healthy lifestyle practice</u> that includes a <u>balanced diet</u> and <u>physical exercise</u>. <u>Screening and lifestyle support programs</u> are also vital.

Critical Reflection Exercise

1. e	3. a	5. d	7. i	9. g
2. c	4. k	6. j	8. h	10. f

Practice Questions

1. c	6. b	11. c	16. d	21. a
2. d	7. d	12. b	17. d	22. d
3. c	8. a	13. c	18. b	23. a
4. d	9. c	14. c	19. b	24. a
5. a	10. b	15. a	20. d	25. d

PRENATAL DEVELOPMENT AND BIRTH

OVERVIEW OF CHAPTER

Human development begins when the genes and chromosomes are passed on to the new individual at the moment of conception. From the time of implantation on, the prenatal environment strongly affects the developing fetus. From conception to birth, prenatal development follows an amazing course that begins with a single cell and ends with a crying—but curious—newborn making his or her debut in the outside world.

Conception

- The first step in the development of an individual human being happens at conception, when a sperm fertilizes an ovum (egg cell). Fraternal twins come from two eggs that are fertilized by two separate sperm; identical twins result when a single fertilized ovum separates into two parts and each develops into a separate individual.

- Assisted reproductive techniques are available to couples that have difficulty conceiving. In Canada, new legislation now regulates assisted human reproduction (AHR) and related research. Many AHR procedures are available to couples that have difficulty conceiving. One is fertility drugs; another is artificial insemination, which has a higher success rate than in vitro fertilization (IVF).

- IVF laboratories create numerous embryos. Newer cryopreservation methods have evolved that freeze embryos instantly. This vitrification protocol improves the survival rate of embryos. IVF has, however, raised ethical concerns.

- Multiple births are more frequent in women who become pregnant using IVFs because several embryos may be implanted. Single embryo transfer (SET) will likely become the international norm in IVF treatment. Canadian guidelines recommend that women under the age of 35 receive no more than two embryos per fertility cycle. Exceptions may be made for older women.

Pregnancy and Prenatal Development

- Pregnancy is a physical condition in which a woman's body is nurturing a developing embryo or fetus. Prenatal development, or gestation, is the process that transforms a zygote into a newborn. Pregnancy is usually divided into trimesters, three periods of 3 months each. The three stages of prenatal development are defined by specific developmental milestones and are not of equal length.

- Because prenatal development is strongly influenced by maturational codes that are the same for both males and females, there are only a few sex differences in prenatal development.

- Prenatal behaviour includes fetal responses to music and other stimuli. Fetal learning conducts research into what fetuses can learn and how this learning may affect later development.

Issues in Prenatal Development

- In Canada, 2 to 3% of newborns are born with a serious congenital anomaly.

- Many disorders appear to be transmitted through the operation of dominant and recessive genes. Autosomal disorders are caused by genes located on the autosomes; the genes that cause sex-linked disorders are found on the X chromosome.

- A variety of problems can occur when a child has too many or too few chromosomes, a condition referred to as chromosomal error or chromosomal anomaly.

- Deviations in prenatal development can result from exposure to teratogens, substances that cause damage to an embryo or fetus. The general rule is that each organ system is most vulnerable to harm at the time when it is developing most rapidly. Teratogens include maternal diseases, such as rubella, HIV, and STDs, and drugs, such as nicotine, alcohol, heroin, and cocaine.

- The mother's diet, age, and mental and physical health can adversely affect prenatal development. With regard to diet, mothers who wish to prevent risks to their unborn child and to themselves may follow the Health Canada's (2002b) guide, *Nutrition for a Healthy Pregnancy: National Guidelines for Childbearing,* for proper nutritional intake.

- Current research suggests that teratogens (which fall into three broad categories: mutagenic, environmental and epimutagenic) can have effects on pre-natal development. Mutagens are agents that cause alterations (mutations) to genomic DNA.

- Little research has been conducted in regards to the father's role in reproductive risk, but of the 60% of malformations otherwise unaccounted for, at least some may be related to paternal factors such as occupation or exposure to toxic substances.

- If a woman is at risk of bearing a child with a congenital defect, genetic counselling is an option in order for her and her family to understand potential outcomes and choices.

- Diagnostic tests such as chorionic villus sampling and amniocentesis, are used to identify problems before birth. The use of ultrasound technology is useful in high-risk pregnancy. Another method of monitoring fetal development is through laboratory tests.

Birth and the Neonate

- Once gestation is complete, the fetus must be born into the world. In industrialized countries, especially in Canada, parents have several choices, including whether to use the services of a doctor or a birth attendant (midwife), whether or not to use drugs during delivery, and whether to have the birth at home or in a hospital.

- Labour is typically divided into three stages. Stage 1 includes dilation and effacement, stage 2 is the delivery of the baby, and stage 3 is the delivery of the placenta and other material from the uterus.

- A baby is referred to as a neonate for the first month following birth. The health of the neonate is assessed with the Apgar scale at 1 minute and 5 minutes after birth. The Brazelton Neonatal Behavioural Assessment Scale is used to track a newborn's development over the first 2 weeks or so following birth. Standard screening procedures have been expanded in Canada to include the new tandem mass spectrometry process and the Nipissing District Developmental Screen (NDDS).

- Classification of a neonate's weight is another important factor in assessment. All neonates below 2500 grams are classified as low birth weight (LBW). Most LBW infants are preterm—born before the 38th week of gestation. Infants that are small-for-date have completed 38 weeks or more of gestation but are still LBW.

LEARNING GOALS

After completing Chapter 3, students should be able to:
1. Explain the basic genetics of conception.
2. Trace the development of the unborn child from conception to birth.
3. List and describe several problems in prenatal development.
4. Examine several preventative measures used to decrease adverse effects in prenatal development.
5. Describe the birth process, and describe the assessment of the neonate.

GUIDED STUDY QUESTIONS

CONCEPTION

The Process of Conception (pp. 62–65)

Objective 3.1: Explain the process of reproduction.

1. Define the following terms:
   a. ovum
   b. fallopian tube
   c. uterus
   d. chromosomes
   e. gametes
   f. zygote
   g. autosomes
   h. sex chromosomes
   i. X chromosome
   j. Y chromosome

2. Trace the paths of the ovum and the sperm in the process of fertilization.

3. Explain how the sex of a zygote is determined.

4. Define the following terms, and distinguish between them:
    a. fraternal twins (dizygotic)
    b. identical twins (monozygotic)

5. Identical twins are always the same sex. Why?

6. Distinguish among the following forms of assisted reproductive techniques.

Technique	Process	Advantages	Disadvantages
Fertility drugs			
In vitro fertilization			
Artificial insemination			

7. State the purpose of Canada's Bill C6 regarding assisted human reproduction.

8. What is the advantage of the vitrification protocol?

9. What are some of the possible effects on women if in vitro fertilization (IVF) fails.

10. State the reason why multiple births are more frequent in women who use (IVF).

11. The _____ will likely become the international norm in IVF treatment.

12. What do the Canadian guidelines recommend for women under the age of 35 and over 39 regarding embryo transfers?

Research Report: Twins in Genetic and Epigenetic Research (p. 64)

Objective 3.2: Summarize the results of research on twin studies.

13. What is the logic upon which twin studies are based?

14. What do the findings of twin studies inform us about intelligence and attitudes?

15. Explain the importance of epigenetic variables that researchers are taking into consideration in monozygotic (identical) twin research.

PREGNANCY AND PRENATAL DEVELOPMENT

The Mother's Experience (pp. 66–68)

Objective 3.3: Describe the mother's experience during the three trimesters of pregnancy.

16.   Define the following terms:
    a. pregnancy
    b. prenatal development or gestation
    c. trimesters

17.   Distinguish between pregnancy and prenatal development.

18.   Define the following terms:
    a. morning sickness
    b. ectopic pregnancy
    c. spontaneous abortion
    d. gestational diabetes
    e. colostrums
    f. toxemia of pregnancy

19.   Summarize the events, discomforts, prenatal care needed, and serious problems frequently associated with each trimester of pregnancy.

Trimester	Events	Discomforts	Prenatal Care	Serious Problems
First				
Second				
Third				

20.   Pregnancy begins when _____.

21.   Prenatal care during the first trimester is critical to the prevention of birth defects because _____

Prenatal Development (pp. 68–72)

Objective 3.4: Outline the milestones of the three stages of prenatal development.

22. Define the following terms:
    a. cephalocaudal principle
    b. proximodistal principle

23. Define the following terms:
    a. germinal stage
    b. blastocyst
    c. placenta
    d. umbilical cord
    e. yolk sac
    f. amnion
    g. embryonic stage
    h. neurons
    i. neural tube
    j. gonads
    k. organogenesis
    l. fetal stage
    m. glial cells
    n. lanugo
    o. vernix
    p. surfactant
    q. viability
    r. engagement

24. Summarize the major events in each prenatal stage, and indicate when they occur.

Prenatal Stage Begins/Ends	Major Events
Germinal	
Embryonic	
Fetal	

Sex Differences (pp. 72–73)

Objective 3.5: List some of the sex differences in prenatal development.

25. Define the following terms:
    a. testosterone
    b. congenital adrenal hyperplasia

26. Why are there only a few sex differences in prenatal development?

27. List some of the documented sex differences in prenatal development.

Prenatal Behaviour (pp. 73–74)

Objective 3.6: Describe some of the research findings about the behaviours of fetuses.

28. List some of the documented behaviours of fetuses.

ISSUES IN PRENATAL DEVELOPMENT

Genetic Disorders (pp. 75–76)

Objective 3.7: Identify some common autosomal disorders and common sex-linked disorders that affect prenatal development.

29. Define the following terms, and distinguish between them:
  a. autosomal disorders
  b. sex-linked disorders

30. Define the following terms:
  a. phenylketonuria (PKU)
  b. sickle-cell disease
  c. Tay-Sachs disease
  d. Huntington's disease
  e. red-green colour blindness
  f. hemophilia
  g. fragile-X syndrome

31. Which of the following dominant-recessive disorders is autosomal or sex-linked, and what are its symptoms?

Disease	*Autosomal or Sex-linked*	*Symptoms*
Fragile-X syndrome		
Hemophilia		
Huntington's disease		
Phenylketonuria (PKU)		
Red-green colour blindness		
Sickle-cell disease		
Tay-Sachs disease		

Chromosomal Errors (pp. 76–77)

Objective 3.8: Identify common trisomy errors and sex-chromosome anomalies that can affect prenatal development.

32. Define the following terms:
     a. chromosomal error or chromosome anomaly
     b. trisomy
     c. trisomy 21 or Down syndrome
     d. Klinefelter's syndrome
     e. Turner's syndrome

33. What is the birth rate of infants with Down syndrome in Canadian women aged 35–39?

34. Indicate whether the likelihood of each of the following disorders is influenced by the mother's age, and list the symptoms for the disorder.

Disease	*Influenced by Mother's Age?*	*Symptoms*
Klinefelter's syndrome (XXY)		
Turner's syndrome (X0)		
Extra X chromosome (XXX)		
Extra Y chromosome (XYY)		

Teratogens: Maternal Diseases (pp. 77–79)

Objective 3.9: Summarize the effects of maternal diseases on the embryo or the fetus.

35. Define the following terms:
     a. teratogens
     b. rubella or German measles
     c. HIV
     d. syphilis
     e. genital herpes
     f. gonorrhea

36. Indicate the period when each teratogen is most likely to cause damage to the fetus. List the symptoms of the disease.

Teratogen	*When Most Vulnerable?*	*Symptoms*
Genital herpes		
Gonorrhea		
HIV		
Rubella		
Syphilis		

37. The general rule is that each organ system is most vulnerable to harm at what point? Why does this make the first 8 weeks of gestation the period of greatest risk for most teratogens?

38. What have Canadian researchers demonstrated regarding HIV-positive pregnant women who take anti-HIV drugs in combination with caesarean section birth and formula feeding?

Teratogens: Drugs (pp. 79–81)

Objective 3.10: Identify drugs taken by the mother during pregnancy that can cause damage to the child, and describe the symptoms the child might exhibit.

39. Define fetal alcohol syndrome.

40. The term _____ is often used to encompass a continuum of effects caused by the consumption of alcohol while pregnant.

41. What is the safest course for pregnant women regarding alcohol?

42. List symptoms of each of the following teratogens.

Teratogen	Symptoms
tobacco	
alcohol	
heroin	
cocaine	

Teratogens: Other Harmful Influences on Prenatal Development (pp. 81–83)

Objective 3.11: List and describe other influences on prenatal development.

43. Define the following terms:
    a. spina bifida
    b. brain stunting
    c. Body Mass Index (BMI)
    d. fetal-maternal medicine

44. How many milligrams of folic acid should the pregnant women be consuming per day?

45. Describe the problems that may occur if the mother has insufficient overall calories and protein, and list the benefits available to her if she follows the Health Canada's (2002b) guide *Nutrition for a Healthy Pregnancy: National Guidelines for the Childbearing Years.*

46. Why is the impact of maternal malnutrition greatest on the developing nervous system? (Hint: consider the principles of development.)

47. List several problems with the fetus that are associated with the mother's age (over 30 and young teens).

48. List several problems with the fetus that are associated with the mother's chronic illness (emotional and physical). What have Canadian researchers found regarding the "immigrant effect"?

49. What does recent evidence suggest for the stressed and/or at-risk pregnant women?

Teratogens: Mutagenic, Environmental, and Epimutagenic (pp. 83–84)

Objective 3.12: Identify and describe the current research regarding the three broad categories of teratogens.

50. What are mutagens? How do they contribute to birth defects?

51. What effects do environmental teratogens have on pre-natal development?

52. Define epimutagens. Explain what effects epimutagens may have on generations.

No Easy Answers: Pregnancy, Epilepsy, and Antieptileptic Drugs (p. 83)

Objective 3.13: Summarize the dilemma associated with pregnant women who have epilepsy.

53. Define the following terms:
    a. epilepsy
    b. anticonvulsant drugs

54. What are the risks of untreated epilepsy? What are the risks of using antieptileptic drugs (AEDs) during pregnancy?

55. What do physicians recommend to pregnant women who have epilepsy?

Paternal Influences: Preconceptual and Prenatal (pp. 84–85)

Objective 3.14: Describe the findings on the father's role in prenatal development.

56. What specific occupations can be associated with higher reproductive risk?

57. Identify factors that can damage DNA.

58. State another serious threat to maternal and child health.

Fetal Assessment and Treatment (pp. 85–86)

Objective 3.15: List various types of prenatal diagnostic tests to detect fetal abnormalities.

59. State the importance of genetic counselling.

60. Define the following terms:
    a. chorionic villus sampling (CVS)
    b. amniocentesis
    c. ultrasonography
    d. alpha-fetoprotein
    e. fetoscopy

61. List the laboratory tests that can indicate chromosomal errors and many genetic disorders prior to birth.

BIRTH AND THE NEONATE

Birth Choices (pp. 88–89)

Objective 3.16: Summarize the choices about birth that may be available in industrialized countries, especially in Canada.

62.   Define midwifery and outline midwifery practice in Canada.

63.   Distinguish among the following drugs that may be used during delivery:
      a.   analgesics
      b.   sedatives or tranquilizers
      c.   anaesthesia

64.   State two sides of controversial evidence about the causal link between the drugs used during delivery and the baby's later behaviour or development.

65.   Describe how natural childbirth practices such as the Lamaze method can help women avoid drugs during delivery.

66.   List the components of natural childbirth.

67.   Describe four location options available in most communities for birth in Canada.

The Physical Process of Birth (pp. 89–92)

Objective 3.17: List and describe what happens in each of the three stages of labour..

68.   Define the following terms:
      a.   dilation
      b.   effacement
      c.   breech presentation
      d.   caesarean section

69.   List the length of each of the phases of stage 1 of labour, and the major events occurring in that phase.

Phase	*Approximate Length of Stage*	*Major Events*
Early		
Active		
Transition		

70.   What events mark the beginning and the end of stage 2 of labour?

71.   What happens in stage 3 of labour?

72.   Define the following terms:
    a. fetal distress
    b. anoxia

73.   List other complications of the process of birth.

Assessing the Neonate (pp. 92–93)

Objective 3.18: Distinguish between the two tools used to assess the health of infants.

74.   Define neonate.

75.   Distinguish between the following scales of assessment of the neonate:
    a. Apgar Scale
    b. tandem mass spectrometry
    c. Brazelton Neonatal Behavioural Assessment Scale
    d. Nipissing District Developmental Screen (NDDS)

Low Birth Weight (pp. 93–94)

Objective 3.19: Describe the risks associated with low birth weight in infants.

76.   Define low birth weight (LBW).

77.   Distinguish between the following terms:
    a. preterm neonate
    b. small-for-date neonate

78.   Define respiratory distress syndrome or hyaline membrane disease.

79.   What are some factors that may impact a LBW neonate's chances of catching up to his or her normal peers within the first few years of life?

CRITICAL REFLECTION EXERCISES

Healthy Pregnancies

Imagine you have a friend who has just discovered that she is pregnant. She is taking a lifespan development course, and the class is discussing all of the things that can go wrong during prenatal development. She is worried that the chances of her baby being born healthy are very slim. Utilizing information from this chapter, answer the following questions from your friend:

1.   What things can I do to minimize the risks to my developing baby? (Provide at least four examples for your friend.)

2.   What if my baby is born low birth weight? Is there anything I can do to minimize the long-term effects of this? (Provide at least three examples for your friend.)

3.   How much smoking or drinking can I do while pregnant? Is there a critical period during which the effects of these would be most harmful?

PRACTICE QUESTIONS

1.   Conception occurs when _____.
     a.   the zygote implants in the uterine wall
     b.   a sperm penetrates an ovum
     c.   an ovum is released from the ovary
     d.   gametes are produced

2.   The technique that involves uniting an ovum and a sperm in a laboratory dish and implanting the resulting embryo in a woman's uterus is called _____.
     a.   cryopreservation
     b.   artificial insemination
     c.   fertility enhancement
     d.   in vitro fertilization

3.   One of the following is a Canadian guideline for women under the age of 35 in regards to embryo transfers per fertility cycle. The woman should receive no more than

     _____.
     a.   four embryos
     b.   three embryos
     c.   five embryos
     d.   two embryos

4.   Researchers suggest that over the course of a lifetime, which one of the following variables can bring changes in epigenetic markers in identical twins?
     a.   water consumption.
     b.   fitness levels
     c.   rest periods.
     d.   sun exposure.

5.   Which of the following statements about pregnancy is true?
     a.   Pregnancy is a physical condition in which a woman's body is nurturing a developing embryo or fetus.
     b.   Pregnancy is the process that transforms a zygote into a newborn.
     c.   Pregnancy is divided into three stages that are defined by specific developmental milestones.
     d.   Pregnancy begins when ovulation occurs.

6. The developmental principle that causes development to proceed from the head down is called the _____.
   a. proximodistal principle
   b. organogenic principle
   c. cephalocaudal principle
   d. distalproximo principle

7. The three stages of prenatal development are, in order, _____.
   a. germinal, embryonic, fetal
   b. viability, organogenesis, germinal
   c. embryonic, fetal, viability
   d. embryonic, germinal, fetal

8. Which statement most accurately represents the sex differences in prenatal development?
   a. There are numerous sex differences in prenatal development.
   b. Female fetuses are more active than male fetuses.
   c. There are only a few sex differences in prenatal development.
   d. Male fetuses are more sensitive to external stimuli than female fetuses.

9. Which statement is true about the behaviour of fetuses?
   a. Newborns do not remember stimuli to which they were exposed prenatally.
   b. Fetuses can distinguish between familiar and novel stimuli as early as the 20th week.
   c. Prenatal behaviour is stable in male fetuses but not in female fetuses.
   d. Fetuses respond to sounds and vibrations with heart rate changes, head turns, and body movements.

10. Which statement correctly illustrates sex-linked transmission?
    a. A girl inherits hemophilia from the father.
    b. A boy inherits hemophilia from the mother.
    c. A girl inherits hemophilia from both parents.
    d. A boy inherits hemophilia from both parents.

11. An anomaly in which a girl receives only one X chromosome and no Y chromosome is called _____.
    a. Klinefelter's syndrome
    b. Turner's syndrome
    c. fragile-X syndrome
    d. Tay-Sachs disease

12. Which one of the following viruses can be passed directly to the infant through breast milk after delivery?
    a. rubella
    b. measles
    c. HIV
    d. genital herpes

13. Which of the following would be considered a teratogen?
    a. Down syndrome
    b. hemophilia
    c. genetic errors
    d. cocaine

14. Infants of mothers who smoke _____ than infants of non-smoking mothers.
    a. are about half a pound lighter
    b. gain weight more rapidly
    c. are more active
    d. learn faster

15. Mothers who follow the *Nutrition for Healthy Pregnancy: National Guidelines for Childbearing* early in their pregnancy and onward will _____.
    a. increase weight gain substantially at the beginning of the pregnancy
    b. experience no effect on their weight gain throughout the pregnancy
    c. decrease their weight towards the end of the pregnancy
    d. maintain the necessary degree of weight throughout the pregnancy

16. Mutagens are agents that cause alterations to the _____.
    a. digestive process of the mother
    b. neural tube in the fetus
    c. genomic DNA
    d. blood components in the fetus

17. There is a higher reproductive risk for men who work in which one of the following occupations?
    a. painter
    b. car dealer
    c. police officer
    d. chef

18. What is the main purpose of genetic counselling?
    a. to assist the mother and family to choose correct fetal assessment procedures
    b. to allow family to normalize their grief while waiting for the outcome
    c. to help the mother and family to understand potential outcomes and choices.
    d. to assist the mother and family to assess their strengths during the period of pregnancy

19. Why should the use of pain medications be kept to a minimum during delivery?
    a. so that the mother can more fully participate in the process
    b. because the drugs can pass through the placenta to the fetus
    c. to allow for faster reaction times to physician requests
    d. because the baby can become addicted to them

20. The flattening out of the cervix is called _____.
    a. dilation
    b. transition
    c. fetal distress
    d. effacement

21. During which stage of labour will the actual delivery take place?
    a. second
    b. transition
    c. third
    d. first

22. Which of the following is *not* a fairly common birth complication?
    a. dislocation of the infant's shoulder or hip
    b. fetal distress
    c. fetus allergic reaction to pollen
    d. mother's blood pressure suddenly increases or decreases

23. The Canadian screening tool designed to assist professionals and parents to identify those aspects of a child's development which may require early intervention is called the _____.
    a. Brazelton Neonatal Behavioural Assessment Scale
    b. tandem mass screening tool
    e. Nipissing District Developmental Screen
    f. Apgar scale

24. Neonates weighing below 2500 grams are classified as:
    a. low-birth-weight infants
    b. preterm infants
    c. breech presentation infants
    d. fetal distress infants

25. Which statement is true about low-birth-weight babies?
    a. Low-birth-weight girls are more likely to show long-term effects than boys.
    b. Low-birth-weight infants show markedly lower levels of responsiveness.
    c. Most low-birth-weight babies never catch up to their normal peers.
    d. Low birth weight is not related to the neonate's health.

CASE STUDY

Marie, who is 16 years old, is pregnant. According to her family doctor she is in her 7th week of pregnancy. Her diet consists mainly of fast foods and she drinks canned sodas frequently throughout the day. According to a few of her friends, her boyfriend, presumably the baby's father, left town without saying goodbye to her.

1.   From your understanding of prenatal development, in which stage would Marie be at 7 weeks of pregnancy? Regarding her diet, what essential nutrient should be taking, and in what amount per day?

2.   What are the consequences for Marie's infant if he/she experiences malnutrition during pregnancy? If you were planning her diet which foods would you include so that she is not malnourished? (Check guide: Nutrition for a Healthy Pregnancy: National Guidelines for the Childbearing Years as well as the new revised Canada's Food Guide).

3.   In what ways would you give Marie the support that she needs when she learns that her boyfriend has left town? (Check Chapter 2, Humanistic Theories).

INVESTIGATIVE PROJECT

Student Project 4: Available Prenatal Services

Basic Questions to Answer

The purpose of the project is to discover what kinds of prenatal services are available to poor mothers in your area.

- What prenatal programs are available through public health, health region/authority, local hospitals, or other clinics?

- What funds are available to support those services from local, municipal, provincial, and federal government sources and non-governmental sources?

- How many women take advantage of such services? Is there a waiting list? Is there any information available about the percentage of local women who receive no prenatal care at all, or receive such care only in the final trimester?

- Has there been any change in the availability of such services in your area in the past decade or two? (This may be difficult to determine, but it is worth a try.)

- What are the infant mortality rate and maternal death rate for your province and for your community? How do these compare to national and international statistics?

Sources

Some of the statistics may be available through Statistics Canada and various web links (i.e., Health Canada) as well as in government documents at the library. Most capital cities have Departments of Vital Statistics that may be helpful. Furthermore, the federal and/or provincial Departments of Health may be useful.

For local information, try the local, city, or provincial public health branches. The Government of Canada pages or the Provincial Government pages of your phone book are good places to start. A visit to the offices of the local Population and Public Health Branch and First Nations and Inuit Health Branch is likely to be fruitful. When you call you should explain that the information you seek is to be part of a class project, and that you will report the information to your class.

INVESTIGATIVE PROJECT

Student Project 5: Investigation of Birth Options

Basic Questions to Answer

- Which of the four main choices of birth options (regular hospital maternity unit, hospital-based birth centre or birthing room, free-standing birthing centre, or home delivery) are available in your area?

- How are the local births distributed among the options?

- Are the deliveries in the birth centre or at home done by midwives? Do midwives deliver babies at hospitals as well?

Sources

The Yellow Pages may be your best first source. If that does not yield information, you might make inquiries at several local obstetricians' offices. You will then need to call hospitals, birthing centres, and midwives or their association for further information, or visit each site to get a firsthand look and obtain written information such as brochures. At all times, you should represent yourself accurately as a student working on a project for a class on human development. Do not present yourself as a pregnant woman looking for a place to deliver. Remember always that your questions may be seen as an intrusion on the busy workdays of your **respondents, so be sensitive to the demands you are placing on them.**

Reporting

Your instructor may want you to report back to the class on your findings, either orally or in writing. In any case, you should prepare a written report of what you did, to whom you talked, and what you found out.

CHAPTER 3 ANSWER KEY

Guided Study Questions

11. The **single** <u>embryo transfer (SET)</u> will likely become the international norm in IVF treatment.

20. Pregnancy begins <u>when the zygote implants itself in the lining of the woman's uterus.</u>

21. Prenatal care during the first trimester is critical to the prevention of birth defects because <u>all of the baby's organs form during the first 8 weeks.</u>

37. The general rule is that each organ system is most vulnerable to harm <u>when it is developing most rapidly</u>. The first 8 weeks of gestation is the period of greatest risk for most teratogens because most organ systems develop rapidly during that time.

40. The term "<u>fetal alcohol spectrum disorders</u>" is often used to encompass a continuum of effects caused by consumption of alcohol while pregnant.

44. Women who become pregnant should be consuming the equivalent of <u>0.4 mg</u> of folic acid per day.

46. The impact of the mother's malnutrition is greatest on the developing nervous system because <u>the nervous system interacts with all the other systems</u> (cephalocaudal principle).

62. Midwifery is a regulated health care profession in most provinces in Canada. Midwife practice includes <u>assessing, supervising, and caring for women prior to and during pregnancy</u>.

Practice Questions

1. b	6. c	11. b	16. c	21. a
2. d	7. a	12. c	17. a	22. c
3. d	8. c	13. d	18. c	23. c
4. b	9. d	14. a	19. b	24. a
5. a	10. b	15. d	20. d	25. b

Case Study

1. See Chapter 3 (p. 70). Marie would be in the embryonic stage of prenatal development.
2. See Chapter 3 (p. 81). Marie should be consuming 0.4 mg of folic acid per day. See *Eating Well Canada's Food Guide – Women of Childbearing Age*, http://www.hc-sc.gc.ca/
3. You can best support Marie by to listening to her and telling her you care about her.

WHAT LEGAL PROTECTION EXISTS FOR THE PREGNANT MOTHER AND HER FETUS?

Learning Objective: Examine the issues contributing to the controversy over legal protection of the pregnant mother and her fetus (pp. 97–98).

1. What issues contribute to the legal dilemma between the pregnant mother and her fetus?

2. What is the controversy in the *Canadian Criminal Code* regarding a fetus?

3. List the historical events contributing to this controversy.

4. State the section in the *Criminal Code* that makes abortions illegal.

5. Specify an event that makes doctors exempt from prosecution for having performed an abortion.

6. What event in 1988 led to the modification of Section 287 in the *Criminal Code*?

7. In what ways might you lobby for changes to the *Criminal Code* and the *Charter of Rights and Freedoms* for legal protection for the pregnant mother and her fetus?

8. In what ways might you and others advocate for the interest of the mother and fetus in your community?

9. Healthy public policy is the policy of the future whose purpose is to enhance the health of individuals, families, and communities in order to create a healthy society (Glass & Hicks, 2000). The development of healthy public policy requires a commitment to multi-sectoral collaboration among government departments, agencies, organizations, interest groups, and the community.

    a. In your opinion in what ways could the development of a healthy public policy assist the pregnant mother and her fetus?
    b. What may be the legal impact of the healthy public policy development process on the pregnant mother and her fetus?

Reference

Glass, H. & Hicks, S. (2000). Healthy public policy in public health reform. In M. Stewart (ed.), *Community Nursing: Promoting Canadian's Health*. Toronto: W.B. Saunders.

PHYSICAL, SENSORY, AND PERCEPTUAL DEVELOPMENT IN INFANCY

OVERVIEW OF CHAPTER

During the first 2 years after birth, infants go from being relatively unskilled newborns to toddlers who can move about efficiently, formulate goals and plans, and use words. There are also many important variations among individuals and across groups.

Physical Changes

- At birth, the midbrain and the medulla are the most fully developed structures of the brain. The cycle of synaptogenesis, followed by synaptic pruning for neurological development, continues throughout the lifespan. Events during this cycle of neurological development have important implications for the infant. Myelinization of the nerve fibres follows the cephalocaudal and proximodistal patterns.

- Adaptive reflexes such as sucking help infants survive. Primitive reflexes, such as the Moro or startle reflex and the Babinski reflex, disappear in about 6 months. Neonates move through five states of consciousness in a cycle that lasts about 2 hours. Infants cry as a way of communicating. Parents across a variety of cultures use very similar techniques to soothe crying infants. Colic, which involves intense bouts of infant crying, may be difficult to cope with but disappears eventually.

- The acquisition of motor skills depends on brain development as well as on substantial changes in bones, muscles, lungs, and heart.

- Babies depend on the adults in their environments to help them stay healthy. Although breast milk has many advantages, in some instances it is not recommended for a baby. Babies need adequate amounts of food, fortified with vitamins and minerals. Canada is a world leader of food fortification. In addition, babies need well-baby care and immunizations.

- Preterm and low-birth-weight infants tend to fall behind their full-term peers in achieving the milestones of development, but they generally catch up by age 2 or 3.

- Although post-term infants present a high risk of fetal and neonatal mortality, the rate of such deliveries has decreased in Canada due to effective medical practices.

- Canada's rate of infant mortality has declined significantly. Sudden infant death syndrome (SIDS) is the leading cause of death for post-neonatal children aged 28 days to 1 year. Rates for First Nations infants are three times the national average.

Sensory Skills

- Color vision is present at birth. Visual acuity and visual tracking skills are relatively poor at birth, but they develop rapidly in the first few months.

- Hearing skills, smell, and taste are well developed at birth. In the infant the senses of touch and motion may be the best developed.

Perceptual Skills

- The nativism/empiricism controversy is a central issue in the study of perceptual development.

- Appropriate visual stimulation in infancy is vital to the later development of visual perception. Depth perception can be judged by using three different kinds of information. Babies use kinetic cues first, then binocular cues, and finally monocular cues by about 5 to 7 months. Babies can recognize their mothers' features in the first few hours after birth.

- Babies appear to attend to, and discriminate among, speech contrasts present in all possible languages. Babies also attend to, and discriminate among, different patterns of sounds, such as melodies or speech inflections.

- The skill by which infants can integrate information from several senses is called intersensory integration. The skill by which the infant can transfer information from one sense to another is called cross-modal transfer.

LEARNING GOALS

After completing Chapter 4, students should be able to:
1. Trace the developing physical changes and abilities of children in the first 2 years after birth.
2. Summarize the concept of sensory skills in infants and outline relevant research findings.
3. Describe the sequence of events during perceptual development in the infant.

GUIDED STUDY QUESTIONS

PHYSICAL CHANGES

The Brain and the Nervous System (pp. 100–102)

Objective 4.1: Trace the development of the brain and the nervous system during the first 2 years.

1. What do the midbrain and the medulla regulate?

2. What are the most fully developed parts of the brain at birth? What is the least developed part of the brain at birth?

3. Define the following terms:
   a. synapses
   b. synaptogenesis
   c. pruning
   d. neuroplasticity

4. Describe the pattern of brain development (cycle of synaptogenesis followed by synaptic pruning).

5. List and explain two implications from the information about neurological development.

6. Define the following terms:
   a. myelinization
   b. reticular formation

7. Give examples of how the sequence of myelinization follows both the cephalocaudal and proximodistal patterns.

8. Describe myelinization of the reticular formation from infancy to the mid-20s.

Reflexes and Behavioural States (pp. 102–104)

Objective 4.2: Describe the reflexes, and behavioural states of an infant.

9. Define the following terms:
   a. adaptive reflexes
   b. primitive reflexes

10. Give examples of the two types of reflexes.

11. Weak or absent adaptive reflexes in neonates suggest that _____..

12. List the states of consciousness, and describe the characteristics of each.

13. How do cultural beliefs play a role in parents' responses to infants' sleep patterns?

14. Describe the differences in an infant's cry for pain, for anger, and for hunger.

15. Research suggests that prompt attention to a crying baby in the first 3 months actually leads to _____.

16. State the findings of a research study regarding colic conducted by a group of University of Western Ontario medical researchers.

Developing Body Systems and Motor Skills (pp. 104–107)

Objective 4.3: Describe the development of bones, muscles, lungs and the heart, and their impact on motor skill development during infancy.

17. During infancy, bones change in _____.

18. Explain how motor development is dependent on ossification.

19. Changes in _____ lead to increases in strength that enable 1-year-olds to   walk, run, jump, climb, and so on.

20. Define stamina, and explain how it is related to the lungs and heart.

21. Trace the development of motor skills by completing the following table.

Age (in months)	Locomotor Skills	Nonlocomotor Skills	Manipulative Skills
1			
2–3			
4–6			
7–9			
10–12			
13–18			

22. State the importance of the Canadian norms being developed as a part of Warren Eaton's ongoing University of Manitoba Infant Milestone Study.

23. The _____ of motor skill development is virtually the same for all children, even those with serious physical or mental handicaps.

24. List some gender differences which are evident during infancy.

Health Promotion and Wellness (pp. 107–110)

Objective 4.4: Identify the health issues of infants.

25. What are the benefits of breast milk over bottle-feeding?

26. Describe some special circumstances in which breast milk may need to be supplemented or replaced.

27. How can malnutrition in infancy impair an infant's brain?

28. Explain Canada's role in food fortification to combat malnutrition.

29. Define the following terms and describe how each is harmful to children:
    a. macronutrient malnutrition
    b. marasmus
    c. kwashiorkor
    d. micronutrient malnutrition

30. Define well-baby care.

31. List the vaccinations that Canadian infants typically receive from 2 months of age to the infant's 1st birthday.

32. How can the timing of respiratory infections that lead to ear infections be important?

The Real World/Parenting: Nutrition from Birth to 1 Year (p. 108)

Objective 4.5: Examine issues regarding nutrition in Canada from birth to 1 year.

33. Describe the recommended nutritional practice for infants from birth to 1 year.

Preterm and Low-Birth-Weight Babies (p. 110)

Objective 4.6: Discuss the developmental issues of infants who are preterm and low birth weight.

34. Infants born before 32 weeks gestation may not have _____.

35. Preterm babies are at a higher risk for _____.

36. Why might breast milk not be the best food for preterm infants?

37. Why do preterm babies move more slowly than normal-term babies through most developmental milestones? When do they catch up to their peers?

Post-Term Infants (pp. 110–112)

Objective 4.7: Discuss the general outcome of post-term infants.

38. Infants born after 42 or more weeks of gestation are considered _____.

39. Why has the rate of post-term deliveries in Canada decreased?

No Easy Answers: When do Preterm Infants Catch Up with Full-Term Infants? (p. 111)

Objective 4.8: Summarize the research findings regarding when preterm infants catch up developmentally with full-term infants.

40. Give an example of "corrected age."

41. List four factors are used in preterm infants to predict development for many years following birth.

42. In what ways do the responses of the parent to the child contribute to the rate at which the child develops?

43. Identify two factors that shape parental responses to preterm infants.

Infant Mortality in Canada (pp. 112–113)

Objective 4.9: Discuss the issue of infant mortality in Canada.

44. In Canada, what is the leading cause of death for post-neonatal children aged 28 days to 1 year?

45. Define sudden infant death syndrome (SIDS).

46. List key evidence or recommendations stated by researchers regarding the causes of SIDS.

Contributor	Evidence or Recommendation
a. low income families	
b. male babies	
c. sleeping position	
d. quilts, soft toys	
e. smoking in the home	

SENSORY SKILLS

Vision (pp. 114–115)

Objective 4.10: Trace the development of vision during infancy.

47. Define the following terms:
    a. visual acuity
    b. tracking

48. Describe the changes in an infant's visual acuity during the first 2 years after birth.

49. Explain why tracking is an important skill for infants to develop.

Hearing and Other Senses (pp.115–117)

Objective 4.11: Trace the development of hearing and other senses

50. Define auditory acuity.

51. How does the auditory acuity of an infant compare to that of an adult?

52. Describe how the ability to determine the location of a sound develops during infancy.

53. Summarize the development of the senses of smell, taste, and touch and motion.

PERCEPTUAL SKILLS

Explaining Perceptual Development (pp.117–119)

Objective 4.12: Summarize the arguments about perceptual development from the nativist, empiricist, and interactionist positions.

54. Define the following terms:
    a. nativist
    b. empiricist
    c. preference technique
    d. habituation
    e. dishabituation

55. Make an argument for each of the following positions.
    a. nativist
    b. empiricist
    c. interactionist

56. Describe the three basic methods used to study what babies experience.

Looking (pp.119–124)

Objective 4.13: Describe the importance of looking behaviour in infants.

57. Briefly state the research findings regarding early visual stimulation.

58. Differentiate the three kinds of cues that infants may use to judge depth.

59. List the ages in which depth perception develops.

60. Trace the development of what babies look at in the first few months, including faces.

Research Report: Babies' Preferences for Attractive Faces (p.122)

Objective 4.14: Summarize the research on the preferences of babies for attractive faces.

61. What were the findings of the Langlois study of the preferences of babies for attractive faces?

Listening (pp.124–125)

Objective 4.15: Describe the listening behaviour of infants.

62. Trace the development of the abilities of infants to discriminate speech sounds, including individual voices.

63. Describe the evidence that infants pay attention to patterns or sequences of sounds.

Combining Information from Several Senses (pp. 125–126)

Objective 4.16: Explain the importance of intersensory integration and cross-modal transfer.

64. Define the following skills:
    a. intersensory integration
    b. cross-modal transfer

65. Describe the development of intersensory integration and cross-modal transfer.

CRITICAL REFLECTION EXERCISES

What Babies Do

1. How would you respond to the following comment from a student colleague? "Babies drive me nuts; all they can do is eat and sleep. They can't do anything for themselves."

2. Your friend has a 10-month old girl whom she is trying to get to feed herself. She is expressing her frustration to you because her daughter keeps throwing her spoon on the floor. Explain to her why her child might be doing this. What suggestions would you have for how your friend can encourage the child to learn, yet keep the floor clean?

3. How could you design a study to see if an infant remembers a toy she saw an hour ago?

Advice for Young Parents

Imagine that you are a social worker and have been assigned the following case. Sara and her partner Jim are both 17. They are the proud parents of Katie, a 4-month-old daughter. Sara and Jim do not have much money, but they want to provide the best they can for their girl. Using information from the chapter, give at least five pieces of advice to these young parents. For each piece of advice you give, cite specific information from the textbook to support that advice.

PRACTICE QUESTIONS

1. The part of the newborn brain that is the *least* developed is the _____.
    a. brainstem
    b. hypothalamus
    c. cortex
    d. thyroid

2. One of the implications from the cyclical synaptogenesis-pruning feature of neurological development is that children will retain a more complex network of synapses in an environment that is _____.
    a. child safe
    b. intellectually challenging.
    c. family oriented
    d. free of violence

3. Neurons that are insulated with the myelin sheath _____.
    a. cannot form new neural connections
    b. can conduct the neural impulse faster
    c. become nerve muscle cells
    d. become rigid and less efficient

4. An infant's primitive reflexes do not disappear by around 6 months of age.
    a. We might suspect a neurological problem.
    b. There is nothing to worry about since they never disappear.
    c. The infant is more likely to be a boy since boys mature more slowly.
    d. It means the infant is not getting enough intellectual stimulation.

5. The typical sequence of the infant's behavioural states is _____.
    a. deep sleep, crying and fussing, active sleep, quiet awake, active awake
    b. active sleep, deep sleep, crying and fussing, active awake, quiet awake
    c. active awake, quiet awake, active sleep, quiet sleep, crying and fussing
    d. deep sleep, active sleep, quiet awake, active awake, crying and fussing

6. The purpose of the Infant Milestone Study is to develop _____.
    a. Canadian norms regarding the infant's motor skills
    b. universal norms regarding the infant's motor skills
    c. Canadian growth charts depicting the infant's age and height
    d. universal growth charts depicting the infant's age and height

7. As Canada is the world leader in food fortification, which one of the following vitamins has been added to fluid milk since the 1960s?
    a. Vitamin B
    b. Vitamin C
    c. Vitamin D
    d. Vitamin E

8. Which one of the following is the most important element of well-baby care?
    a. assessment of behavioural states
    b. screening for adaptive reflexes
    c. assessment of bone ossification
    d. vaccination against a variety of diseases

9. By what age will a preterm infant be likely to catch up developmentally with his or her peers?
    a. within the first 10 months
    b. usually between 12 and 18 months
    c. by age 2 or 3 years
    d. it depends on the gender of the preterm infant

10. One factor that has contributed to the decrease in the rate of post-term deliveries in Canada is _____.
    a. a supply of nutritious foods.
    b. the practice of inducing post-term pregnancies.
    c. genetic counselling to the pregnant mother.
    d. the practice of alternative therapies.

11. A brief period when a baby's breathing stops is called _____.
    a. apnea
    b. marasmus
    c. dyspnea
    d. arrythmia

12. Each of the following is a factor related to SIDS (sudden infant death syndrome) *except*
    _____.
    a. smoking in the home.
    b. infants sleeping in a prone position.
    c. infants attending day care.
    d. soft toys left in crib.

13. The ability to see details at a distance is called _____.
    a. visual acuity
    b. habituation
    c. intersensory ability
    d. preference technique

14. If you clap your hands near the newborn, she can judge the general direction from which the sound originates by _____.
    a. turning her head in roughly the right direction toward the sound
    b. smiling when she hears the sound
    c. crying when she hears the sound
    d. becoming passive and quiet when she hears the sound

15. Babies appear to be especially sensitive to touches on each of the following *except* the
    _____.
    a. abdomen
    b. soles of the feet
    c. face
    d. legs

16. _____ argue that perceptual skills are learned.
    a. Interactionists
    b. Evolutionists
    c. Empiricists
    d. Nativists

17. Learning to respond to a familiar stimulus as if it is new is called _____.
    a. interposition
    b. habituation
    c. intersensory integration
    d. dishabituation

18. Pictorial information, sometimes called _____, requires input from only one eye.
    a. linear perspective
    b. binocular cues
    c. monocular cues
    d. kinetic cues

19. A baby's visual attention is focused on where objects are in his world _____.
    a. between 2 and 3 months
    b. after 6 months
    c. in the first 2 months
    d. between 4 and 6 months

20. Before 2 months, babies seem to look mostly at _____.
    a. a person's mouth
    b. the internal part of a face
    c. the edges of a face
    d. a person's eyes

21. Babies seem to prefer the mother's face _____.
    a. from 1 month after birth
    b. from 3 months after birth
    c. from the earliest hours of life
    d. from 6 months after birth

22. A Canadian psychologist found that as early as 6 months of age babies listen to which one of the following?
    a. melodies and recognize patterns
    b. animal sounds and recognize patterns
    c. people's inflections and recognize who they are
    d. nursery rhymes and recognize patterns

23. The skill known as intersensory integration is best illustrated when infants _____.
    a. know what mouth movements go with which sounds
    b. sense what a babysitter will say when she approaches them
    c. know what eye movements go with which sounds
    d. sense what father will do when he picks the infant up

24. The transfer of information from one sense to another is called _____.
    a. intersensory perception
    b. cross-modal perception
    c. habituation
    d. transfer technique

25. Empirical findings indicate that cross-modal transfer is possible as early as _____ and becomes common by_____.
    a. 3 months; 1 year
    b. 1 month; 6 months
    c. 6 months; 1 year
    d. 1 month; 9 month

RESEARCH PROJECT

Student Project 6: Observation in a Newborn Nursery

You can get a feeling for what newborn babies are like, as well as learn something about observational techniques, by arranging to visit a newborn nursery in a local hospital. Your instructor will have made arrangements with one or more hospitals for permission for such observations. You will need to sign up for a specific observation time.

At all times, remember that newborn nurseries are complex and busy, and they cannot tolerate lots of questions or intrusions. So be unobtrusive and undemanding and do as you are told.

Procedure

Position yourself at one side of the window outside the newborn nursery, leaving room at the window for others to see their newborns. From this vantage point, observe one baby for approximately half an hour. Proceed in the following way:

BABY'S STATES

30-second intervals	Deep Sleep	Active Sleep	Quiet Awake	Active Awake	Crying & Fussing
1					
2					
3					

1. Set up a score sheet that looks something like the one shown above, continuing the list for 60 30-second intervals.

2. Reread the material in Table 4.1 (p. 103 in the text) until you know the main features of the five states as well as possible. You will need to focus on the eyes (open versus closed, rapid eye movement), the regularity of the baby's breathing, and the amount of body movement.

3. Select an infant in the nursery and observe that infant's state every 30 seconds for half an hour. For each 30-second interval, note on your score sheet the state that best describes the infant over the preceding 30 seconds. Do not select an infant to observe who is in deep sleep at the beginning. Pick an infant who seems to be in an in-between state (active sleep or quiet awake), so that you can see some variation over the half hour observation.

4. If you can arrange it, you might do this observation with a partner, each of you scoring the same infant's state independently. When the half hour is over, compare notes. How often did you agree on the infant's state? What might have been producing the disagreements?

5. When you discuss or write about the project, consider the following issues: Did the infant appear to have cycles of states? What were they? What effect, if any, do you think the nursery environment might have had on the baby's state? If you worked with a partner, how much agreement or disagreement did you have? Why?

You may find yourself approached by family members of the babies in the nursery, asking what you are doing, why you have a clipboard and a stopwatch. Be sure to reassure the parents/partners or grandparents that your presence does not in any way suggest that there is anything wrong with any of the babies. Let them know that you are doing a school project on observation. You may even want to show them the text describing the various states.

Alternative Project

The same project can be completed in a home setting with any infant under 1 or 2 months of age, with appropriate permission obtained from the baby's parents/partners. You should observe the infant when he or she is lying in a crib or another sleeping location where it is possible for the child to move fairly freely (an infant seat won't do, nor will a baby carrier of any kind).

CHAPTER 4 ANSWER KEY

Guided Study Questions

11. Weak or absent adaptive reflexes in neonates suggest <u>that the brain is not functioning properly and that the baby requires additional assessment.</u>

15. Research suggests that prompt attention to a crying baby in the first 3 months actually <u>leads to less crying later in infancy.</u>

17. During infancy, <u>bones change in size, number, and composition.</u>

19. Changes in <u>muscle composition</u> lead to increases in strength that enable 1-year-olds to walk, run, climb, and so on.

23. The <u>sequence</u> of motor skills development is virtually the same for all children, even those with serious physical and mental handicaps.

28. <u>Micronutrients</u> have been added to Canada's food supply for about 50 years.

34. Infants born before 32 weeks of gestation may not have <u>adaptive reflexes</u> that are sufficiently developed to enable them to survive.

35. Preterm babies are at a higher risk for <u>neurological impairments, respiratory difficulties, infections, and neonatal and infant mortality.</u>

38. Infants born after 42 or more weeks of gestation are considered <u>post-term.</u>

39. The rate of post-term deliveries in Canada has decreased in part because of the effective use of <u>ultrasound dating and the practice of inducing post-term pregnancies.</u>

Practice Questions

1. c	6. a	11. a	16. c	21. c
2. b	7. c	12. c	17. d	22. a
3. b	8. d	13. a	18. c	23. c
4. a	9. c	14. a	19. c	24. b
5. d	10. b	15. d	20. b	25. b

COGNITIVE DEVELOPMENT IN INFANCY

OVERVIEW OF CHAPTER

Cognitive development in infancy includes changes in thinking, learning and remembering, and the emergence of language skills. This chapter also discusses measuring infants' intelligence.

Cognitive Changes

- In Piaget's sensorimotor stage, infants begin with schemes they are born with and accommodate them to their experiences. The development of object permanence is the most important cognitive milestone.

- Recent research suggests that Piaget underestimated infants' capabilities and their inborn abilities.

- A few developmental researchers have investigated object permanence within the more general context of infants' understanding of what objects are and how they behave. The term "object concept" refers to this understanding.

Learning, Categorizing, and Remembering

- From the first moments following birth, babies are capable of learning in a variety of ways, such as classical, operant conditioning, and schematic learning.

- Infants use categories to organize information. The sophistication of these categories increases over the first 2 years.

- Babies as young as 3 months of age can remember specific objects and their own actions with those objects over period of as long as a week. This remembering ability must have some form of internal representation at a time well before Piaget supposed. With age, their memories become increasingly less tied to specific cues or contexts.

- Recent research has indicated that habituation tasks have a high potential as measures of infant intelligence.

The Beginnings of Language

- Behaviourists claim that babies learn language by being reinforced for making word-like sounds. On the other hand, nativists argue that children's comprehension and production of language is innate. Constructivists say that language development is a subprocess of cognitive development.

- An eclectic approach includes elements of all three perspectives, and seems to fit with research showing that both environmental and internal variables affect language development.

- Babies' earliest sounds are cries, followed by cooing, then by babbling. The importance of babbling has been studied in regards to language development. At 9 months, babies typically use meaningful gestures and can understand more words than they can produce.

- The first spoken words typically occur at about 1 year, after which children acquire words slowly. At about 24 months, they add new words rapidly and generalize them to many more situations.

- Simple two-word sentences appear in children's expressive language at about 18 months.

- The rate of language development varies from one child to another. Some toddlers   display an expressive style while others show a referential style.

- The sequence of language development seems to hold true for babies in all cultures. The word order of a child's telegraphic speech is dependent on what language the child is learning.

LEARNING GOALS

After completing Chapter 2, students should be able to:
1. Describe how thinking changes in the first 2 years after birth.
2. Describe how babies learn and remember.
3. Detail the language skills that babies develop during their first 2 years.
4. Describe how psychologists measure intelligence in infants.

GUIDED STUDY QUESTIONS

COGNITIVE CHANGES

Piaget's View of the First 2 Years (pp. 131–134)

Objective 5.1: Explain Piaget's view of sensorimotor intelligence.

1. Define the following terms:
   a. sensorimotor stage
   b. primary circular reactions
   c. secondary circular reactions
   d. means-end behaviour
   e. tertiary circular reactions
   f. object permanence
   g. deferred imitation

2. Fill in the following table indicating the name of each of the sensorimotor substages and characteristics of each:

Substage	Name	Characteristic
1 (0–1 month)		
2 (1–4 months)		
3 (4–8 months)		
4 (8–12 months)		
5 (12–18 months)		
6 (18–24 months)		

3. Trace the development of object permanence across the first year.

4. Trace the development of deferred imitation in infancy.

Development in the Information Age: What Do Babies Really Learn from Watching Television? (p. 134)

Objective 5.2: Summarize the research on what babies learn from watching television.

5. What do infants really learn from watching television?

Challenges to Piaget's View (pp. 134–136)

Objective 5.3: Identify the challenges to Piaget's view.

6. Describe the recent research about object permanence that challenges Piaget's findings.

7. List two important exceptions to the general confirmation of Piaget's sequence of imitation.

8. List three reasons why the findings about deferred imitation are significant.

Alternative Approaches (pp. 136–139)

Objective 5.4: Summarize the research findings of object permanence within the context of infants' global understanding of objects.

9. Compare the research findings of Spelke, Baillargeon, and Xu in regard to object permanence

10. What was the main conclusion arrived at by the researchers regarding Piaget and object permanence?

LEARNING, CATEGORIZING, AND REMEMBERING

Conditioning and Modeling (pp. 139–140)

Objective 5.5: Describe how infants learn through classical conditioning, operant conditioning, and modelling.

11. Give examples of the ways infants learn through the following processes:
    a. classical conditioning
    b. operant conditioning
    c. modelling:

Schematic learning (pp. 140–141)

Objective 5.6: Give examples of schematic learning.

12. Define schematic learning.

13. Describe how infants build and use categories as they take in information, including the concepts of superordinates and hierarchical categorization.

Memory (pp. 141–142)

Objective 5.7: Summarize the recent research on infants' memory.

14. What do the research findings on infants' memory demonstrate?

Measuring Intelligence in Infancy (pp. 142–143)

Objective 5.8: Summarize the research on measuring intelligence in infancy.

15. Define Bayley Scales of Infant Development and state the scales' usefulness and drawbacks.

16. How have habituation tasks been of value as measures of infant intelligence?

17. Describe the usefulness of the Fagan Test of Infant Intelligence for special populations.

THE BEGINNINGS OF LANGUAGE

Theoretical Perspective (pp. 143–145)

Objective 5.9: Differentiate among the theoretical perspectives of the development of language.

18. Define the following terms:
    a. language acquisition device
    b. motherese (or infant directed speech)
    c. constructivists

19. Differentiate among the following perspectives on the development of language. Include examples *of each.*

Theory	Proponent(s)	Description and Examples
Behaviourist		
Nativist		
Constructivist		

20. List two examples of evidence in support of the constructivist view.

An Eclectic Approach to Language Development (pp. 145–146)

Objective 5.10: Describe the eclectic approach to language development.

21. State the effects of poverty on exposure to language.

22. Give examples of factors that contribute to a child's language development.

23. Give examples of how adults use expansion (or recasting) when speaking to infants.

24. List characteristics of motherese that seem attractive to babies.

25. List the four steps of language development that supports the integration of the nativist and constructivist position.

Speech Perception (p. 147)

Objective 5.11: Describe the research on babies' perception of speech sounds.

26. Give examples of babies' perception of speech sounds.

Sounds, Gestures, and Word Meanings (pp. 147, 148–150)

Objective 5.12: Trace the pattern of pre-language development in infants.

27. Give examples of the development of sounds that babies produce.

28. List two important reasons for babies' babbling.

29. Define receptive language.

30. List the series of changes that seem to come together at 9 or 10 months.

Research Report: Setting the Stage for Language Acquisition and Word Learning (pp. 148–149)

Objective 5.13: Summarize the research on speech perception and language development.

31. Describe the developmental stages for speech perception and language development.

32. Differentiate between grammatical words and lexical words.

33. State the importance of the research that demonstrates that infants show a clear preference for lexical words.

The First Words (pp. 150–151)

Objective 5.14: Describe the research about the infant's first words.

34. Define the following terms:
     a. expressive language
     b. holophrases
     c. naming explosion

35. State what Choi (2000) found regarding infants patterns of learning nouns and verbs.

The First Sentences (pp. 151–152)

Objective 5.15: Describe the development of a child's first sentence.

36. Define the following terms:
     a. telegraphic speech
     b. inflections

37. Describe the distinguishing features of babies' first sentences.

Individual Differences in Language Development (pp. 152, 154–155)

Objective 5.16: Discuss the research findings about individual differences in language development.

38. Define the following terms:
     a. mean length of utterance
     b. expressive style
     c. referential style

39. Describe the subset of children who talk late and who do not catch up.

40. Differentiate between expressive style and referential style, and give examples of how they are related to a child's cognitive development.

No Easy Answers: One Language or Two? (p. 153)

Objective 5.17: Summarize the advantages and disadvantages of learning two languages.

41.   Define metalinguistic ability.

42.   List at least four advantages of growing up bilingual.

43.   List at least two disadvantages of growing up bilingual

Language Development Across Cultures (pp. 155–156)

Objective 5.18: Describe the cross-cultural differences in language development in infancy.

44.   List four similarities in language development across cultures.

45.   Give examples of cross-cultural differences in learning language.

PRACTICE QUESTIONS

1.   Piaget's first stage, when infants use information from their sense and motor actions to learn about the world, is called _____.
     a.   sensorimotor stage
     b.   preoperational stage
     c.   concrete operational stage
     d.   formal operational stage

2.   Means-end behaviour is _____.
     a.   randomly displayed
     b.   carried out in a pursuit of a specific goal
     c.   oriented around external objects
     d.   carried out to learn more about the world

3.   Which of the following is an example of a tertiary circular reaction?
     a.   You touch the child's cheek, and he turns his head the opposite direction.
     b.   The child verbally imitates the actions of others.
     c.   A child repeatedly throws food on the floor to see what will happen.
     d.   The child no longer needs a pacifier to be comforted.

4.   The understanding that a toy exists even if we roll it under the couch is called
     _____.
     a.   object permanence
     b.   conservation
     c.   concept consistency
     d.   schematic processing

5.   The best thing that babies learn from watching television is _____.
      a.   phonological awareness
      b.   the behaviour of watching television
      c.   reading recognition
      d.   the acquisition of object permanence

6.   A criticism of Piaget's theory is that _____.
      a.   Piaget underestimated the cognitive abilities of infants
      b.   development is set in the formative years
      c.   Piaget did not measure the infant's ability to carry out a motor behaviour
      d.   object permanence could be simply explained

7.   Each of the following statements is true of the recent findings about deferred imitation
      except that _____.
      a.   babies may be more skillful than Piaget thought
      b.   infants learn specific behaviours through modeling, even when they have no chance to
           imitate the behavior immediately
      c.   more abilities than Piaget suggested may be built in from the beginning and may
           develop continuously rather than in stages in infancy
      d.   deferred imitation begins at 14 months

8.   A few developmentalist researchers have investigated object permanence within the more
      general context of infants' understanding of what objects are and how they behave. Which
      one of the following terms refers to this understanding?
      a.   object concept
      b.   objectivity of single objects
      c.   object accommodation
      d.   subjectivity of single objects

9.   Newborns learn by operant conditioning through the use of reinforcers. Which one of the
      following reinforcer is the most effective for mother-infant interaction?
      a.   sweet liquids
      b.   mother's heartbeat
      c.   mother's voice
      d.   background music

10.   Infants can learn by watching models, especially in the _____.
      a.   2nd year
      b.   first 6 months
      c.   1st year
      d.   beginning of their 3rd birthday

11. Schematic learning assumes that _____.
    a. babies attempt to categorize their experiences
    b. children cannot learn unless the information is organized for them
    c. babies will only learn if they are reinforced for exploring
    d. learning is sequential and orderly

12. Which of the following is an accurate statement about infant memory?
    a. Infants younger than 6 months old do not retain memories.
    b. The expansion of memory is pre-programmed.
    c. Infants develop very general memories for information.
    d. Early infant memory is specific to the context in which it was learned.

13. The psychologist would use Bayley Scales of Infant Development to measure which one of the following infant skills?
    a. auditory
    b. habituation
    c. motor and sensory
    d. cognitive

14. Infants who suffer from _____ cannot perform many of the tasks required by Bayley Scales.
    a. cerebral palsy
    b. eating disorders
    c. depression
    d. colic

15. Which one of the following is the most accurate statement about infant intelligence tests?
    a. Babies who habituate quickly when they are 4 or 5 months old are likely to have higher intelligence test scores at later ages.
    b. The Bayley Scales of Infant Development accurately predict a child's intelligence at age 10.
    c. None of the infant intelligence tests correlate with intelligence test scores at later ages.
    d. Infant intelligence tests are based on individual differences in cognitive abilities.

16. The theory of language development that proposes that infants learn language because they are guided by an innate language processor called LAD is known as the _____.
    a. holophrase acquisition
    b. behaviourist explanation
    c. nativist explanation
    d. language acquisition device

17. Another name for motherease is _____.
    a. infant-directed speech
    b. metalinguistic ability
    c. babbling
    d. expressive language

18. Very young infants can discriminate among all sounds that appear in any language. What happens to this ability as they age?
    a. They get even better at it because they are learning to speak.
    b. There is very little change.
    c. There are modest improvements but nothing dramatic.
    d. They lose this ability after 6 months to 1 year.

19. Which one of the following best signifies the importance of babbling?
    a. indicates generic oral-motor behaviour
    b. related to the beginnings of language production
    c. includes only the sounds that the baby hears
    d. indicates the knowledge of vowel sounds

20. A child points to Daddy's shoe and says, "Daddy." This is an example of _____.
    a. referential style
    b. expressive style
    c. holophrase
    d. personification

21. Johnny, age 18 months, informs you that he "eat cookie." You know that this type of speech is called _____.
    a. adaptive
    b. receptive
    c. threshold
    d. telegraphic

22. Inflections are _____.
    a. examples of the dialogic reading style
    b. grammatical markers
    c. metalinguistic ability
    d. recasting

23. A child's early vocabulary that uses words linked to social relationships rather than objects is called _____.
    a. hierarchical style
    b. referential style

    c. expressive style

    d. metalinguistic ability

24. In a wide variety of cultures babies begin to use their first words when they are how many months old?

    a. 12

    b. 15

    c. 14

    d. 13

25. Which statement is true about language development across cultures?

    a. Babies the world over coo before they babble.

    b. Telegraphic speech precedes holophrases in every language.

    c. Babies speak language before they really understand it.

    d. Not all cultures have expressive-style toddlers.

CASE STUDY

You are visiting your neighbour whose child, Bobby, is around 15 months old. He is sitting in a high chair. His mother gives him a toy which he throws on the floor to one side of the high chair while laughing. Meanwhile, his mother is holding his 10-month-old cousin Jennifer, who is stretching out her hand making whimpering sounds demanding the toy. You notice that mother is repeatedly picking up the toy and giving it back to Bobby. Each time she returns the toy he laughs or grimaces and throws it on the floor, sometimes on one side of the high chair sometimes on the other. Each time she gives him the toy her voice escalates and she scolds him for the behaviour. Jennifer meanwhile continues to whine and reach out.

1. From your understanding of the sensorimotor stage, what substage is Bobby portraying by his repetitive actions?

2. What type of language is Jennifer using?

3. From your understanding of Piaget's sensorimotor stage what can you say about Bobby to his mother?

CHAPTER 5 ANSWER KEY

Practice Questions

1.	a	6.	a	11.	a	16.	c	21.	d
2.	b	7.	d	12.	d	17.	a	22.	b
3.	c	8.	a	13.	c	18.	d	23.	c
4.	a	9..	c	14.	a	19.	b	24.	a
5.	b	10.	a	15.	a	20	c	25.	a

Case Study

See Chapter 5, p. 132.

1. Bobby is exploring the environment and is demonstrating tertiary circular reaction.
2. Jennifer is using gestural language (p. 150).
3. The child is behaving naturally, and in doing so he is using different facial expressions and behaviour.

CHAPTER 6

SOCIAL AND PERSONALITY DEVELOPMENT IN INFANCY

OVERVIEW OF CHAPTER

Developmentalists of different theoretical orientations agree that the formation of a strong emotional connection to a primary caregiver early in life is critical to healthy child development and has important implications across the entire lifespan.

Theories of Social and Personality Development

- Freud believed that the weaning process in the oral stage of development influenced the development of personality. Erikson emphasized the role of the family in providing for all of the infant's needs, thereby instilling a sense of trust.

- Ethologists believe that the first 2 years constitute a sensitive period for attachment in human infants, and that infants who fail to form a close relationship with a primary caregiver are at risk for future social and personality problems.

Attachment

- The development of synchrony, a set of mutually reinforcing and interlocking behaviours that characterize most interactions between parent and infant, is essential to the development of the parents' attachment to the infant.

- Canadian researchers found that both mothers and fathers can be equally sensitive to the needs of their children. Fathers tend to initiate more physically playful behaviours with their children than do mothers.

- According to Bowlby, the baby's attachment to the parents emerges gradually across three stages: nonfocused orienting and signalling; proximity promoting; and secure base behaviour.

- Children differ in the security of their first attachments and in the internal working model that they develop. The secure infant uses the parent as a safe base for exploration and can be readily consoled by the parent.

- Caregiver characteristics such as age, depression, and a history of abuse can affect attachment quality.

- Preterm and low-birth-weight (LBW) infants are at a greater risk for developing insecure attachments.

- Children who were securely attached to their mothers in infancy are more sociable and more positive in their behaviour toward friends and siblings than those who were insecurely attached. The internal model of attachment that individuals develop in infancy affects how they parent their own babies.

Personality, Temperament, and Self-Concept

- A few key dimensions appear in the lists of dimensions described by many of the key researchers. They are activity level, inhibition, negative emotionality, and effortful control/task persistence.

- Strong evidence exists that temperamental differences have a genetic component. However, temperament is not totally determined by heredity or by ongoing physiological processes. A child's built-in temperament shapes her interactions with the world and affects others' responses to the child.

- Infant temperament may affect security of attachment. The goodness-of-fit between an infant's temperament and the ways the surrounding environment responds to him is the real factor in correlations between temperament and attachment.

- The infant develops the awareness of a separate self and the understanding of self-permanence (called the subjective self) and an awareness of herself as an object in the world (the objective self). In addition, the infant begins to develop awareness that other people have separate thoughts and intentions. An emotional self develops in the first year as the range of emotions develops, as well as the ability to use information about emotions.

Effects of Nonparental Care

- The nonparental care of children has evolved as more women have entered the work force. Since 2000, Canada's *Federal Employment Insurance Act* has extended the duration of benefits for parental leave. Consequently, approximately 50% of mothers remained with their babies for a period of 1 to 2 years. Interestingly, in 2007, 55% of fathers took time out from work for their children. However, still more mothers than fathers are taking leave.

- More Canadian mothers have now met the global breastfeeding standard set by public health organizations, including the World Health Organization (WHO).

- Comparing parental care to nonparental care is difficult because there are so many kinds of nonparental care arrangements.

- Nonparental care of children is now a part of the Canadian way of life. The most common pattern, especially for infants and toddlers, is for the child to be cared for by a nonrelative. Income levels are one factor determining the placement of children.

- High-quality daycare has beneficial effects on many children's overall cognitive development. This is especially helpful for disadvantaged children but confers some benefits on middle-class children.

- Some studies show that children with a history of daycare are more aggressive in their peer relationships whereas other studies show them to be more socially skilful.

- Some studies indicate a small difference in security of attachment between infants who enter daycare, and those reared at home; other studies show little difference.

LEARNING GOALS

After completing Chapter 5, students should be able to:
1. Summarize the key points of the major theoretical perspectives.
2. Discuss the development of attachment in infancy.
3. Explain the development of personality, temperament, and self-concept.
4. Describe the effects of nonparental care.

GUIDED STUDY QUESTIONS

THEORIES OF SOCIAL AND PERSONALITY DEVELOPMENT

Psychoanalytic Perspectives (p. 162)

Objective 6.1: Describe the psychoanalytic perspective of social and personality development.

1. Define the following terms:
   a. oral stage
   b. symbiotic relationship
   c. trust versus mistrust stage

2. What was Freud's belief about the importance of the oral stage? Why was the weaning process important?

3. Describe the importance of the symbiotic relationship between the mother and the infant.

4. How does Erikson's theory differ from Freud's? Why is the trust versus mistrust stage so important?

Ethological Perspectives (pp. 162–163)

Objective 6.2: Describe the ethological perspective of social and personality development.

5. Define the following terms:
   a. attachment theory
   b. affectional bond

    c. attachment

    d. reactive attachment disorder

6. What was Bowlby's argument?

7. Distinguish between affectional bonds and attachment. Give examples of each.

8. Ethologists believe that the first 2 years of life constitute a _____. They claim that infants who fail to form a close relationship with a primary caregiver are at risk for _____.

No Easy Answers: Adoption and Development (p. 163–164)

Objective 6.3: Summarize the issues involved with adoption and development.

9. Why are the child's circumstances prior to adoption important to consider?

10. Many potential difficulties exist in parenting adopted at-risk children. There are a few important facts that parents who adopt them should keep in mind. List three of these important facts.

ATTACHMENT

The Parents' Attachment to the Infant (pp. 165–166)

Objective 6.4: Describe the development of the parent's bond to the infant.

11. Define synchrony and give examples.

12. Give an example of how the degree of synchrony in parent-infant interactions seems to contribute to cognitive development.

13. Past the first few weeks, what are the signs of a kind of specialization of parental behaviours with infants and toddlers?

14. Canadian researchers found that fathers can be _____.

15. State the differences in ways that infants respond to mothers compared to how they respond to fathers.

The Infant's Attachment to the Parents (pp. 166–168)

Objective 6.5: Describe the development of the infant's bond to the parents.

16. Complete the following table with information about the three stages that Bowlby suggested in the development of the infant's attachment:

Stage	Name of Stage	Age	Attachment Behaviours
1			
2			
3			

17. Define the following terms:
    a. stranger anxiety
    b. separation anxiety
    c. social referencing
    d. affect dysregulation

18. How do infants express stranger anxiety? Separation anxiety?

19. How do babies between 8 and 24 months typically respond when they are frightened or under stress?

Variations in Attachment Quality (pp. 168–170)

Objective 6.6: List and describe the variations in attachment quality.

20. Define the internal model, and give examples.

21. By age five, most children have clear internal models of _____, _____, and a model of _____. Once formed, such models _____ __.

22. Define the following terms:
    a. Strange Situation
    b. secure attachment
    c. avoidant attachment
    d. ambivalent attachment
    e. disorganized/disoriented attachment

23. List, in order, the eight episodes in the Strange Situation to measure attachment.

24. What is the new way of measuring attachment developed by two Canadian researchers?

25. Define the following terms, and give examples of each:
    a. emotional availability
    b. contingent responsiveness

26. A low level of _____ appears to be an ingredient in any type of insecure attachment.

27. What are the distinct antecedents for each pattern of insecure attachment?
    a. avoidant
    b. ambivalent
    c. disorganized/disoriented

28. What may happen to the consistency of security or insecurity if the child's circumstances change in some major way? Give examples.

29. How does the quality of the child's relationship with each parent determine the child's security with that specific adult?

Caregiver Characteristics and Attachment (pp. 170–171)

Objective 6.7 Describe how the characteristics of the caregiver influence attachment.

30. How might marital status affect attachment?

31. Differentiate caregiving behaviours between adolescent and older mothers.

32. How might a mother's depression affect an infant's nutrition?

33. List the three problematic behaviour patterns that may occur when depressed mothers interact with their infants. Describe the responses of the babies to their mother's behaviour patterns.

34. How does the behaviour of a mother with panic disorder affect the synchrony with her infant?

Preterm and Low-Birth-Weight Infants (pp. 171–172)

Objective 6.8: Identify the factors of preterm and low-birth-weight babies that put them at risk for developing insecure attachment patterns.

35. Why are very ill preterm and low-birth-weight babies considered to be at a significantly greater risk for developing insecure attachments than are those babies who are healthy?

36. Give examples of the temperamental characteristics of preterm infants that place them at risk of insecure attachment.

37. Why is insecure attachment an additional risk for preterm and low-birth-weight babies?

Long-Term Consequences of Attachment Quality (p. 172)

Objective 6.9: Summarize the research on the long-term consequences of attachment quality.

38. List six behaviours of children who were rated as securely attached to their mothers in infancy.

39. List five behaviours of adolescents who were rated as securely attached to their mothers in infancy.

40. List two behaviours of adolescents who were rated as insecure attachments—
    particularly those with avoidant attachments—in infancy.

41. How does attachment in infancy predict sociability in adulthood?

42. Give examples of how an adult's internal model of attachment affects his or her
    parenting behaviours.

43. How does attachment history affect parental attitudes?

PERSONALITY, TEMPERAMENT, AND SELF-CONCEPT

Dimensions of Temperament (p. 173)

Objective 6.10: Explain the dimensions of temperament.

44. Define the following terms:
    a. personality
    b. temperament

45. Identify and describe the three types of temperament proposed by Thomas and Chess.

46. Describe each of the following key dimensions of temperament:
    a. activity level
    b. inhibition
    c. negative emotionality
    d. effortful control/task persistence.

Origins and Stability of Temperament (pp. 174–176)

Objective 6.11: Describe the research on the inheritance of temperament.

47. Describe the evidence that temperamental differences are inborn.

48. Explain how each of the following physiological patterns might account for
    temperamental differences.
    a. differing thresholds for arousal in parts of the brain
    b. function of the neurotransmitters dopamine and serotonin
    c. frontal lobe symmetry

49. List three temperament/environment interactions that tend to strengthen built-in
    qualities. Give examples of each.

50. List the characteristics of temperament that seem to be consistent over rather long
    periods of infancy and childhood.

Temperament and Attachment (pp. 176–177)

Objective 6.12: Explain the relationship between temperament and attachment.

51. Describe the meaning of the temperament dimension in infancy called effortful control.

52. Individual differences in infant temperament may also be related to _____.

53. Give examples of how infant temperament may be related to security of attachment. Include the importance of synchrony.

54. Define goodness-of-fit; and give examples of its importance in attachment.

Research Report: Gender Differences in Temperament (pp. 177–178)

Objective 6.13: Summarize the gender differences in temperament.

55. List the differences in temperament found in some research studies.

56. Describe how temperamental stereotyping may affect the quality of the parent-infant relationship.

Self-Concept (pp. 178–181)

Objective 6.14: Trace the steps in the process of the development of the self-concept.

57. During the same months that the baby is creating an internal model of attachment and expressing his or her own unique temperament, he or she is also developing an

   _____.

58. State the finding of a recent Canadian study regarding the timing of the emergence of an infant's capacity to differentiate objects.

59. Define the subjective, or existential, self.

60. Define the objective, or categorical, self.

61. Describe the research on the point by which a child has developed the initial self-awareness that defines the beginning of the objective self.

62. In Bowlby's language, a child apparently creates a/an _____.

63. Development of the emotional self begins when _____.

64. Trace the development of the emotional self by completing the following table:

Age	*Behaviour*	*Emotions Expressions*
2–3 months		
5–7 months		
End of 1st year		
Near the middle of 2nd year		

65. Explain the meaning of the term "joint attention" by giving an example.

EFFECTS OF NONPARENTAL CARE

Difficulties in Studying Nonparental Care (pp. 183–184)

Objective 6.15: List the issues involved in studying nonparental care.

66. List at least five factors that may be involved in the issue of daycare that confound the question of how much impact nonparental care has on infants and young children.

67. What is the most common pattern of nonparental care?

Effects on Cognitive Development and Peer Relations (pp. 184–186)

Objective 6.16: State the advantages and disadvantages of daycare on cognitive development and peer relations.

68. There is a good deal of evidence to indicate that_____
    has beneficial effects on many children's overall _____. This
    effect is particularly strong for children from _____.

69. Describe the findings of the effects of a high quality daycare experience on cognitive development in middle-class children.

70. Describe the evidence that researchers have found on the impact of daycare on children's personalities.

71. What evidence is there that daycare has a negative impact on peer relations?

72. What is one possible resolution of the conflicting evidence?

Effects on Attachment (p, 186)

Objective 6.17: Describe the research on the impact of daycare on the effects of children's attachment to parents.

73.   State the findings that are contributing to the current controversy regarding the impact of daycare on children's attachment to parents.

74.   What are some possible explanations for this controversy?

The Real World/Parenting: Choosing a Daycare Centre (p. 187)

Objective 6.18: Identify the criteria for choosing a high-quality daycare setting.

75.   Identify 14 criteria, as suggested by the Canadian Child Care Federation, for choosing either a centre or home daycare.

CRITICAL REFLECTION EXERCISE

Attachment

Imagine that you work in a daycare centre. You notice that one parent is having a difficult time dropping off his son. The child clings to the father, in apparent fear of being left behind. He kicks and screams when the father walks away and then seems fine. You also notice that the child seems very angry at his father when the father returns to pick him up. The boy refuses to look his father in the eye, does not want to be picked up, and will not answer the father's questions about how the boy's day went. Using information from the text, provide answers to the following questions:

1.   According to Ainsworth's categories of attachment, what kind of attachment bond seems to have developed between this parent and child?

2.   What types of interaction between the parent and child seem to lead to this type of attachment bond?

3.   What effects might this attachment bond have on the child's developing sense of self? Why?

4.   What things might you do, when interacting with this child in the daycare, to ensure that this same type of relationship does not develop between you and this child? Discuss at least four things that you might do.

PRACTICE QUESTIONS

1. The theorist who proposed that infants must resolve their conflict of trust versus mistrust was_____.
    a. Ainsworth
    b. Bowlby
    c. Erikson
    d. Freud

2. A relatively long-enduring tie in which the partner is important as a unique individual and is interchangeable with no other is called _____.
    a. trust versus mistrust
    b. an affectional bond
    c. personality theory
    d. reactive attachment

3. The mutual, interlocking pattern of attachment behaviours between a parent and an infant is called _____.
    a. synchrony
    b. attachment
    c. temperament
    d. conversation

4   When Robbie, an infant, is interacting with his father he will_____.
    a. smile gradually and subtly
    b. laugh and wiggle with delight
    c. initially cry and squirm
    d. snuggle immediately

5. An infant's internal model includes each of the following elements except the child's
    _____.
    a. expectation of affection or rebuff
    b. sense of assurance that the other is really a safe base for exploration
    c. confidence (or lack of it) that the attachment figure will be available or reliable
    d. anticipation of affect dysregulation

6. A child who does not seek much contact with the mother after she returns from a short absence is probably _____.
    a. securely attached
    b. attached/avoidant
    c. attached/ambivalent
    d. attached/disorganized/disoriented

7. What pair of factors seems to be the most important in developing a secure attachment between parent and child?
   a. acceptance of the infant; contingent responsiveness
   b. whether the baby was a planned child; the educational level of the parents
   c. the relative temperament of the child; parental self-esteem
   d. emotional connection to the child; the age of the parents

8. Which of the following statements about the relationship between the mother's age and attachment is most accurate?
   a. The mother's age is not a factor in attachment.
   b. Adolescent mothers are more likely to describe their babies as "difficult."
   c. Mothers in their 30s are more likely to describe their babies as "difficult."
   d. Training in child development has no effect on the mother's ability to interpret an infant's behaviour.

9. Which one of the following statements about the relationship between the mother's depression and attachment is most accurate?
   a. Depressed mothers are always less sensitive and responsive to their babies' needs than nondepressed mothers.
   b. When mothers are depressed, the babies' own facial expressions and behaviours suggest that they are depressed as well.
   c. All depressed mothers interact with their babies in the same way.
   d. Children of depressed mothers are more likely to form a secure attachment than are children of nondepressed mothers.

10. Which one of the following statements about preterm and low-birth-weight babies is most accurate?
    a. Parents of a very ill preterm baby are more attached to the baby because it might die than are parents of a full-term infant.
    b. Preterm infants do not display temperamental characteristics that place them at risk for insecure attachment.
    c. Most preterm and low-birth-weight babies seem to differ little, compared to full-term infants, in their attachment patterns.
    d. Preterm and low-birth-weight babies are more cuddly than are full-term babies.

11. Secure attachments in childhood have been linked to _____ in adolescence.
    a. self-esteem problems
    b. rebellious backlash
    c. earlier sexual experiences
    d. more intimate friendships

12. Parents with a history of insecure attachments are more likely to view their infants in a/an _____ way.
    a. indifferent
    b. clinging
    c. positive
    d. negative

13. Which of the following is *not* a dimension of temperament described by many of the key researchers?
    a. activity level
    b. emotional maturity
    c. inhibition
    d. negative emotionality

14. Which statement is most accurate about where temperament qualities come from?
    a. Temperament is developed in response to parental style.
    b. Gender differences can account for most differences in temperament.
    c. Temperament differences in infancy appear to be genetically based.
    d. Early differences in temperament are a combination of the infant's mood and parental style.

15. Developmentalists propose that it is not temperament per se that influences attachment. Rather it is the _____ between the infant's temperament and her environment.
    a. self-concept
    b. niche-picking
    c. synchrony
    d. goodness-of-fit

16. According to Piaget, what cognitive skill seems linked to the child's understanding of his subjective self?
    a. object permanence
    b. conservation
    c. reversible thinking
    d. transformative thinking

17. The _____ is sometimes called the categorical self because once the child achieves self-awareness, the process of defining the self involves placing the self in a whole series of categories.
    a. subjective self
    b. objective self
    c. emotional self
    d. developmental self

18. At about what age should we expect a child to demonstrate self-related emotions such as pride or shame?
    a. 30 months
    b. birth
    c. 24 months
    d. 12–18 months

19. Betty, age 2, wants to redirect her mother's attention to her new doll. She will attempt to do so by _____.

a. grabbing her mother's clothing
b. pointing her finger
c. throwing a temper tantrum
d. crying out loud

20. The family income of Jane, age 3, is in excess of $100,000 per year. Jane's family is most likely to place her, for care, with:
    a. her grandmother
    b. her aunt
    c. a nonrelative
    d. her godmother

21. Which of the following is probably *not* one of the difficulties encountered in studying nonparental care?
    a. Infants enter these care arrangements at different ages.
    b. Nonparental care varies hugely in quality.
    c. Most nonparental care occurs in daycare centres.
    d. Too many arrangements are all lumped under the title nonparental care.

22. What has been discovered about the effects of daycare on cognitive development?
    a. Children spending time in daycare exhibit more emotional problems.
    b. Children from poorer families are especially disadvantaged by daycare.
    c. There are no consistent findings about the effects of daycare.
    d. Cognitively enriched daycare experiences tend to positively affect children.

23. Which of the following statements is true about the effects of daycare on peer relations?
    a. All children in daycare are much more sociable, more popular, and have better peer-play skills than do those reared primarily at home.
    b. All kindergarten children who have spent time in daycare are more aggressive and less popular with their peers by school age than are children who have been reared entirely at home.
    c. It is not daycare itself that is at issue, but the child's actual experience on a day-to-day basis.
    d. The age at which children enter nonparental care is more important than the total length of time in daycare.

24. Which of the following is the central question concerning the effects of nonparental care on attachment?
    a. Do children in daycare form a stronger bond to their daycare caregiver than to their parents?
    b. Can an infant or toddler develop a secure attachment to her mother or father if she is repeatedly separated from them?
    c. How many hours a week can children be in daycare without it affecting their attachment to their parents?
    d. What is the best age to start children in daycare so as not to affect their attachment to their parents?

25. Which one of the following characteristics, as suggested by the Canadian Child Care Federation, should be considered for choosing either a centre or a home daycare?
    a. the written program policies and plans
    b. the gender of the child and the gender of the daycare personnel
    c. the number of days the child is in a daycare environment
    d. whether the daycare personnel have children of their own

INVESTIGATIVE PROJECT

Student Project 8: Observation of Turn Taking

This observation is designed to examine "turn taking" in the feeding interaction. You will observe a single feeding—breast or bottle—of an infant not older than 1 month, preferably younger. Naturally, you will need to obtain the appropriate written permission from the parents for this observation. Tell them that the purpose of your observation is simply for you to develop better observational skills. You will not be interfering in any way, and there are no "right" or "wrong" ways to go about the task.

Procedure

Observe for a total of about 10 minutes. Keep a running record of behaviours demonstrated by the child and by the parent. To make the task manageable, focus on only three of the behaviours listed below for each member of the pair. Use an appropriate abbreviation letter for each behaviour:

Infant behaviours
- sucking (S)
- fussing or crying (C)
- other vocalizing (grunt, any other non-crying sounds) (V)

Parent behaviours
- jiggling (J)
- vocalizing (any talking to the infant, other sounds such as singing or cooing) (V)
- stroking or touching (T)

To record these behaviours, you will need a sheet with 2 columns of boxes on it: one column for the infant and one for the parent, such as:

Infant	Parent

Begin your observation a few minutes after the feeding has begun so that the infant and parent can adapt to your presence and settle into some kind of interaction pattern. Then start recording whatever behaviour is occurring.

- If the infant is doing nothing, but the parent is jiggling or talking or touching, then put the relevant letter in the parent box for the first row.

- If the infant is doing something and the parent is simultaneously doing something, record each in the adjacent boxes in a single row.

- If the infant is doing something but the parent is not, then put the relevant letter in the infant box for that row and leave the parent box blank.

When either member of the pair changes behaviour, move to the next row in your record sheet.

- If the baby sucks and then stops, and after the baby stops the mother jiggles and then says something, and then the baby sucks again, the chart would look like this:

Infant	Parent
S	
	J
	V

- If the baby sucks and the mother talks at the same time, and then the infant stops sucking and the mother keeps talking, it would look like this:

Infant	Parent
S	V
	V

For this observation, you should pay no attention to the duration of an activity. For the purposes of this exercise, it doesn't matter if the child sucks for three seconds or for 30 seconds before some change occurs.

When you have completed 10 minutes of observation, or when the feeding is completed, whichever comes first, stop recording. You will need to remain seated and quiet until the feeding is over so as not to distract the parent or the infant. Be sure to thank the parent, and feel free to show the parent your observational record if he or she asks.

Analysis and Report

In examining your observational record, see if you can detect any signs of "turn taking" in the patterns of interaction. Does the parent jiggle or talk primarily during the pauses of the infant's sucking; or does the parent talk and jiggle at the *same time* as the sucking? Can you devise some way of scoring the sequence of interactions that would yield a measure of "turn taking?" What are the difficulties involved in interpreting such a score?

RESEARCH PROJECT

Student Project 9: Assessment of Daycare Centres

You will obtain a considerably better sense of the extent and type of variation to be encountered in the quality of daycare centres if you personally visit some selected daycare centres. Your instructor might arrange for visits to several such centres; and you may need to sign up for designated times. Try to arrange to visit a daycare centre in a First Nations community.

Procedure

Immediately upon your arrival at the centre you must present yourself at the office. Identify yourself as a student in Professor (name your professor)'s (name the course) class, and that you understand that arrangements have been made for your visit. Enquire about what special ground rules are in effect, and which places in the centre you may not visit.

Arrange to spend at least an hour at the centre, sitting as unobtrusively as possible at the side of the room or on the edge of the playground. If you need to walk around so that you can see the full setting, feel free to do so, but do not intrude on the process. As you observe, imagine that you are a parent of a youngster and you are looking for a care setting for that child. With that frame of reference, record the following information for each centre:

• What is the teacher–child ratio? Does this ratio vary depending on the age of the child?

• How many children are cared for in each group in the centre? (Some centres will care for all children as a single "group." Others will have groups for children of different ages. What you want to know is the number of children cared for together.)

In addition, you should rate the centre on a series of 5-point scales, where 1 always means "poor" or "low" and 5 always means "optimum".

Activity	Score
Amount of individual one-on-one contact between adults and children	1 2 3 4 5
Amount of verbal stimulation from adults to children	1 2 3 4 5
Richness and complexity of verbal stimulation from adults to children	1 2 3 4 5
Cleanliness of environment	1 2 3 4 5

Activity	Rating
Colourfulness of environment	1 2 3 4 5
Adequacy of space	1 2 3 4 5
Summary rating of centre	1 2 3 4 5

Analysis

Compare the results for all of the centres you observed. If you had a young child, would you be willing to place your child in these centres? Why or why not? Having observed these centres, can you suggest other criteria that might be helpful for a parent? What research questions need to be asked to determine the importance of these features for a child's development?

INVESTIGATIVE PROJECT

Student Project 10: Investigation of Daycare Options

Almost any parent can tell you that it is not easy to obtain good information about available daycare options. The purpose of this investigation project is, therefore, not only to discover as much as possible about the options in your community, but to identify good sources and good strategies for obtaining such information.

Basic Questions to Answer

*   What types of daycare settings are available?

*   What types of prior vocations might the operators of the centres have?

*   How many, and of what ages of children do these centres accommodate?

*   What are the operating costs of such centres?

*   What is the cost per child per day in these centres?

*   What is the best way for someone to learn about these care options?

*   What daycare options are available? How does one locate them? Is there a registry? A regulated licensing process? Are all daycare providers listed in such registries?

*   Are after-school care settings available? What are the qualifications of those who operate them? What is the cost of after-school settings?

*   Is care available for children in the evening and at night (as might be needed by a parent who works evenings or on the night shift)?

Sources

Much of the information you'll need can be obtained on the phone. The Yellow Pages list daycare centres, usually under "Child-Care Services." Data on daycare is much more difficult to obtain (both for you and for parents). For information on licensing, especially the licensing of home-care or daycare providers, you will want to talk to relevant agencies. To locate individual care providers, bulletin boards are one data source. They are often located in places parents are likely to be, such as grocery stores, laundromats, etc.

A person or group doing this project should check out such stores in some systematic fashion, and then call the providers whose names they find, to find out how many children are cared for, their ages, their hours of operation, and what fee is charged at the daycare centre.

Analysis and Report

Your instructor may want you to prepare an oral or a written report for your class. In any case, you should prepare a written description of the steps you followed and the answers to the questions listed above.

CHAPTER 6 ANSWER KEY

Guided Study Questions

8. Ethologists believe that the first 2 years of life constitute a <u>sensitive period for attachment in human infants</u>. They claim that infants who fail to form a close relationship with a primary caregiver are at risk for <u>future social and personality problems.</u>

14. Canadian researchers found that <u>fathers can be as sensitive to the needs of their child as mothers.</u>

21. By age five, most children have clear internal models of <u>the mother (or other caregiver), a self-model</u>, and a model of <u>relationships</u>. Once formed, such models <u>shape and explain experiences, and affect memory and attention.</u>

26. A low level of <u>caregiver responsiveness</u> appears to be an ingredient in any type of insecure attachment.

52. Individual differences in temperament may also be related to <u>security of attachment.</u>

57. During the same months that the baby is creating an internal model of attachment and expressing his or her own unique temperament, he or she is also developing an <u>internal model of self.</u>

62. In Bowlby's language, what seems to be happening here is that the child is creating an <u>internal model of self, just as he or she creates an internal model of relationships.</u>

63. Development of the emotional self begins when <u>the baby learns to identify changes in emotion expressed in others' faces.</u>

68. There is a good deal of evidence that <u>high-quality cognitively enriched daycare</u> has beneficial effects on many children's overall <u>cognitive development</u>. This effect is particularly strong for children from <u>poor families, who show significant and lasting gains in IQ and later school performance after attending highly enriched daycare throughout infancy and childhood.</u>

Practice Questions

1. c	6. b	11. d	16. a	21. c
2. b	7. a	12. d	17. b	22. d
3. a	8. b	13. b	18. a	23. c
4. b	9. b	14. c	19. b	24. b
5. d	10. c	15. b	20. c	25. a

PHYSICAL AND COGNITIVE DEVELOPMENT IN EARLY CHILDHOOD

OVERVIEW OF CHAPTER

In the years from 2 to 6, the period known as early childhood, the child changes from being a dependent toddler, able to communicate only in very primitive ways, to being a remarkably competent, communicative, social creature, ready to begin school. Subtle physical changes happen during this period, as well as a number of advances in cognitive and language development. Issues involved in intelligence testing are also discussed.

Physical Changes

- Changes in height and weight are far slower in the preschool years than in infancy. Motor skills continue to improve gradually, with marked improvement in large muscle skills, but with slower advances in small muscle skills. Developmentalists at the University of Manitoba, who studied children's motor activity levels and behavioural self-control, uncovered some interesting findings. One such finding was that children who display higher motor activity have the ability to control their behaviour better, allowing for more successful task achievement.

- Brain growth, synapse formation, and myelinization continue in early childhood, although at a pace slower than in infancy. Neurological milestones such as lateralization and handedness develop between 2 and 6 years of age.

- Health promotion and wellness issues include diet, illness, stress, and accidents. Unintentional injuries are a major cause of harm and death for preschoolers. Parenting, cognitive, and social factors affect injury rates

- Physical abuse, sexual abuse, physical neglect, and emotional maltreatment constitute child maltreatment in Canada. Certain characteristics of both children and parents increase the risk of abuse. Children who are frequently or severely abused may develop post-traumatic stress disorder. Education, the identification of families at risk, and keeping abused children from further injury are three ways to help prevent abuse.

Cognitive Changes

- According to Piaget, the 18- to 24-month-old child begins to use mental symbols and enters the preoperational stage. Despite this advance, the preschool child still lacks many sophisticated cognitive characteristics. A child of this age is still egocentric, lacks an understanding of conservation, and is often fooled by appearances.

- Research challenging Piaget's findings makes it clear that young children are less egocentric than Piaget thought.

- By the end of early childhood, the child has developed a new and quite sophisticated theory of mind. The child understands that other people's actions are based on their thoughts and beliefs.

- Information-processing theory explains early childhood cognitive development in terms of limitations on young children's memory systems. Vygotsky's sociocultural theory asserts that children's thinking is shaped by social interaction through the medium of language.

- By integrating the theory of mind and the social interaction approaches, it seems that cognitive processes develop in unison.

Changes in Language

- Fast-mapping enables language development to increase at a rapid pace between the age of 2 and 4, beginning with simple two-word sentences.

- Between the ages of 3 and 4, the child's advances in grammar are extraordinary. Inflections, questions and negatives, and over-regularizations lead to the use of complex sentences.

- Phonological awareness, a child's sensitivity to the sound patterns that are specific to his or her own language, is highly important to the child's ability to learn to read and write. Children seem to acquire this skill through word play and dialogical reading.

- Individual rates of language development vary greatly. Cross-linguistic studies have shown both consistencies and inconsistencies in language development among children in different groups.

Differences in Intelligence

- Today, one test used frequently by psychologists is the Wechsler Intelligence Scale for Children, called the WISC-IV.

- Scores on early childhood intelligence tests are predictive of later school performance and are at least moderately consistent over time.

- Arguments about the origins of difference in IQ nearly always boil down to a dispute about nature versus nurture. However, twin and adoption studies provide evidence that half the variation in IQ scores are due to genetic differences.

- Environmental influences such as home environments and family interactions are not the only sources that can significantly influence the child's intellectual development. Programs like Head Start can modify the path of a child's intellectual development. In Canada, two programs used to assist children are the Aboriginal Head Start and High/Scope programs.

LEARNING GOALS

After completing Chapter 7, students should be able to:
1. Describe the physical changes in early childhood.
2. Summarize the cognitive changes in preschoolers.
3. Trace the factors that affect language development in young children.
4. Summarize the issues surrounding the use of intelligence testing in early childhood.
5. Describe the factors that can influence intellectual differences in children.

GUIDED STUDY QUESTIONS

PHYSICAL CHANGES

Growth and Motor Development (pp. 192–194)

Objective 7.1: Summarize the changes in growth and motor development in preschool children.

1. What are the typical changes in height and weight in the preschool years?

2. Compare the milestones of motor development from age 2 to age 6 by completing the following table:

Age	Locomotor Skills	Nonlocomotor Skills	Manipulative Skills
18–24 months			
2–3 years			
3–4 years			
4–5 years			
5–6 years			

3. Describe the research findings of Campbell, Eaton, and McKeen, from the University of Manitoba, regarding children's activity levels and behavioural self-control.

4. What are the implications of training effects for children in writing letters?

The Brain and Nervous System (pp. 194–196)

Objective 7.2: List and describe the developmental milestones of the brain and the nervous system in early childhood.

5. Define the following terms:
    a. corpus callosum
    b. lateralization
    c. hippocampus
    d. handedness

6. Describe the interaction of maturation and experience in the development of lateralization.

7. Define the hippocampus and describe how it is involved in memory.

8. How does handedness develop?

Health Promotion and Wellness (pp. 196–197)

Objective 7.3: Identify the most common health issues of children in early childhood.

9. Examine health issues of preschool children.

    a. For each of the following health issues of children in early childhood, identify possible causes of concern:

Issue	*Possible Causes of Concern*
Medical check-ups	
Diet	
Illness	
Stress	
Accidents	

    b. State the percentage of children aged 1 to 4 years in Canada who have had an accident that requires hospitalization.

Research Report: Unintentional Injuries in Canadian Preschoolers (p. 197)

Objective 7.4: State Canadian data and research findings related to unintentional injuries in preschoolers.

10. State the only technique, as identified by researchers, that reliably lowered risk-taking behaviour and resulted in a fewer injuries in children.

Child Maltreatment in Canada (pp. 198–200)

Objective 7.5: Summarize the issues involved in child maltreatment in Canada.

11.   State the forms of child maltreatment.

12.   List, in descending order, the common forms of substantiated cases of child maltreatment.

13.   What type of parents account for the largest portion of alleged maltreatment?

14.   What differentiates abusive from non-abusive parents, according to this model, is:

_____ .

15.   Give examples of each of the following broad categories of explanation for why abuse occurs.

Categories	*Examples*
Sociocultural factors	
Characteristics of the child	
Characteristics of the abuser	
Family stresses	

16.   Define post-traumatic stress disorder (PTSD), and explain why some abused children develop it.

17.   List ways each of the following may help prevent abuse:
      a.   education
      b.   identification of families at risk
      c.   protection from further injury

Research Report: Traumatic Events and Neurobiological and Functional Changes in the Brain (p. 199)

Objective 7.6: Describe the research findings obtained in studies of traumatic events and neurobiological and functional changes in the brain.

18.   What structures of the brain, as revealed by brain imaging studies, can be affected in adults who were traumatized as children?

19. State the reason that Functional Magnetic Resonance Imaging (MRI) was used in the research study by Lanius et al.

20. Examine the research findings of Lanius et al., comparing the brain functioning of people who had developed PTSD, to those who had not in the aftermath of comparable traumatic events.

COGNITIVE CHANGES

Piaget's Preoperational Stage (pp. 200–203)

Objective 7.7: Describe Piaget's view of cognitive development during the preschool period.

21. Define the following terms, and give examples of each:
    a. preoperational stage
    b. egocentrism
    c. centration
    d. conservation

22. Explain Piaget's use of the following terms, and give an example of each:
    a. locomotion
    b. animism

23. Explain, by using each of the characteristics listed, how children demonstrate their understanding of conservation:

Characteristics	*Explanation of Conservation*
Identity	
Compensation	
Reversibility	

Challenges to Piaget's View (p. 203)

Objective 7.8: Summarize the challenges to Piaget's view.

24. List and give examples of the two levels of perspective-taking ability proposed by John Flavell.

25. Give an example of how preschoolers' understanding of emotion has challenged Piaget's description of the young child's egocentrism.

26. Define the false belief principle, and give an example.

27. State the recent findings of a Canadian study conducted to clarify the boundaries of the false belief principle in young children.

Theories of Mind (pp. 205–207)

Objective 7.9: Summarize the research on theories of mind.

28. Define theory of mind.

29. Describe the progression of children's understanding of other people's thoughts, desires, and beliefs by completing the following table.

Age	*Examples of Understanding*
18 months	
3–5 years	
4–5 years	
6 years	
5–7 years	

30. List at least four correlates of a child's theory of mind.

Alternative Theories of Early Childhood Thinking (pp. 207–210)

Objective 7.10: Describe the alternative theories of early childhood thinking.

31. Define the following terms:
     a. short-term storage space (STSS)
     b. operational efficiency
     c. metamemory
     d. metacognition

32. How does information-processing theory explain why the 7-year-old is better able to handle the processing demands of conservation than the 4-year-old?

33. Describe the research on training children in matrix classification skills.

34. Examine the Flexible Item Selection Task (FIST) described by Jacques at Dalhousie University.

35. Describe the research study conducted by Bisanz and his colleagues at the University of Alberta to study the development of arithmetic skills in preschoolers.

36. Give examples of how children's metamemory and metacognitive skills improve during the early childhood period.

37. Briefly describe Vygotsky's views on development, using the example of the puzzle.

38. Define the following terms:
    a. zone of proximal development
    b. scaffolding

39. Vygotsky proposed four stages that represent steps toward the child's internalization of the ways of thinking used by adults in his or her society. Complete the following table to trace this development.

Stage	*Examples of Internalization*
Primitive stage	
Naive psychology stage	
Egocentric speech stage	
Ingrowth stage	

CHANGES IN LANGUAGE

Research Report: Early Long-Term Memories in Children (pp. 211–212)

Objective 7.11: Examine the research on early long-term memories in children.

40. Define infantile amnesia.

41. Compare and contrast the two longitudinal studies conducted by Peterson and her colleagues on early long-term memories of children regarding their injuries.

42. List factors that facilitate the memory of traumatic events.

43. State the importance of the method of inquiry used to interview children.

Fast-Mapping (p. 212)

Objective 7.12: Explain how children use fast-mapping to increase their vocabularies.

44. Define fast-mapping and explain how it enables children's to learn new words.

The Grammar Explosion (pp. 212–214)

Objective 7.13: Summarize the increase in the effective use of grammar during the preschool years.

45. Children seem to add inflections and more complex word orders in fairly predictable sequences. Give examples of each of the following:
    a. adding -*ing* to a verb
    b. preposition
    c. plural
    d. irregular past tense
    e. possessives
    f. articles
    g. plural to third-person verbs
    h. regular past tense
    i. auxiliary verbs

46. List the sequence in the child's development in the use of questions and negatives.

47. Define over-regularization, or over-generalization, and give examples.

Phonological Awareness (pp. 214–215)

Objective 7.14: Describe the development of phonological awareness in the preschool years.

48. Define the following terms, and give examples of each:
    a. phonological awareness
    b. invented spelling

49. Numerous studies have shown that the greater a child's phonological awareness before he or she enters school, _____.

50. Describe how phonological awareness develops through word play.

51. The evidence suggests that one of the best ways parents and preschool teachers can help young children to prepare for formal instruction in reading is to _____
    _____.

Individual and Cross-Linguistic Variations (pp. 215, 217)

Objective 7.15: Identify some of the individual and cross-linguistic variations in language development.

52. State several factors that Canadian researchers have found that influence language and cognitive development in children up to age 3.

53. Describe several similarities in the pattern of language development across cultures.

The Real World/Teaching: Strengthening Language Skills in Preschoolers (pp. 216–217)

Objective 7.16: Summarize the findings and outcomes of the research studies conducted to strengthen language skills in preschoolers.

54. Differentiate between receptive and expressive vocabulary.

55. State eight tips for dialogic reading that may be used for children to enhance their language-skills development.

DIFFERENCES IN INTELLIGENCE

Measuring Intelligence (pp. 219–221)

Objective 7.17: Identify the issues involved in measuring intelligence.

56. Define the following terms:
    a. Stanford-Binet
    b. intelligence quotient (IQ)
    c. WISC-IV

57. What was the practical purpose of the first IQ test?

58. How was IQ computed from the Stanford-Binet? State the formula and give examples.

59. What is the current process for IQ score calculations?

60. Children who score above _____ are often called gifted; those who score below ___ are referred to by terms such as intellectually delayed or as having a development disability. In order to classify a child as having a development disability the child will also tend to have problems with _____.

61. Describe the Wechsler Intelligence Scale for Children (WISC-IV).

62. Describe how IQ scores can be stable yet show wide fluctuations in individual scores.

63. List at least three limitations of IQ tests.

Origins of Individual Differences in Intelligence (pp. 221–225)

Objective 7.18: Describe the issues surrounding the origins of the differences in intelligence.

64. Both twin studies and studies of adopted children show _____.

65. List five behaviours of family interactions that foster higher scores.

66. How do programs like Head Start or other quality preschool experiences supplement home environments and family interactions? Include IQ scores as well as other measures in your answer.

67. Describe the Abecedarian project. What were the findings of IQ scores in children who were enrolled in the special program?

68. List the domains of school readiness measured by Eleanor Thomas, who conducted a major Statistics Canada Study.

69. Two programs in Canada that target high-risk children are _____ and _____.

70. Describe the results of the two programs listed in the above statement.

CRITICAL REFLECTION EXERCISES

Kindergarten

You are about to enter your first day of teaching kindergarten. Based on the information provided in the text, provide detailed responses to the following questions:

1. At what level of language development will most of these children be? What language skills will they have?

2. How might the child's perception of you and the classroom experience be related to culture? What things might you do to minimize any potential negative effects of cultural differences; but, at the same time, support these differences?

3. How would a child's cognitive development influence his or her play?

Intelligence

Based on the discussion of intelligence in the text, how would you define "intelligence"? There is not a "right versus wrong" definition. Using the concepts discussed what definition makes sense to you? Why? How would you use this definition if you were raising a child in the 2 to 6 age range?

PRACTICE QUESTIONS

1. Which of the following statements is true concerning growth and motor skill development in the preschool years?
   a. Changes in height and weight are at the same rate as in infancy.
   b. Changes in motor development are as dramatic as in infancy.
   c. The most impressive changes are in small muscle skills.
   d. Changes in height and weight are far slower in the preschool years.

2. The tendency to rely primarily on the right or left hand is called _____.
   a. lateralization
   b. handedness
   c. mixed dominance
   d. non-locomotor development

3.   The _____ is involved in the transfer of information to long-term memory.
    a.   corpus callosum
    b.   hippocampus
    c.   cerebral cortex
    d.   cerebellum

4.   Unintentional injuries resulting in death for children age 1 to 4 years are more likely to happen _____.
    a.   at home
    b.   on a family vacation
    c.   at school
    d.   in a neighbour's car

5.   Which of the following is a manifestation of post-traumatic disorder (PTSD) in a child?
    a.   mild levels of anxiety
    b.   enuresis
    c.   nightmares
    d.   poor appetite

6.   According to Piaget, the preschool child is in the _____ stage of cognitive development.
    a.   sensorimotor
    b.   preoperational
    c.   concrete operational
    d.   formal operational

7.   A child who thinks that ten pennies in a row is more money than ten pennies in a stack is unable to understand _____.
    a.   object permanence
    b.   conservation
    c.   law of small numbers
    d.   law of large numbers

8.   Johnny is 4½ years old. He is beginning to understand that ice can transform into water and back into ice. He is therefore beginning to under stand conservation of _____.
    a.   identity
    b.   reversibility
    c.   compensation
    d.   centration

9.   A child who develops a whole series of complex rules to explain exactly what the other person sees or experiences is _____.
    a.   at level 2 of perspective taking
    b.   exhibiting ethnocentrism
    c.   at level 1 of perspective taking
    d.   at least 6 years old

10. A set of ideas that explains other people's ideas, beliefs, desires, and behaviours is called _____.
    a. false belief principle
    b. theory of mind
    c. metamemory
    d. matrix classification

11. Klein and Bisanz developed a novel method of studying arithmetic skills in preschoolers by using _____ in lieu of counting.
    a. toy cars
    b. cookies
    c. poker chips
    d. blocks

12. Sally is listening to a story but soon realizes she has forgotten the name of the main character. Which one of the following processes will allow her to ask the reader the name of the character?
    a. metacognition
    b. theory of mind
    c. cognitive dissonance
    d. self-concept

13. Bobby, aged 3, is walking down a flight of stairs and says to himself "Be careful." According to Vygotsky's Sociocultural Theory, a child who uses language as a guide to solve problems is in which one of the following stages of cognitive development?
    a. naïve psychological stage
    b primitive stage
    c. egocentric speech stage
    d. ingrowth stage

14. The ability to link new words categorically to real-world referents is called which one of the following?
    a. fast-tracking
    b. invented spelling
    c. fast-mapping
    d. categorizing

15. Which of the following inflections is the child likely to add first to his words?
    a. the suffix *-ing*
    b. the suffix *-ed*
    c. auxiliary verbs
    d. plurals

16. A child who says "foots" instead of "feet" is _____.
    a. probably in danger of developing language deficits
    b. exhibiting over-regularization
    c. not a native speaker of English
    d. at least 5 years old

17. A child's sensitivity to the sound patterns that are specific to her own language is called _____.
    a. metacognition
    b. over-regularization
    c. metamemory
    d. phonological awareness

18. Which of the following statement defines receptive vocabulary?
    a. words that are understood when heard
    b. words whose meaning is used correctly when speaking
    c. words that have a pictorial representation
    d. words that have no meaning when spoken

19. All of the following techniques are included in dialogic reading for children except for _____.
    a. follow your own interests
    b. expand on what the child said
    c. praise and encourage the child
    d. ask "wh" questions

20. Canadian researchers, comparing children from various socioeconomic levels, found several factors that influence language and cognitive development in children up to 3 years of age. One such factor is _____.
    a. that children of teenage mothers displayed especially superior levels of language development.
    b. the number of linguistic and social toys available to the child.
    c. the duration of a father's vocalization when his infant was 6 and 18 months of age.
    d. that children who are reared in large homes are prone to difficulties in cognitive development.

21. The practical use of the first modern intelligence test was to _____.
    a. help children identify their school career potential
    b. identify children who might have difficulty in school
    c. sort out children who were gifted and needed extra assignments
    d. label children as "smart" and "not smart"

22. The working memory index of the WISC-IV, which measures intelligence, taps into:
    a. long-term memory
    b. repressed memory
    c. procedural memory
    d. short-term memory

23. Which of the following types of families tend to have children with higher IQs?
    a. families that avoid excessive restrictiveness
    b. families that set extremely high performance standards
    c. families that do not place high demands on their children
    d. families that encourage competition between siblings

24. Thomas, using National Longitudinal Survey of Children and Youth (NLSCY-cycle 5) data, measured the following domains of school readiness *except*:
    a. academic skills
    b. moral values
    c. language and communication skills
    d. social competence and independence

25. Which of the following is a benefit for students of the High/Scope program in Canada?
    a. They spent more time in special education programs.
    b. They had average high school graduation rates.
    c. They had better school readiness.
    d. They had average employment income upon graduation.

CASE STUDY

Maria is a young mother with three children. Sarah is 4 years old and loves sweets. Lately she has not been eating well and Maria is concerned. Robbie is 2½ and has a dog. When you come to visit he tells you that "doggie running" and "I playing". Maria and her husband have been thinking about sending Sarah to a day care. She has been informed that the teachers in one of the day care centres are engaged in a training program for the development of fine motor skills. She knows that you are taking a Growth and Development course and asks you what you know about the training program.

1. From your understanding of food intake for the preschooler, what can you share with Maria?

2. What grammatical marker is Robbie using when he speaks?

3. What is your understanding of the importance of these training programs for young children?

INVESTIGATIVE PROJECT

Student Project 11: Assessing the Child's Theory of Mind

For this project, you will need to locate a child between the ages of 3 and 5. You must obtain written permission from the child's parents, following whatever procedure your instructor specifies. The testing should be done in a quiet place in the child's home.

The task that has most often been used to assess the child's theory of mind has been called the Smarties task because it uses a box of Smarties, a common Canadian candy. This recent research, conducted by Philip Zelazo and Janet Boseovski (2001) of the University of Toronto, helps to clarify the boundaries of the false belief principle.

Procedure

Find a quiet place where you and the child can sit down at a table or on the floor. Tell the child:

> *We're going to play a game where I show you some things and ask you questions about them.*

Bring out your Smarties box and ask the child to look at it. Then open the box and show the child that there is a string inside. Ask:

> *What's inside the box?*

If the child doesn't say "string," ask again, *What's inside the box?* When it is clear that the child knows that it is a string, put the string in the box and close it. Now ask the child the following questions and write down the child's answers carefully.

> *Does it look like this box has a string in it or does it look like it has candies in it?*

> *What's really inside the box? Is there really a string inside it, or are there really candies inside it?*

> *When you first saw the box, before we opened it, what did you think was inside it? Did you think there was a string inside it, or did you think there were candies inside it?*

> *Your mom hasn't seen inside this box. If your mom sees the box all closed up like this, what will she think is inside it? Will she think there is a string inside it, or will she think there are candies inside it?*

When you are done, thank the child, compliment the child on his or her answers, and stay long enough to play with the child at some game the child chooses.

Analysis and Report

In analyzing and reporting on your result, compare your child's answers to those reported in the text. Did your child understand the difference between appearance and reality? Did she or he understand false belief principle?

RESEARCH PROJECT

Student Project 12: Beginning Two-Word Sentences

Some of you have been around young children a lot, and already have some sense of the delightful quality of their early language, but you would benefit from some additional listening. Locate a child who is still in the earliest stages of sentence formation, or just beginning to add a few inflections. This is most likely to be a child of 20 to 24 months, but a child between 24 and 30 months may do well. The one essential aspect is that the child must be speaking at least some two-word sentences. If you are unsure, ask the parent; he or she can nearly always tell you whether the child has reached this stage or not.

Procedure

As usual, begin by following whatever procedures your instructor requires for obtaining appropriate informed consent from the parents of your subject for you to observe. Then arrange to spend enough time with the child at his or her home, or in any other convenient setting, so that you can collect a list of 50 different spontaneous utterances, including both one-word and two-word sentences. By spontaneous, we mean those that the child speaks without prompting. Try to avoid getting into a situation in which the mother or some other adult actively tries to elicit language from the child, although it is certainly acceptable if you collect a sample from a time when the child is playing with an adult, or doing some activity with a parent or older sibling. The most fruitful time is likely to be when the child is playing with someone. You may ask the mother to play with the child, but not to play the sort of game in which the object is to get the child to talk. Whenever you can, make notes about the context in which each sentence occurred, so that you can judge the meaning more fully.

Analysis and Report

When you have your list of 50 utterances, try describing the child's language in any terms from the text. For example, is the child using any grammatical inflections? Which ones? Does the pattern conform to what was described? What about questions or negatives? And what about the different meanings expressed? What is the child's mean length of utterance (MLU)? To calculate the MLU you will need to count the number of meaningful units in each sentence. Each word is a meaningful unit, but so is each grammatical inflection, like the -*s* for a plural, the -*ed* ending for a past tense, etc. Some specific rules to follow in calculating the MLU are:

1. Do not count such sounds as "uh," "um," or "oh," but do count "no," "yeah," and "hi."

2. All compound words, like "birthday," "choo-choo," "night-night," and "pocketbook" should be counted as single words.

3. Count all irregular past tenses as single words, such as "got," "did," "want," and "saw," but count as two words any regular past tense, such as "play-ed," or any erroneous extension of the past tense, such as "went-ed."

4. Count as one word all diminutives, such as "doggie" or "mommy."

127

5.   Count as one word all combinations, such as "gonna," "wanna," or "hafta."

6.   Count as one word each auxiliary, such as "is," "have," "will," "can," and "must," and as one word each inflection, such as the "s" for plural or possessive, the "s" for third person singular verb form, and the "ing" on a verb.

RESEARCH PROJECT

Student Project 13: Conversation Between Mother and Child

This project focuses on the social environment—what is said to the child as well as the child's response. Find a child around age 2, though it's acceptable to go up to about 3½. (It can be the same child you listened to in the previous project, but you should collect the two sets of observations separately.)

Procedure

After obtaining the appropriate informed consent, spend some time with the child while the mother or father is around. As with project 12, the interaction should be as spontaneous as possible. It is fine if the adult and child play together as long as they aren't playing "repeat after me" naming games.

Record the conversation between the parent and the child, making sure that you have the sentences of the two people in the right order. Continue to record the conversation until you have at least 25 sentences for each. You may use a tape recorder if you wish, but you'll find it helpful to write down the sentences as they occur as well.

Analysis and Report

Did the adult adapt his or her language to that of the child? Did the adult repeat the child's utterances with minor modifications? Was there any obvious reinforcement or shaping going on? Did the adult attempt to correct the child's speech, and if so, what was the effect? Include your record of the conversation in your report, along with a page or two of comments.

CHAPTER 7 ANSWER KEY

Guided Study Questions

14. What differentiates abusive from non-abusive parents, according to this model, is <u>the presence of a number of risk factors that shape how they respond to the ordinary stresses of parenting.</u>

49. Numerous studies have shown that the greater a child's phonological awareness before he or she enters school, <u>the faster he or she learns to read.</u>

51. The evidence suggests that one of the best ways parents and preschool teachers can help young children to prepare for formal instruction in reading is to <u>engage them in activities that encourage word play and invented spelling.</u>

60. Children who score above <u>130</u> are often called gifted; those who score below <u>70</u> are referred to by terms such as intellectually delayed or are considered to have a development disability. A child classified as having a developmental disability will also tend to have problems with <u>"adaptive behaviour"</u>.

64. Both twin studies and studies of adopted children show <u>strong hereditary influences on IQ.</u>

69. Two programs in Canada that target high-risk children are the <u>Aboriginal Head Start</u> and <u>High/Scope</u> programs.

Practice Questions

1. d	6. b	11. c	16. b	21. b
2. b	7. b	12. a	17. d	22. d
3. b	8. b	13. c	18. a	23. b
4. a	9. a	14. c	19. a	24. b
5. c	10. c	15. a	20. b	25. c

Case Study

1. See Chapter 7 (p. 196). Tell Maria that children grow more slowly during early childhood years and seem to eat less than when they were babies. Nutritionists recommend keeping a variety of nutritious foods on hand and allowing a child's appetite to be a guide to how much food a child should eat.
2. See Chapter 7 (p. 213). Inflections are grammatical markers attached to words. The earliest inflection used among children learning English is adding "ing" to a verb. Robbie is demonstrating a grammatical marker.

3.   See Chapter 7 (p. 193). Researchers have found that early training, beginning at about age 2, can accelerate the rate at which young children acquire school-refined fine motor skills such as writing letters. However, older preschoolers, those beyond age 3, benefit more than younger children. Sarah will benefit from attending such a day care.

SOCIAL AND PERSONALITY DEVELOPMENT IN EARLY CHILDHOOD

OVERVIEW OF CHAPTER

Children between the ages of 2 and 6 undergo remarkable changes in their social skills. They go from being nay-saying, oppositional toddlers, who spend most of their play times alone, to being skilled, cooperative playmates by the age of 5 or 6.

Theories of Social and Personality Development

- Freud and Erikson each described two stages of personality development in early childhood. Both suggested that the key to this period is the balance between the child's emerging skills and desire for autonomy, and the parent's need to protect and control the child's behaviour. More recent psychoanalytic approaches, however, include relationships with peers and siblings.

- Social-cognitive theorists emphasize that advances in social and personality development are associated with cognitive development. They focus on three areas of interest: person perception, understanding of others' intentions, and understanding of rule categories.

Family Relationships

- Although the child's attachment to the parents remains strong, many attachment behaviours become less visible. Young preschoolers may show more refusals and defiance of parental influence attempts than infants do; but as they gain language and cognitive skills, they generally comply fairly readily.

- Different approaches to parenting result in differences in children's development. Authoritative parenting, which combines warmth, clear rules, and communication with high maturity demands, is associated with the most positive outcomes for children. One important aspect of parenting is that of the effective utilization of child discipline. The most important purpose of discipline is for the child to develop self-control, moral character, and proper conduct.

- Ethnicity and socioeconomic class are linked to parenting style. Studies suggest that the parenting style adopted may be dependent upon the cultural context in which the parents and children reside. Consequently, as the cultural context changes the best corresponding type of parenting style changes with it.

Family Structure and Divorce

- Family structure affects social and personality development. Two-parent blended families have increased in number in Canada. Studies reveal that children from lone-parent families are more susceptible to problems. For children raised by gay and lesbian parents, or for those conceived by artificial insemination, developmental outcomes are predicted by how parents interact with them.

- Following a divorce, children typically show disruptive behaviour. Many effects of divorce are associated with problems that existed before the marriage ended.

- A number of variables are involved with family structure and divorce, such as a change in family income and the upheaval of subtracting or adding new adults to the family system. Ultimately, it is the parenting style rather than any particular disruption that is significant for the child. Many families construct social networks that are beneficial for the child.

Peer Relationships

- Preschoolers participate in various kinds of play that are related to the development of social skills. Children who are unskilled at the social skill of group entry are often aggressive and tend to be rejected by their peers.

- Physical aggression toward peers increases and then declines during these years, whereas indirect aggression increases among some children more than others. Researchers at one Canadian university report that many preschool children bully other children. Some children develop a pattern of aggressive behaviour that continues to cause problems for them throughout childhood and adolescence.

- Children display prosocial behaviour at as young as age 2 and the behaviour seems to grow as the child's ability to take another's perspective increases. In studying the role of empathy on prosocial behaviour, Canadian researchers have indicated several findings. One finding revealed that the links between child and parental characteristics predicted two-thirds of children's empathy. Stable friendships develop between children in this age range.

Personality and Self-Concept

- As young children gain more understanding of the social environment, their temperaments ripen into true personalities.

- Two aspects of self-concept, the categorical self and the emotional self, continue to develop between ages 2 and 6, and the social self is added. Children make major strides in the development of self-control, as well as in their understanding of their own social roles.

- Canadian researchers found that aggressive students initiated more interactions with teachers than did shy children, and that children who were more sociable interacted more with other students than they did with teachers.

The Gender Concept and Sex Roles

- Social learning theorists who emphasize the role of parents in shaping children's sex-role behaviour and attitudes ignore the role of cognitive development. Social-cognitive theories suggest that children's understanding of gender is linked to gender-related behaviours.

- Children seem to develop gender constancy, the understanding that gender is an innate characteristic that cannot be changed, in three steps: labelling their own and others' gender, understanding the stability of gender, and comprehending the constancy of gender at about age 5 or 6.

- A Canadian study reveals that children begin to learn early what goes with being a boy or a girl. By age 5 or 6, most children have developed fairly rigid rules about what boys or girls are supposed to do or be.

- Sex-typed behaviour—different patterns of behaviour among girls and boys—develops earlier than ideas about sex roles, beginning as early as 18 to 24 months of age. Girls tend to adopt an enabling style of behaviour whereas boys are likely to show a constricting or restrictive style. Cross-gendered behaviour is more common among girls than boys.

LEARNING GOALS

After completing Chapter 8, students should be able to:
1. Distinguish the theories of social and personality development.
2. Describe the changes in family relationships of preschoolers.
3. Discuss the impact of family structure and divorce on young children.
4. Identify the issues involved in the peer relationships of preschool-aged children.
5. Summarize the development of personality in early childhood.
6. Explain the process of development of the gender concept and sex roles.

GUIDED STUDY QUESTIONS

THEORIES OF SOCIAL AND PERSONALITY DEVELOPMENT

Psychoanalytic Perspectives (pp. 229–230)

Objective 8.1: Summarize the key points of the psychoanalytic theories that are relevant to early childhood.

1. Freud and Erikson's psychoanalytical perspective offered key insights into

   _____.

2. What did Erikson emphasize in his psychosocial stages of development?

3. List and describe the two stages of Erikson's theory during the preschool years.

4. List and describe the two kinds of relationships that Hartup emphasized.

5.   Why does Hartup suggest that both kinds of relationships are needed for the child to develop effective social skills?

Social-Cognitive Perspectives (pp. 230–233)

Objective 8.2: Summarize the key points of the social-cognitive perspective that are relevant to early childhood.

6.   Define the following terms:
     a.   social cognitive theory
     b.   person perception.

7.   Give examples of how young children's observations and people categories are far less consistent than those of older children.

8.   Give examples of how preschoolers categorize others on the basis of observable characteristics.

9.   Give examples of how preschoolers use classification skills to begin to understand the difference between social conventions and moral rules.

10. Give examples of how young children demonstrate their understanding of intentions.

The Real World/Learning: Storybooks and Learning to Classify Personality (p. 231)

Objective 8.3: Describe how storybooks and learning might contribute to shaping an understanding of emotion and personality in early childhood.

11. One particular source of early exposure to psychology may have been from the raspy-voiced narration of _____.

12. Shea and her colleagues contend that the characters of the A.A. Milne stories display
     _____.

13. In light of analysis of Shea et al., what thoughts may occur regarding exposure to these stories?

FAMILY RELATIONSHIPS

Attachment (p. 234)

Objective 8.4: Describe the preschool-aged child's attachment to his or her parents.

14. Compare a 2- or 3-year-old child's attachment to his or her parents with that of an infant.

15. Give examples of how attachment quality predicts behaviour during the preschool years.

16. According to Bowlby, how does the attachment relationship change at about age 4? Give examples.

17. How do advances in the internal working model lead to new conflicts?

Parenting Styles (pp. 234–238)

Objective 8.5: Discuss the impact of styles of parenting on the social and personality development of the preschool child.

18. Complete the following table by listing the four aspects of family functioning, and stating how each is related to various child behaviours.

Aspect of Family Functioning	Relationship to Child's Behaviours

19. Define the following terms:
    a. permissive parenting style
    b. authoritarian parenting style
    c. authoritative parenting style
    d. uninvolved parenting style

20. According to Maccoby and Martin, what are the two dimensions of family characteristics?

21. Complete the following table to describe how parenting style affects the child's behavioural outcomes:

Parenting Style	Likely Behavioural Outcomes
Authoritarian	
Permissive	
Authoritative	
Uninvolved	

22. Describe two key problems in establishing what constitutes effective discipline.

23. State what Canadian childcare advocates agree upon regarding discipline.

24. Define inductive discipline, and give examples.

25. List the four dimensions of parent-child interactions found in the NLSCY that Canadian researchers have been measuring and that complement Baumrind's classification of parenting style.

Ethnicity, Socioeconomic Status, and Parenting Styles (pp. 238–240)

Objective 8.6: Identify the ethnicity and socioeconomic variables that interact with parenting styles.

26. Describe the parenting characteristics that are used in Asian American and Aboriginal child-rearing practices.

27. Explain the relationship of cultural context to parenting style.

28. List some reasons why the effect of socioeconomic status (SES) is important to consider in child development.

FAMILY STRUCTURE AND DIVORCE

Family Structure (pp. 241–243)

Objective 8.7: Explain how the structure of children's families may influence the children's development.

29. Describe the changing family profile that has emerged in recent years.

30. Describe the profile of a lone-parent family.

31. Most children being raised in lone-parent families are doing fairly well by all measures, but there is a subset of these families in which children are _____.

32. Describe the type of research available on custodial grandparenting.

33. Researchers who have conducted comprehensive reviews of studies regarding cognitive and social development of children from gay and lesbian parents, found that _____
_____.

34. Describe the research available on children who were conceived by artificial insemination.

Divorce (pp. 243–245)

Objective 8.8: Describe the impact of divorce on children in the preschool years.

35. Some of the negative effects of divorce are due to factors that were present _____ _____ the divorce such as _____ .

36. List several negative effects of divorce for children, adolescence and adults.

37. How might divorce affect boys and girls differently?

38. Explain how age differences in children may reflect the severity of a child's reaction to a divorce.

Understanding the Effects of Family Structure and Divorce (p. 245)

Objective 8.9: Identify explanations for the effects of family structure and divorce.

39. List and describe three key reasons that explain the negative findings about divorce.

40. Define extended family, and give examples of how it assists single and divorced mothers.

PEER RELATIONSHIPS

Relating to Peers through Play (pp. 246–247)

Objective 8.10: Trace a child's changing relationship with his or her peers through play.

41. Define and describe the following types of play:
     a. solitary play
     b. parallel play
     c. associative play
     d. cooperative play

42. Define the following terms:
     a. social skills
     b. group entry

43. How does the social skill of group entry predict children's relationships with their peers?

44. What are the sex differences in the reasons for and consequences of poor group-entry skills?
     a. for girls
     b. for boys

45. Describe social-skills training.

Aggression (pp. 247–250)

Objective 8.11: Identify the key factors in aggressive behaviour in preschool children.

46. Define the following terms:
    a. aggression
    b. physical aggression
    c. indirect aggression

47. Summarize the findings from the following Canadian research studies on physical (PA),   and indirect aggression (IA):

Researcher	Physical Aggression	Indirect Aggression
Tremblay (2000)		
Côté, Vaillancourt, LeBlanc, Nagin & Tremblay (2006)		
Côté, Vaillancourt, Varker, Nagin & Tremblay (2007)		
Strayer (1980)		

48. How does the emergence of dominance hierarchies affect the display of physical aggression? Why?

49. Summarize the findings about the key factors in aggressive behaviours by completing the following table.

Factor	Research Findings
Frustration	
Reinforcement	
Modelling	

50. State the research findings from the NLSCY data regarding childhood aggression and the family environment.

Prosocial Behaviour and Friendships (pp. 251–252)

Objective 8.12: Trace the development of prosocial behaviour through the preschool years.

51. Define the following terms:
    a. prosocial behaviour
    b. altruism

52. Give examples of prosocial behaviour for children aged 2 or 3 and for older children.

53. State research findings, in the Canadian studies regarding the roles of empathy and prosocial behaviour in children.

54. Define attributions.

55. Describe examples of parental behaviour that contributes to the development of prosocial behaviour by completing the following table.

Parental Behaviour	*Examples*
Providing a loving and warm climate	
Providing prosocial attributions	
Looking for opportunities for children to do helpful things	
Modelling prosocial behaviour	

56. These early peer interactions are still quite primitive. However, it is noteworthy that preschool friend pairs nonetheless show _____ _____ _____ than is true between non-friend pairs at this age, all signs that these relationships are more than merely passing fancies. Moreover, having had a friend in early childhood is related to _____.

PERSONALITY AND SELF-CONCEPT

From Temperament to Personality (p. 253)

Objective 8.13: Explain the relationship between a young child's temperament and his or her developing personality.

57. Describe the link between a difficult temperament and concurrent and future behaviour problems.

58. Give an example of the processes through which temperament becomes modified into personality during the early preschool years.

59. How is the transition from temperament to personality influenced by parental responses to a young child's temperament?

Self-Concept (pp. 254–255)

Objective 8.14: Trace the development of the self-concept during early childhood.

60. State the findings of a research study mentioned in the text conducted by Bosacki at Brock University in Canada.

61. Describe, and give examples of, the development of the categorical self in the preschool years.

62. In a Canadian study of children's emotional knowledge, preschool girls scored _____than _____in the ability to correctly label emotions and understand complex emotions.

63. How does a child's temperament affect the process of gaining self-control?

64. How are parents' age-based expectations and parenting behaviours important in the process of gaining self-control?

65. Define social "scripts" and give an example.

66. Give examples of how role scripts help young children become more independent.

67. Describe the Canadian research findings regarding three patterns of child-teacher interactions.

THE GENDER CONCEPT AND SEX ROLES

Explaining Gender Concept and Sex-Role Development (pp. 256–257)

Objective 8.15 Distinguish among the theories that explain gender concept and sex-role development.

68. Define the following terms:
    a. gender concept
    b. sex role
    c. gender constancy theory
    d. gender constancy
    e. gender schema theory

69. Summarize the theoretical views of gender-concept and sex-role development by completing the following table.

Social Learning Theory
Role of parents:
Evidence that social-learning theory is insufficient:
Social-Cognitive Theories
Kohlberg's theory:
Difficulty with gender constancy theory:
Gender schema theory:
Key difference between gender schema and Kohlberg's theory:

The Gender Concept (pp. 257–258)

Objective 8.16: Identify the steps in the development of gender constancy.

70. Define the following terms:
    a. gender identity
    b. gender stability

71. Describe the three steps in the development of gender constancy.

72. How is gender constancy related to the concept of conservation?

Sex-Role Knowledge (pp. 258–259)

Objective 8.17: Describe how preschoolers acquire knowledge of sex roles.

73. Define sex-role stereotypes, and give examples of commonly stereotyped traits for men and for women.

74. Give an example, found in a large Canadian study, of children's ideas about how men and women (or boys and girls) ought to behave..

Sex-Typed Behaviour (pp. 259–261)

Objective 8.17: Describe the sex-typed behaviour of young children.

75. Define the following terms:
    a. sex-typed behaviour
    b. enabling style
    c. constricting, or restrictive, style
    d. cross-gender behaviour

76. Give examples of girls' use of the enabling style and boys' use of the restrictive style.

77. Give examples of cross-gender behaviour of girls and boys and state how peers and adults react to it.

78. It cannot be assumed that the prevalence of sex-typed play among boys is strictly the result of adult and peer influence. List three pieces of evidence for the statement.

CRITICAL REFLECTION EXERCISE

Social and Personality Development

Based on the information in the text, respond to the following question about social and personality development during the age range of 2 to 6 years:

1. Why is the development of self-control so important during these ages? Be sure to include evidence from the text to support your answer.

2. How would you utilize the information from this chapter of the text in a preschool? What kind of issues would you confront as the teacher (discuss at least three issues)? How would you utilize the information from this chapter to address these issues?

PRACTICE QUESTIONS

1. The text suggests that both Freud and Erikson believed that the key to the social development of 2- to 6-year-olds is _____.
   a. striking a balance between the child's emerging skills and parents' need for control
   b. the successful development of peer relationships
   c. whether potty training goes smoothly
   d. the ability of the parents to give the child freedom to grow

2. Which of the following represents a complementary relationship?
   a. becoming friends with someone who is older than us
   b. developing attachments with persons that are our equals
   c. an increase in attachment
   d. attachment to someone who has greater social power than we do

3. The ability to classify others is called _____.
   a. social-cognitive perception
   b. the Oedipus conflict
   c. complementary perception
   d. person perception

4. Developmental psychologists believe that 2-year-olds _____.
   a. are more compliant than at any other age
   b. comply with parents' requests more often than not
   c. are more likely to comply with self-care requests than other requests
   d. will generally say "no" to everything but then comply

5. Baumrind focused on the following four aspects of family functioning: warmth or levels of nurturance, level of expectations or "maturity demands," clarity and consistency of rules, and _____.
   a. communication
   b. responsibilities
   c. friendliness
   d. standards

6. A Canadian study of children in high-risk families, conducted by Landy and Tam, found that the incidence of problems decreased if parenting practices were

   _____.
   a. positive and controlling
   b. positive and permissive
   c. positive and questioning
   d. positive and supportive

7. Which parental style is linked to the best outcomes for most children?
   a. permissive
   b. authoritarian
   c. authoritative
   d. oligarchic

8. According to the Canadian Paediatric Society (CPS) the goal of effective and positive discipline is to _____.
   a. teach and guide children
   b. lessen emotional temper tantrums in children
   c. correct behaviour in children
   d. lessen risk-taking behaviour in children

9. Parenting characteristics in Aboriginal child-rearing practices are similar to a(n)_____.
    a. permissive parenting style
    b. authoritarian parenting style
    c. uninvolved parenting style
    d. authoritative parenting style

10. What do we know about the effects of family structure on a child?
    a. Family structure appears to affect girls more negatively than boys.
    b. It does not matter who reared the child, but what matters is how the child is reared.
    c. The structure does not matter, but the temperament of the child does.
    d. The optimum family structure includes both natural parents that rear a child.

11. A family structure that includes parents, grandparents, aunts, uncles, cousins, and so on is best called _____.
    a. involved parenting
    b. lone parenting
    c. an extended family
    d. a reconstituted family

12. Tommy's parents have been divorced. Which one of the following behaviours will he likely exhibit?
    a. decreased likelihood of depression
    b. declines in school performance
    c. less defiance
    d. decreased aggression

13. Two children who are playing side by side with their own toys but who are not interacting are _____.
    a. probably 24 months old
    b. exhibiting coordinated play
    c. demonstrating enabling play
    d. exhibiting parallel play

14. Tremblay (2000) found in his study that physical aggression (PA) tends to _____.
    a. decline during the preschool years
    b. increase dramatically until age 12
    c. decline in toddlers
    d. increase for girls but not for boys

15. In regard to aggression, when a group of children arrange themselves in a well-understood pecking order of leaders and followers, this phenomenon is referred to as _____.
    a. leader-follower dichotomies
    b. dominance hierarchies
    c. role management
    d. interactional synchrony

16. When Shelly's mother says to her, "You are such a helpful child", the statement is an example of _____.
    a. a dominance hierarchy
    b. interactional synchrony
    c. a prosocial attribution
    d. a manipulative device

17. The process of acquiring self-control requires _____.
    a. the ability to role-play
    b. sensorimotor thought
    c. shifting control from the parents to the child
    d. a shift in maturity level on the part of the child

18. The knowledge of what behaviours go with being a boy or a girl is called _____.
    a. gender concept
    b. gender constancy
    c. gender identity
    d. sex role

19. Social-cognitive theory suggests that _____.
    a. children's understanding of gender is linked to gender-related behaviour.
    b. parents have a role in shaping children's sex role behaviour
    c. children show sex behaviour appropriate for their behaviour at birth
    d. parents are key motivators in facilitating gender scripts for their child

20. The understanding that gender is an innate characteristic that cannot be changed is called _____.
    a. sex role
    b. gender schema
    c. gender constancy
    d. cross-gender behaviour

21. Gender schema theory is derived from _____.
    a. Freud's theory
    b. social-learning theory
    c. Kohlberg's theory
    d. the information-processing approach

22. The first step in developing gender constancy is _____.
    a. gender stability
    b. gender identity
    c. sex-role behaviour
    d. gender scripts

23. The assumption that "girls should like dolls" illustrates a _____.
    a. sex-role stereotype
    b. cultural truism
    c. genetic constant
    d. sex-role attitude

24. Girls tend to use an enabling style when interacting. This means _____.
    a. fostering equality and intimacy
    b. critiquing the partner so improvements can be made
    c. discussing one's own attributes more than the partner's
    d. contradicting, interrupting, boasting, and other forms of self-display

25. Which of the following statements is true about sex-typed play among boys?
    a. It is easy to change boys' play preferences with modelling and reinforcement.
    b. Boys prefer the company of a boy who engages in cross-gender activity to a girl who is a tomboy.
    c. Sex-typed play preferences do not appear until middle childhood.
    d. By age three, boys are likely to show an actual aversion to "girl" activities.

INVESTIGATIVE PROJECT

Student Project 14: Observation of Altruistic Behaviour

In this project, take an "anthropological" approach to an observation of preschool-age children. Your instructor will have arranged for you to observe in a preschool, or other group-care setting, containing children between 18 months and 4 years of age. Usually, permission will have been obtained though the centre itself, but you will need to follow whatever process is required to obtain the appropriate informed consent.

Procedure

For this observation, assume you are a researcher who has become interested in the earliest forms of altruistic behaviour in children and that there has not yet been any research on this subject. You want to begin by simply observing. You have no preconceived ideas about how frequently this type of behaviour might occur, or the circumstances in which it might occur.

Observe for at least 2 hours in a group-care setting. Note in narrative form any episode that appears to you to fit some general criteria of "altruistic" or "compassionate" behaviour. For each episode, record the circumstances involved, the gender of the child, the approximate age of the child, the other children present, and the words used (if any).

Analysis and Report

After the observation, look over your notes and try to answer the following questions:

1. What definition of altruism guided your observations? Did your definition change as a result of observing the children? Were there several types of observed altruistic actions that seem to be conceptually distinct?

2. Based on the episodes you have observed, what tentative hypotheses about the early development of altruism might you propose for further study? For example, are there hints of sex differences or age differences? Did the specific setting seem to have an effect? Was such behaviour more common in pairs of children than in larger groups? Did this behaviour occur primarily when one child was hurt or upset, or did it occur in other situations as well?

3. How might you test these tentative hypotheses with further research?

CHAPTER 8 ANSWER KEY

Guided Study Questions

1. Freud and Erikson's psychoanalytic perspective offered key insights into <u>the emotional components of development in the early childhood years</u>.

11. One particular source of early exposure to psychology may have been from the raspy-voiced narration of <u>"Winnie-the-Pooh" stories</u>.

12. Shea and her colleagues contend that the characters of A. A. Milne stories display <u>a wide range of serious emotional conditions</u>.

31. Most children being raised in lone-parent families are doing fairly well by all measures, but there is a subset of these families in which children are <u>more vulnerable to a range of problems</u>.

33. Researchers, who conducted comprehensive reviews of studies regarding cognitive and social development of children from gay and lesbian parents, found that <u>the majority of studies suggest that children raised by gay and lesbian parents do not differ from those raised by heterosexual parents</u>.

35. Some of the negative effects of divorce are due to factors that were present <u>before</u> the divorce, such as <u>difficult temperament in the child or excessive marital conflict between the parents</u>.

56. These early peer interactions are still quite primitive. However, it is noteworthy that preschool friend pairs nonetheless show <u>mutual liking, more reciprocity, more extended interactions, more positive and less negative behaviour, and more supportiveness in a novel situation</u> than is true between non-friend pairs at this same age, all signs that these relationships are more than merely passing fancies. Moreover, having had a friend in early childhood is related to <u>social competence during the elementary school years</u>.

62. In a Canadian study of children's emotional knowledge, preschool <u>girls</u> scored higher than <u>boys</u> did in the ability to correctly label emotions and understand complex emotions.

Practice Questions

1. a	6. d	11. c	16. c	21. d
2. d	7. c	12. b	17. d	22. b
3. d	8. a	13. d	18. d	23. a
4. b	9. a	14. a	19. a	24. a
5. a	10. b	15. b	20. c	25. d

POLICY QUESTION II

HOW SHOULD WE DISCIPLINE OUR CHILDREN?

Learning Objective: Examine the issues regarding child discipline (pp. 265–266).

1.   Describe the various meanings given to the term discipline.

2.   State the findings of a Canadian research study at McMaster University regarding the outcomes in later life of children who were slapped and/or spanked.

3.   Examine the findings from other researchers regarding spanking and detrimental outcomes.

4.   Describe the Canadian cases involving the use of corporal punishment to discipline children.

5.   What are your own thoughts and feelings regarding the use of corporal punishment?

6.   State the January 2004 Canadian Supreme Court ruling regarding discipline.

7.   What is the controversy regarding physical punishment made by child psychologist Joan Durrant (2004), at the University of Manitoba?

8.   What, in your estimation, are alternative forms of effective discipline?

9.   Explain, in your own terms, the "Joint Statement on Physical Punishment of Children and Youth."

10. Describe the findings regarding physical punishment administered by parents.

11. What steps would you take to begin to develop a health-teaching plan to inform parents on discipline? Outline a health-teaching plan that you have designed.

POLICY QUESTION III

WHAT ARE THE EFFECTS OF CHILDHOOD POVERTY IN CANADA?

Learning Objective: Summarize the issues about childhood poverty in Canada (pp. 267–269).

1. Compare and contrast child poverty rates in Canada and Sweden.

2. Suggest reasons to account for the poverty rates that occurred during the late 1990s for families within different sectors.

3. Poverty rates for Aboriginal children were more than _____.

4. Outline the effects of poverty on families and children.

5. List the negative consequences created by poverty that place children at greater risk.

6. Considering different family forms at risk, list the negative consequences created by poverty.

7. Differentiate the types, quality, and extent of treatment available to children in the working class or middle class and in low-income families.

8. Parents who are poor but who nonetheless feel that they have enough social support are _____.

9. Some of the differences in child-rearing patterns between low-income and high-income parents may also result from _____, and some may be a _____.

10. State the research findings regarding the effect of living in a concentrated pocket of poverty.

11. Dr. Fraser Mustard and the Honourable Margaret McCain co-authored a report for the Ontario Government called _____.

12. State a significant point of the report and its outcome.

13. Social policy issues:
    a. What is your definition of low-income?
    b. How do you know whether or not there are low-income families living in your town/city? What kinds of resources are available in your area to assist children living in poverty?

c. How can responsible citizens assist in the creation of opportunities for children who live in poverty?

d. What policies are in effect to assist children living in poverty? What social policies need to be created to assist children living in poverty?

14. List the several initiatives launched in order to progress towards dealing with the serious inequities and barriers that block opportunities for children's success.

15. What, in your opinion, may be additional initiatives needed to assist Canadian children living in poverty to reach their maximum potential?

POLICY QUESTION III ANSWER KEY

3. Poverty rates for Aboriginal children were more than <u>twice the rate for non-Aboriginal children (CCSD, 2003b)</u>.

8 Parents who are poor but who nonetheless feel that they have enough social support are <u>much less likely to be harshly punitive, or unsupportive of their children</u>.

9. Some of the differences in child-rearing patterns between low-income and high-income parents may also result from <u>straightforward modelling of the way the parents themselves were reared</u>, and some may be <u>a product of ignorance of children's needs</u>.

11. Dr. Fraser Mustard and the Honourable Margaret McCain co-authored a report for the Ontario government entitled "<u>Early Years Study—Reversing the Real Brain Drain</u>."

CHAPTER 9

PHYSICAL AND COGNITIVE DEVELOPMENT IN MIDDLE CHILDHOOD

OVERVIEW OF CHAPTER

Development in middle childhood, ages 6 to 12, is marked by major physical changes, including those in the brain. Cognitive advances occur in these years, and the patterns and habits established during this time affect not only adolescent experiences, but also adulthood. Formal education affects development, and a variety of factors such as learning disabilities, attention problems, language proficiency, gender, race, and culture shape academic achievement.

Physical Changes

- Growth from 6 to 12 is steady and slow. Coordination of both large muscles and fine motor continue to improve. Sex differences in bone and skeletal maturation may lead boys and girls to pursue different activities.

- Major growth spurts occur in the brain in 6- to 8-year-olds and in 10- to 12-year-olds. Neurological development leads to improvements in selective attention, information processing speed, and spatial perception.

- School-aged children require a regular medical check-up. Unintentional injuries and obesity are among the most significant health hazards of this age group.

Cognitive Changes

- Language development continues at an astonishing rate, with vocabulary growth, improvements in grammar, and an understanding of the social uses of language.

- The school-aged child discovers or develops a set of immensely powerful schemes that Piaget called concrete operations, such as reversibility, addition, subtraction, multiplication, division, and serial ordering. The child develops the ability to use inductive logic but does not yet use deductive logic.

- Piaget understood that it took children some years to apply the new cognitive skills to all kinds of problems, a phenomenon he called "horizontal decalage". The "operations" may actually be rules for solving specific types of problems.

- Children in middle childhood clearly make improvements in processing efficiency, automaticity, executive and strategic processes, and expertise.

Schooling

- Literacy, the ability to read and write, is the focus of education in the 6- to 12-year-old period. Reading skills include improvements in phonological awareness, automaticity, learning word parts, comprehension strategies, and exposure to good literature. Writing techniques include outlining, paragraph development, and language mechanics, as well as children's ability to edit their own and others' written work.

- School has a significant effect in fostering the 6- to 12-year-old's shift to more advanced cognitive skills. Children who lack school experience show fewer such skills.

- School progress of children with exceptionalities is sometimes assessed using both IQ tests and achievement tests. Both types of tests can overlook important aspects of intellectual functioning.

- In Canada, the trend is towards evaluating a student in terms of age-appropriate provincial or territorial standards.

- Effective schools have many of the same qualities of authoritative parenting, such as clear rules and goals, good control, good communication, and high nurturance. Parent involvement is important in high-quality schools. Some parents choose to educate their children at home, but research examining the cognitive and social effects of home-schooling is sparse.

Individual and Group Differences

- In Canada, 10 to 15% of the population may experience learning problems that are a continuation of learning disabilities from early childhood. A general trend exists away from the use of labels for learning problems and toward a focus on child's academic strengths and style of processing information. The Learning Disabilities Association of Canada (LDAC) has developed a national definition of learning disabilities.

- Many children with attention-deficit hyperactivity disorder (ADHD) have problems in school but do not fit well into typical special education categories.

- Children with limited English skills perform as well as English-speaking peers when they receive specific kinds of support in school.

- The official languages of Canada are English and French. In the Canadian education system, French Immersion programs have become a successful component of the school system

- There are no sex differences in overall IQ, but recent Canadian studies reveal that girls do somewhat better on reading, writing, and math tasks. There is no clear agreement about how to explain such differences.

LEARNING GOALS

After completing Chapter 8, students should be able to:
1.   Trace the physical changes in middle childhood.
2.   Summarize the cognitive changes in the school years.
3.   Discuss ways in which schools influence cognitive development for ages 6 to 12.
4.   Discuss the learning disability concept.
5.   Describe some of the individual differences that have an impact on school-aged children.

GUIDED STUDY QUESTIONS

PHYSICAL CHANGES

Growth and Motor Development (pp. 271–272)

Objective 9.1: Identify the changes in growth and motor development from ages 6 to 12.

1.   Between 6 and 12, children grow _____ centimetres and add about _____ kilograms each year.

2.   List some of the skills that improve as a result of gains in large muscle coordination and in fine muscle coordination.

3.   Give examples of how the sex differences in skeletal and muscular maturation cause girls to be better coordinated but slower and somewhat weaker than boys.

The Brain and Nervous System (pp. 272–273)

Objective 9.2: Describe how the growth spurts of the brain in middle childhood affect cognitive development.

4.   Define the following terms:
     a.   selective attention
     b.   association areas
     c.   spatial perception
     d.   relative right-left orientation
     e.   spatial cognition

5.   Describe the site and result of the two growth spurts by completing the following table.

Site of Growth Spurt	Area of Improvement

6. Give an example of how the myelinization of linkages between the frontal lobes and the reticular formation work together to develop selective attention.

7. How does the myelinization of the association areas contribute to increases in information-processing speed?

8. Give an example of the development of the lateralization of spatial perception, and describe a behavioural test of spatial perception lateralization that neuroscientists often use.

9. What evidence suggests that visual experience affects the development of spatial perception? Give an example of how visual experiences might explain sex differences in spatial perception and spatial cognition.

Health Promotion and Wellness (pp. 273–276)

Objective 9.3: Identify the health risks to children in middle childhood.

10. Define the following terms:
    a. obesity
    b. body mass index (BMI)

11. At what age should children be vaccinated for Hepatitis B if it was missed during infancy?

12. State the most frequent cause of fatal and non-fatal unintentional injuries to school-aged children.

13. Aside from unintentional injuries, the most significant health risk of the middle childhood period concerns _____.

14. _____ contributes to obesity in children just as it does in adults. However, both twin and adoption studies suggest that _____
    _____.

15. Describe data from Cycle 3 of NLSCY regarding the participation of children and adolescents in physical exercise. What recommendations, by CAHPERD and CMA, have been given regarding physical exercise for children in kindergarten through Grade 12?

16. Describe the effects of a lack of physical exercise in children.

Development in the Information Age: The Effects of Video Games (p. 274)

Objective 9.4: Summarize the issues involved with video games and the development of spatial cognition.

17. What are the positive effects, and the dark side, of video games?

18. What are some effects of watching violent video games?

COGNITIVE CHANGES

Language (p. 277)

Objective 9.5: Trace the pattern of language development in the school years.

19. Across the middle years, children also learn how to _____
_____.

20. Define derived words, and give examples.

21. According to Anglin, what do children learn about the structure of language at about age 8 or 9?

Piaget's Concrete Operational Stage (pp. 277–278)

Objective 9.6: Explain Piaget's view of concrete operations.

22. Define the following terms:
    a. concrete operations
    b. decentration
    c. operations
    d. reversibility

23. Why did Piaget believe that the concept of reversibility was the most important?

24. Define and differentiate between the following:
    a. inductive logic
    b. deductive logic

Direct Tests of Piaget's View (pp. 278–280)

Objective 9.7: Summarize the research testing Piaget's ideas.

25. Piaget understood that it took children some years to apply these new cognitive skills to all kinds of problems, a phenomenon he called _____.

26. Give examples of research that has found that Piaget was correct in his assertions that concrete operational schemes are acquired gradually across the 6- to 12-year-old period.

27. Define class inclusion, and give an example.

28. Describe Robert Siegler's research with a balance scale, through which he discovered the rules for problem solving.

29. Describe the four steps of rule formation Siegler found by completing the following table.

Rule	Description
Rule I	
Rule II	
Rule III	
Rule IV	

30.   According to Siegler, what determines the progression from one rule to the next?

Advances in Information-Processing Skills (pp. 280–283)

Objective 9.8: Explain advances in information-processing skills in the school years.

31.   Define the following terms:
   a.   processing efficiency
   b.   automaticity
   c.   executive processes
   d.   memory strategies

32.   State evidence that cognitive processes become more efficient.

33.   Explain why automaticity is critical to efficient information-processing.

34.   Give an example of the importance of the increase of executive processes during middle   childhood.

35.   Explain how expertise can make a difference in how efficiently the information-processing system works.

SCHOOLING

Literacy (pp. 283–284)

Objective 9.9: Describe the skills involved in learning to read and write.

36.   Define the following terms:
   a.   literacy
   b.   phonological awareness

37. Complete the following table by providing an example of each of the following skills.

Skill	Example
automaticity	
oral reading	
word parts	
comprehension strategies	
good literature	

38. Describe the skills involved in learning to write.

39. Describe some techniques to assist poor readers.

Schooling and Cognitive Development (pp. 284–285)

Objective 9.10: Describe the influences that school has on cognitive development.

40. What have cross-cultural studies concluded regarding school experience and cognitive skills?

41. Attending school helps children _____, precisely what it is intended to do.

Measuring and Predicting Achievement (pp. 285–287)

Objective 9.11: Describe means of evaluating students in the educational system in Canada.

42. State the purpose of the creation of the Council of Ministers of Education Canada.

43. Define the following terms:
     a. standardized achievement test
     b. assessment
     c. evaluation

44. Describe the process of evaluating the academic performance of students in Canada.

45. Complete the following table by listing and briefly describing the eight types of intelligence, according to Howard Gardner:

Type of Intelligence	Description

46. List and give an example of the three components of Sternberg's triarchic theory of intelligence by completing the following table.

Component	Example

47. Describe three components of Goleman's theory of emotional intelligence, and explain why it is important.

Component	Importance

48. Children's ability to exercise _____ in early childhood is strongly related to _____.

School Quality, Parent Involvement, and Homeschooling (pp. 288–289)

Objective 9.12: Describe how school quality, parent involvement, and homeschooling affect achievement.

49.   Define an effective school and list its characteristics.

50.   How are the characteristics of an effective school similar to those of authoritative parenting?

51.   List the benefits of parental participation in school activities.

52.   List reasons why some parents choose to homeschool their children.

INDIVIDUAL AND GROUP DIFFERENCES

Learning Disabilities (pp. 289–292)

Objective 9.13: Describe the issues involved with learning disabilities.

53.   State the national definition of learning disability that the Learning Disabilities Association of Canada (LDAC) has developed.

54.   Discuss the controversial debate regarding causes of learning disabilities.

55.   Restate a neurological explanation of how learning disabilities might occur.

56.   Define the term "dyslexia."

The Real World/Schooling: Canadian Special Education Practices (p. 290)

Objective 9.14: Outline the Canadian Special Education practices for exceptional children.

57.   Describe three educational practices developed to meet the special needs of exceptional children.

Attention-Deficit Hyperactivity Disorder (pp. 292–293, 295)

Objective 9.15: Summarize the issues involved with attention-deficit hyperactivity disorder.

58.   Define attention-deficit hyperactivity disorder (ADHD).

59.   Give examples of findings that children with ADHD are neurologically different from their peers.

60.   Describe the association between sleep problems and ADHD that the researchers at OISE have been investigating.

61.   List and describe the two types of ADHD.

62.   List the kinds of problems ADHD children may have in school.

63. Describe parent training that may be useful in helping parents cope with children who have ADHD.

64. Identify the pros and cons of giving children ADHD stimulant medication, like methylphenidate (Ritalin), by completing the following table:

Pros	*Cons*

65. State the reason why Canadian pediatricians caution about the long-term effectiveness of stimulant medications beyond 4 weeks of treatment.

Second-Language Learners (pp. 295–296)

Objective 9.16: Identify the issues related to children who are second-language learners.

66. Define the following terms:
    a. limited English proficient (LEP)
    b. bilingual education
    c. English-as-a-second-language (ESL)

67. Why is submersion probably not the best approach for second language learners?

68. How does LEP students' performance in school compare to that of English-speaking children?

69. State the cautionary note regarding LEP students, and explain why it is necessary.

Bilingual Education (pp. 296–297)

Objective 9.17: Summarize the issues regarding bilingual education.

70. What are several benefits of French Immersion programs in Canadian schools?

71. There is a particular need to preserve the languages of Canadian Aboriginal peoples, since their culture is based on _____.

Sex Differences in Achievement (p. 297)

Objective 9.18: Summarize the findings about sex differences in achievement.

72. What differences between boys and girls exist in the results of provincial standards tests?

73. What are some explanations for the gender differences in test achievements?

CRITICAL REFLECTION EXERCISE

Developing Cognitive Skills

Imagine that you are a schoolteacher working with children ranging in age from 6 to 8 years. You want to make sure that you develop classroom activities that provide children with practice with their developing cognitive skills. First, describe three skills that children are developing during these ages. Second, suggest one activity for each of these skills that you could use in the classroom to enhance the child's use of each skill.

PRACTICE QUESTIONS

1. School-aged children will show the most dramatic increase in _____.
   a. jumping ability
   b. intelligence
   c. running speed
   d. fine motor coordination

2. The ability to identify and act on the relationships of objects in space is called
   _____.
   a. relative right-left orientation
   b. an association area
   c. spatial perception
   d. information-processing speed

3. George, age 9, has the ability to understand the difference between statements such as, "It's on your right," and "It's on my right". This ability to differentiate right and left from multiple perspectives is called_____.
   a. handedness
   b. an executive process
   c. spatial cognition
   d. relative right-left orientation

4. Harry, age 7, has a BMI above the 95th percentile and is classified as obese. To combat his obesity, his parents can encourage Harry to do the following except:
   a. begin dieting
   b. limit time on computers
   c. be involved in an exercise program
   d. take part in a school-based nutrition education program

5. A derived word is one that _____.
   a. was slang but is now considered acceptable
   b. has a basic root to which a prefix or suffix is added
   c. means dramatically different things in different cultures
   d. is offensive to individuals of particular cultural groups

6. The understanding that both physical actions and mental operations can be reversed is called _____.
   a. addition and subtraction
   b. conservation
   c. reversibility
   d. reverse object rotation

7. Which one of the following correctly illustrates inductive logic?
   a. demonstrating an ability to go from a specific experience to a general principle
   b. thinking up examples that illustrate the concept of equality
   c. knowing how to take a general principle and predict a specific outcome
   d. demonstrating an ability to process abstract ideals within a short time-frame

8. Which of the following statements illustrates an understanding of class inclusion?
   a. cats and dogs are not the same
   b. a rose is a flower and that flowers are plants
   c. not all objects are alive
   d. objects stay the same even if their appearance changes

9. The ability to recall information from long-term memory without using short-term memory capacity is called _____.
   a. horizontal decalage
   b. conservation
   c. automaticity
   d. memory strategies

10. Which of the following represents an executive process?
    a. making a decision, carrying it out, and sticking with it
    b. deferring a decision to someone who you feel has more expertise
    c. being able to pull information from long-term memory
    d. planning to write a paper and considering alternative methods for doing so

11. The ability to read and write is called _____.
    a. phonological awareness
    b. literacy
    c. long-term memory
    d. intelligence

12. Oral reading is critical to success in the early years because_____ _____.
    a. it exposes children to good literature
    b. it enables children to learn to edit their own and others' written work
    c. it provides instruction in identifying the purpose of a particular text
    d. it provides an opportunity to practice translating written language into spoken words

13. In Canada, age-appropriate provincial and territorial tests offer the student _____.
    a. a more valid measure of achievement
    b. an increased comfort level regarding school achievement
    c. a true score of academic success
    d. a comparison of achievement with others'

14. Tracy, age 13, has frequent emotional outbursts. Her scholastic achievement is decreasing and she does not want to go to school anymore. Which one of the following theories indicates a relationship between self-control and achievement in adolescence?
    a. Robert Sternberg's triarchic theory of intelligence
    b. Daniel Goleman's theory of emotional intelligence
    c. Robert Rosenthal's Pygmalion in the classroom theory
    d. Howard Gardner's theory of multiple intelligences

15. The text suggests that effective schools do most of the things that _____.
    a. allow the children maximum freedom to explore and learn
    b. authoritative parents do
    c. allow children to learn rule-governed behaviour
    d. the parents should be doing but are not

16. When parents attend parent-teacher conferences and get involved in school, research shows that their children _____.
    a. tend to adapt better to school and get better grades
    b. become resentful and performance tends to drop
    c. have higher performance if the child is a daughter but lower performance if the child is a son
    d. drop out of school at an early age

17. The Learning Disabilities Association of Canada provides interventions for individuals with learning disabilities to include which one of the following?
    a. commending individuals and their families
    b. developing specific skill instructions
    c. developing brief contracts
    d. implementing a critical path for an individual

18. A child who has a reading difficulty has a problem skill called _____.
    a. literacy
    b. dyslexia
    c. learning disability
    d. limited English proficient

19. All of the following are Canadian special education practices for exceptional children, except _____.
    a. Group Educational Plan
    b. program accommodation
    c. Individual Education Plan
    d. modified program

20. Research indicates that sleep-deprived children may display _____, which could be mistaken for ADHD
    a. lethargy
    b. spatial difficulties
    c. compliance
    d. lack of coordination

21. A child who exhibits two types of ADHD usually produces school work that is _____.
    a. well organized
    b. neat and tidy
    c. filled with errors.
    d. creative and graphic

22. The term used to describe both non-English-speaking immigrant children and native-born children who do not speak English is _____.
    a. English-as-a-second-language (ESL)
    b. submersion
    c. limited English proficient (LEP)
    d. bilingual education

23. The processes of learning to read, write, and speak a second language instils an _____.
    a. appreciation for another culture
    b. individualistic style towards the world
    c. understanding of artistic programs
    d. analytical style towards the solution of problems

24. Which one of the following languages may be endangered in Canada?
    a. Ukrainian language
    b. German language
    c. Aboriginal language
    d. Chinese language

25. In Canada, girls seem to outperform boys in which one of the following skills?
    a. speed of information processing
    b. bilingual fluency
    c. vocabulary skills
    d. reading and writing

CASE STUDY

Derek is 7 years old. At his last physical check-up his BMI was above the 85th percentile. He mainly plays indoors and loves to play video games especially of the educational variety. He is beginning to develop much knowledge about dinosaurs. While he plays the video games he munches on potato chips and cheezies and drinks high-calorie pop. Lately, Derek says that he hates school because the students make fun of him. His parents have decided to opt for home schooling.

What are some of the benefits of educationally based video games that Derek views?

Define BMI and explain your understanding of what is meant when a child, like Derek, is above the 85th percentile.

What do you think is contributing to Derek's high BMI?

If you were Derek's parents, what strategies would you suggest to Derek to have him start losing weight?

Would you suggest homeschooling for Derek? What does the research indicate on home schooling.

RESEARCH PROJECT

Student Project 15: Conservation of Mass, Number, and Weight

For this project, you need to locate a child between the ages of 6 and 10, and obtain permission from the parents, or from both the parents and the child, following the procedures specified by your instructor. You will be testing this child for three kinds of conservation: mass, number, and weight.

Recall that the concept of conservation involves the understanding that some features of objects remain invariant despite changes in other features. The weight of an object remains the same regardless of how its shape is changed; the number of objects in a row remain the same regardless of how widely spaced the objects are. Typically, children learn (or discover) number and mass conservation at about age 5 or 6, while they learn conservation of weight later, at perhaps 8 or 9. A child between 6 and 8 may be able to manage the first two conservation tasks, but not the last.

Procedure

The testing can ordinarily be done most easily in the child's home, although other settings are also acceptable. Present the child with the three tasks in the order given here, following instructions precisely.

Conservation of Mass

You will need two equal balls of clay or modelling dough, each a size that can be readily handled by a child's palm. Handle them yourself, rounding them into balls, and then hand them to the child, asking:

> *Is there the same amount of clay in each of these balls? Are they the same?*

If the child agrees that they are the same, proceed. If not, say to the child: "Make them the same." The child may want to squish them a little or may actually shift some clay from one ball to the other. That is all right. When the child is ready, ask again:

> *Is there the same amount of clay in each of these balls? Are they the same?*

Once the child has agreed that they are the same, say:

> *Now I'm going to squash this one into a pancake.*

Squash one of the two balls into a pancake and place the two objects—the remaining ball and the pancake—in front of the child. Read the following questions exactly as written and record precisely what the child says:

Is there the same amount of clay in this one (pointing to the ball) *as there is in this one* (pointing to the pancake), *or is there more here* (pointing to the ball) *or more here* (pointing to the pancake)?

Depending on the child's answer to the first question, follow up by asking:

Why are they the same? or *Why is there more here?*

Now mould the pancake back into a ball and set the two balls aside for the moment.

Conservation of Number

For this part of the process you will need 14 pennies or identical buttons. Start with 10 items and place them between yourself and the child (preferably on a table, but the floor will do), spaced in two rows of five, as follows:

X X X X X

X X X X X

Ask the child:

Are there the same number of pennies (buttons) *in this row as in this row, or are there more here* (pointing to the child's row) *or more here* (pointing to your row)?

The child may want to move the objects around a bit before he or she agrees that the two rows are the same, which is fine. Once the child has agreed that they are the same, spread the objects in your row so that it is now noticeably longer than the child's row but still contains only five objects, i.e.:

X   X   X   X   X

X X X X X

Now ask the following questions, and record the child's exact answers:

Are there the same number of pennies in this row as in this row, or are there more here, or more here?

Depending on the child's answer, ask either of the following probe questions:

Why are they the same? or *Why are there more here?*

Now spread out the child's row and add two objects to each row, so that your row and the child's row are again exactly matched, with seven items equally spaced in each. Repeat the questions above, and record the child's answer precisely.

Now move the objects in your row closer together, so that the child's row is now longer. Ask the questions again, and record the answers.

Conservation of Weight

Put away the pennies (or give them to the child), and bring out the two balls of clay again, saying;

> *Now we're going to play with the clay again.*

Hand the balls to the child and ask:

> *Do these two balls weigh the same? Do they have the same amount of weight?*

If the child agrees that they weigh the same, proceed. If not, say "Make them the same," and let the child manipulate the balls until she agrees. Once she has agreed say:

> *Now I am going to make this ball into a hot dog.*

Roll one of the two balls into a hot-dog shape. When you have completed the transformation, put the two pieces of clay in front of the child and ask:

> *Does this one* (pointing to the hot dog) *weigh the same as this one* (pointing to the ball), *or does this one weigh more, or does this one weigh more?*

Depending on the child's answer to the question, ask one of the following probe questions and record the answers carefully:

> *Why do they weigh the same?* or *Why does this one weigh more?*

This ends the procedure, so you should praise and thank the child. You might also want to play a bit with the child with some other toy of the child's choosing, to make sure that the whole process is pleasant for the child.

Analysis and Report

For each of the crucial questions, decide whether or not the child "conserved." To be regarded as having conserved, the child must have (1) said the two objects were the same after transformation and (2) given a valid reason, such as:

> *You haven't added any or taken any away, so they have to be the same.*

> *One is longer, but it is also skinnier, so it is still the same.*

> *If I made it back into a ball, it would be the same.*

Compare the child's performance on the three types of conservation. Did the child conserve in all three exercises? If not, was the child's performance consistent with the typically observed sequence of acquisition? (If the child conserved weight, but not mass or number, that would be contrary to research data). What else, other than the child's basic comprehension of conservation, might affect the child's answers in the test of this kind? Was the child interested or bored? Were there distractions in the environment? Might the sequence in which the items were given have any effect? Do you think it would have mattered, for example, if conservation of weight had been tested before conservation of mass? If one were designing a study to examine the acquisition of these conservations, would one want to have all children given the items in the same order, or should the order be randomized?

If several students have completed this project, you may want to combine your data and analyze children's success on these three conservations as a function of age. Do your collective findings match the results of existing research?

INVESTIGATIVE PROJECT

Student Project 16: Investigation of IQ Testing in Local Schools

As a follow-up to the information given in the text on the pros and cons of using IQ test scores in the schools, one student, or a small group of students, may wish to investigate the policies on the uses of IQ testing in your local school area.

Basic Questions to Answer

- Is there a provincial or territorial policy on the use of IQ tests in public or private schools? Is there a local area policy instead of, or in addition to, a provincial or territorial policy? What input does a school board have into testing students?

- If individual IQ tests are used in the school area, who administers them? For what purposes are the scores used? What other types of information are used as part of the academic placement process?

Sources of Information

The best sources are the department of education and local school area administrative offices. In school areas, you will have to use some ingenuity to determine which person or office is the best to talk to. Naturally, you should identify yourself as a student and make it clear that this information you seek is for a class report.

CHAPTER 9 ANSWER KEY

Guided Study Questions

1. Between 6 and 12, children grow <u>5 to 8</u> centimetres and add about <u>2.75</u> kilograms per year.

13. Aside from unintentional injuries, the most significant health risk of the middle childhood period <u>concerns body weight</u>.

14. <u>Overeating, or eating too much of the wrong foods</u>, contributes to obesity in children just as it does in adults. However, both twin and adoption studies suggest that <u>obesity probably results from an interaction between a genetic predisposition, epigenetic modifications set early in life for obesity, and environmental factors that promote overeating or low levels of activity</u>.

19. Across the middle years, children also learn how to <u>maintain the topic of conversation, how to create unambiguous sentences, and how to speak politely or persuasively</u>.

25. Piaget understood that it took children some years to apply these new cognitive skills to all kinds of problems, a phenomenon he called <u>horizontal decalage</u>.

41. Attending school helps children <u>learn to think</u>, precisely what it is intended to do.

48. Children's ability to exercise <u>control over their emotions</u> in early childhood is strongly related to <u>measures of academic achievement in high school</u>.

71. There is a particular need to preserve the languages of Canadian Aboriginal peoples, since their culture is based on <u>oral tradition and is expressed most fully through their primary heritage language</u>.

Practice Questions

1. d	6. c	11. b	16. a	21. c
2. c	7. a	12. d	17. b	22. c
3. d	8. b	13. a	18. b	23. a
4. a	9. c	14. b	19. c	24. c
5. b	10. d	15. b	20. d	25. d

Case Study

Answer: Chapter 9 (p. 274). Educationally based video games have several benefits; such as they increase knowledge in various subjects like health, history or science.

Chapter 9 (p. 275). The body mass index (BMI) is a measure that estimates a child's proportion of body fat. A child whose BMI is above the 85th percentile for his or her sex and age is considered to be overweight.

Chapter 9 (p. 275). Decreased activity and the consumption of high-caloric foods are factors leading to obesity.

Chapter 9 (p. 276). One main strategy is to increase physical activity. Several others strategies are for a child to develop good eating habits and limit time on videogames.

Chapter 9 (p. 289). Some parents homeschool to protect their children from negative peer influence or school based crimes. In addition, children with disabilities who are homeschooled don't have to deal with teasing from peers. In this particular case, the parents need to realize that Derek's lifestyle may need changing before opting for homeschooling. Presently, the research on homeschooling is sparse.

SOCIAL AND PERSONALITY DEVELOPMENT IN MIDDLE CHILDHOOD

OVERVIEW OF CHAPTER

The social and personality development in children ages 6 to 12 includes changes in social relationships and the expansion of self-concept. Influences beyond the family and school include after-school care, poverty, and television.

Theories of Social and Personality Development

- Freud believed that children repress sexual desires between ages 6 and 12, a period he called the latency stage. Erikson claimed that children in middle childhood acquire a sense of industry by achieving goals determined by their culture.

- Between ages 6 and 12, children's understanding of others' stable, internal traits improve.

Dimensions of Moral Development

- Psychoanalytic theorists emphasize emotions, such as guilt, shame, and pride in explaining moral development. More recent examinations of moral emotion have focused on empathy and the delay of gratification.

- Cognitive-development theorists focus on moral reasoning. Piaget and Kohlberg claim that moral reasoning develops in stages that correlate with Piaget's cognitive stages.

- According to behavioural theorists, moral development is a function of reward, punishment, and modelling.

Social Relationships

- Middle childhood is a period of increasing independence of the child from the family with fewer attachment behaviours. Yet attachment to parents and siblings continues to be important.

- The biggest shift in relationships in the middle childhood years is the increasing importance of peers, particularly close friendships. Children's selection of friends depends on variables such as trustworthiness as well as play preferences and gender.

- Gender segregation of peer groups is at its peak in the school-aged years in every culture. Boys' and girls' friendships differ in specific ways.

- Research on Canadian children reveals that physical aggression declines in middle childhood, although verbal aggression increases. Boys show higher levels of physical and direct verbal aggression, and higher rates of conduct disorders than girls. Relational aggression, aimed at hurting others, is expressed especially in girls.

- There are three groups of social status: popular children, rejected children, and neglected children. Aggressive children, or those who bully, are often rejected, but some aggressive children are popular. Neglected children may suffer from loneliness and depression.

Personality and Self-Concept

- The Big Five personality traits are identifiable and stable in middle childhood. They may be useful in identifying children who are in need of interventions to prevent anti-social behaviour.

- The psychological self develops in middle childhood. As a result, self-descriptions begin to include traits such as intelligence and friendliness along with physical characteristics.

- One aspect of the self-concept that is complex and understudied is the spiritual self. Several educational ways exist, such as storytelling, to help the preadolescent learn to trust his/her intuition and emotions to search for meaningful existence and to develop the spiritual aspects of the self-concept.

- The self-concept of the 6- to 12-year-old contains an evaluative aspect called self-esteem. It is shaped by the degree of discrepancy a child experiences between goals and achievements, and the degree of perceived social support from peers and parents.

Influences Beyond Family and School

- After school self-care is associated with many negative effects, but children who have parental monitoring are less likely to be affected.

- Large regional differences across Canada exist in the television viewing patterns of children. Television has positive educational effects, such as opportunities for learning vocabulary and prosocial behaviour, but heavy TV watching is associated with lower scores on achievement tests and reduced physical activity. Experts agree that watching violence on television also increases the level of personal aggression shown by a child.

LEARNING GOALS

After completing Chapter 10, students should be able to:
1. Distinguish the theories of social and personality development.
2. Explain the dimensions of moral development.
3. Describe the changes in the social relationships of children ages six to twelve.
4. Summarize the development of personality and self-concept in school-aged children.

5.   Identify the influences beyond the family and school on social and personality development in middle childhood.

GUIDED STUDY QUESTIONS

THEORIES OF SOCIAL AND PERSONALITY DEVELOPMENT

Psychoanalytic Perspectives (pp. 301–302)

Objective 10.1: Describe the key points of the psychoanalytic perspectives relevant to middle childhood.

1.   Define the following terms:
      a.   latency stage
      b.   industry versus inferiority stage

2.   What is the focus of Freud's psychosexual theory during middle childhood?

3.   What is the focus of Erikson's psychosocial theory during middle childhood?

Social-Cognitive Perspectives (pp. 302–303)

Objective 10.2: Summarize the key points of the social-cognitive perspectives relevant to middle childhood

4.   Define the following terms:
      a.   behavioural comparison
      b.   psychological constructs

5.   Give examples of how the child's description of others moves from the concrete to the abstract during middle childhood.

6.   How do behavioural comparisons and psychological constructs change throughout the school years?

DIMENSIONS OF MORAL DEVELOPMENT

Moral Emotions (pp. 303–304)

Objective 10.3: Trace the development of moral emotions across the middle childhood period.

7.   Define the following terms:
      a.   conscience
      b.   ego ideal

8.   According to Freud, how does a child learn moral rules?

9.   According to Freud, what causes a child to feel guilt? What causes a child to feel shame?

10.   How does Erikson's view of moral development differ from Freud's?

11.   What do researchers state about children who experience shame?

12.   How does cognitive development affect the connection between moral emotions and moral behaviour?

Moral Reasoning (pp. 305–306)

Objective 10.4: Trace the development of moral reasoning across the school-aged period.

13.   Define the following terms:
   a.   moral reasoning
   b.   moral realism stage
   c.   moral relativism stage

14.   Describe Piaget's two-stage theory of moral development, and give examples of each stage.

15.   Briefly describe Kohlberg's theory of moral development.

The Real World/Parenting: Encouraging Moral Reasoning (p. 306)

Objective 10.5: List suggestions for helping children learn mature moral reasoning.

16.   Give examples of each of Lickona's suggestions to help children achieve more mature levels of moral reasoning

Moral Behaviour (pp. 306–307)

Objective 10.6: Summarize how learning theory explains the development of moral behaviour.

17.   According to Skinner, how do consequences teach children to obey moral rules? Give examples.

18.   Give examples of how punishment may actually interfere with moral development.

19.   How would parents who use inductive discipline respond to a 7-year-old child who has stolen a candy bar?

20. How does social-learning theorist Albert Bandura explain how children learn moral reasoning?

SOCIAL RELATIONSHIPS

Family Relationships (pp. 308–310)

Objective 10.7: Describe the changes in family relationships across the school years.

21. Give an example of how school-aged children are better than younger children at predicting family roles and relationships.

22. Why does the agenda of issues between parent and child change during middle childhood?

23. Define self-regulation.

24. Give an example of cultural differences in parental expectations of self-regulation.

25. Give an example of sex differences in parental expectations of self-regulation.

26. List two parenting variables that contribute to the development of self-regulation and give an example of how the parenting variables are associated with the authoritative style of parenting

27. State the findings of a study of Canadian mothers conducted to determine if maternal methods of control were related to childhood aggression and social withdrawal.

28. List and give an example of each of the patterns, or styles, of sibling relationships by completing the following table.

Pattern/Style	Example

29. What is stated by the research from other countries regarding children without siblings?

Friendships (pp. 310–312)

Objective 10.8: Trace the development of the friendships of the elementary school child.

30. Give an example of how preschoolers and young school-aged children would describe the way that people make friends. Give an example of how a 10-year-old would describe the way people make friends.

31. List several examples of evidence of the centrality of friends to social development in middle childhood.

32. Canadian researchers have found that social competence is closely related to a

    _____.

Gender Segregation (pp. 312–313)

Objective 10.9: Describe gender segregation in middle childhood.

33. Give examples of how shared interests and activities play a critical part of friendship in the early years of middle childhood.

34. Compare ways that girls' and boys' friendships differ, and list characteristics that they have in common by completing the following table:

Differences	*Commonalties*

35. Define controlling speech, and give examples.

36. Compare and contrast the aspect of close friendships in Canadian children between grade 6 and 10.

Patterns of Aggression (pp. 313–315)

Objective 10.10: Identify the patterns of aggression in school-aged children.

37. Define the following terms:
    a. relational aggression
    b. retaliatory aggression

38. What happens to the level of physical aggression in Canadian children during the middle childhood years? Describe the exception to the general pattern.

39. Explain the difference between girls' and boys' tendency to express aggression.

40. How does the level of retaliatory aggression change across the middle childhood years?

41. Describe a technique to help children learn non-aggressive ways to manage the kinds of situations that lead to retaliatory aggression.

42. Tremblay et al. (1996) found_____ in rates of aggression in children.

43. What is a strong predictor of aggression in boys and girls?

Social Status (pp. 315–318)

Objective 10.11: Describe the characteristics of children that influence their social status in middle childhood.

44. Define social status, and list the three groups of social status.

45. How do developmentalists measure popularity and rejection?

46. Give characteristics of each of the following groups of children by completing the following table. Include behaviour as well as appearance or temperament.

Group	Characteristics
Popular children	
Withdrawn/rejected children	
Aggressive/rejected children	
Neglected children	

47. Not all aggressive children are rejected. Among girls, _____

_____.

Among boys, however, _____

_____.

48. Describe the research findings regarding friends of aggressive boys in grades 4 through 6.

No East Answers: Bullies and Victims (pp. 316–317)

Objective 10.12: Summarize the research on bullies and victims.

49. List the consistent roles related to bullies and victims, which children assume in middle childhood.

50. List the characteristics of victims.

51. List four characteristics of bullies.

52. List four child-rearing factors that lie behind the development of bullying behaviour.

PERSONALITY AND SELF-CONCEPT

The Big Five Personality Traits (pp. 318–319)

Objective 10.13: Summarize the research on the Big Five personality traits.

53. Define the following terms:
    a. the Big Five
    b. extraversion
    c. agreeableness
    d. conscientiousness
    e. neuroticism
    f. openness/intellect

54. State the research findings of the Big Five personality traits in children and adolescents in both Western and non-Western cultures.

55. Give examples of how school-aged children's scores on the dimensions of the Big Five personality traits predict academic achievement and social skills in adolescence and adulthood.

The Psychological Self (pp. 319–321)

Objective 10.14: Trace the development of the psychological self during middle childhood.

56. Define the psychological self, and give examples of how it becomes increasingly complex and abstract during middle childhood.

57. As a child moves through the concrete operational period, her psychological self becomes _____.

58. What is the importance of the development of the spiritual self in the formation of the preadolescent self-concept?

59. List educational strategies that foster the development of the spiritual aspect of the self-concepts of preadolescents.

The Valued Self (p. 321)

Objective 10.15: Describe the development of the evaluative aspect of the self-concept in middle childhood.

60. Over the years of elementary school and high school, children's evaluations of their own abilities become _____
   _____
   _____.

61. Define self-esteem.

62. How does the acquisition of more sophisticated information-processing skills impact their self-esteem?

63. What is the key to self-esteem?

64. State several influences on a child's self-esteem.

65. Describe the results of Susan Harter's research on self-esteem.

66. How stable are self-esteem judgements over time?

67. Describe the correlation between the child's level of self-esteem and depression.

68. List and describe the three sources of differences in self-esteem.

INFLUENCES BEYOND FAMILY AND SCHOOL

After-School Care (pp. 324–325)

Objective 10.16: Explain how after-school care affects the social and personality development of school-aged children.

69. Define the term "self-care children."

70. List the variables associated with the effects that self-care has on a child's development.

71. Why is parental monitoring so important in self-care arrangements? Give examples of effective parental monitoring.

Television (pp. 325–328)

Objective 10.17: Identify the influences that television has on the development of children.

72. Describe the regional difference across Canada in the television viewing patterns of children.

73. Describe the positive educational effects and the negative effects on cognitive skills of television by completing the following table:

Positive Effects	*Negative Effects*

74. Describe the three types of research evidence of a causal link between television and aggression by completing the following table.

Research Type	*Evidence*

75. What is the clear message to parents from the research on television?

CRITICAL REFLECTION EXERCISE

Self-Concept

Using information from the text, provide detailed answers to the following questions:

1. What three factors do you think are the most important in influencing a child's developing self-concept during the 6- to 12-year-old age range? What role does each of these factors play? Why do you think they are so important?

2. You have been hired to teach a parenting class. Design an exercise that you could do with this class to illustrate the important effect that parents have on the developing self-concept of their children. List and discuss three things that parents might do that would have a negative effect on the child's self-concept. Provide suggestions for how to alter each of these negative effects into a positive one.

PRACTICE QUESTIONS

1. Harry, age 7, is concentrating on developing friendships with members of the same sex and on learning academic and social skills. According to Freud this period of development is called the _____stage.
    a. oral
    b. anal
    c. genital
    d. latency

2. According to Erikson, the psychosocial task of children between the ages of 6 and 12 is the development of _____, or the willingness to accomplish tasks.
    a. identity
    b. industry
    c. isolation
    d. initiative

3. Which of the following statements describing others is an example of a behavioural comparison?
    a. "She draws the best in our whole class."
    b. "He's a real stubborn idiot."
    c. "She is mean."
    d. "He is so kind."

4. According to Freud, the superego has two parts, _____.
    a. an ego ideal and a Freudian slip
    b. the id and the conscience
    c. the ego and the id
    d. a conscience and an ego ideal

5. Sally, age 10, has just learned that her parents have decided to let her stay out until 9 p.m. instead of 8 p.m. She has learned that people can agree to change rules if they want to. According to Piaget, which one of the following stages of moral development is Sally in?
    a. moral emotional
    b. moral relativism
    c. moral judgmental
    d. moral realism

6. Which of the following statements is *not* one of the suggestions for encouraging moral reasoning?
    a. encourage children to base obedience on fear
    b. teach children about reciprocity
    c. require children to give reasons for what they want.
    d. challenge children's egocentrism

7. How would a parent who uses inductive discipline help a child learn that stealing a candy bar is wrong?
    a. severely punish the child for stealing
    b. embarrass the child in front of her friends
    c. require the child to admit the crime and pay for the candy
    d. publicly spank the child to teach him a lesson

8. One way in which parents can remain connected with their middle-aged children is by _____.
    a. having family meals together
    b. playing sports together
    c. visiting extended family on weekends
    d. going to church together

9. A child's ability to maintain friendships with peers is strongly related to _____.
    a. the number of siblings in the family
    b. attachment to his parents
    c. the stability of the parents' marriage
    d. her grades in school

10. Which parental style is linked to self-regulation in school-aged children?
    a. permissive
    b. authoritative
    c. authoritarian
    d. neglecting

11. A study of Canadian mothers and children found that mothers of aggressive children were generally _____.
    a. over-controlling
    b. indifferent
    c. punishing
    d. overly permissive

12. Rival or critical relationships are more likely when siblings are _____.
    a. close together in age
    b. of the opposite gender
    c. far apart in age
    d. of the same gender

13. Selman suggested that elementary school children begin to view friends as persons who
    _____.
    a. are similar to them
    b. will do good things for them
    c. help and trust one another
    d. will protect each other

14. Which of the following illustrates controlling speech?
    a. "Let's work on this together."
    b. "If you let me borrow your toy, you can look at mine."
    c. "That's not right!"
    d. "I wish I had that toy, too."

15. Physical aggression _____ across middle childhood in Canadian children.
    a. becomes even more common for girls
    b. goes up dramatically for boys but down for girls
    c. is directed more toward inanimate objects
    d. becomes even less common

16. Which of the following is an example of relational aggression?
    a. "What a nut."
    b. "Bite your tongue."
    c. "You're stupid."
    d. "What's your problem?"

17. Which one of the following characteristics is common of victims who are bullied?
    a. high self-esteem
    b. popular
    c. lack of humour
    d. confident

18. The Big Five personality traits are _____.
    a. openness/intellect, agreeableness, conscientiousness, neuroticism, curiosity
    b. extraversion, agreeableness, conscientiousness, neuroticism, openness/intellect
    c. conscientiousness, efficiency, organization/control, responsibility, persistence
    d. enthusiasm, extraversion, sociability/sympathy, emotionality, insightfulness

19. Children's "Who am I?" responses, as they move through the concrete operational stage, become more _____ across middle childhood.
    a. positive
    b. rigid
    c. focused on physical characteristics
    d. complex and comparative

20. One educational strategy that may strengthen the development of the spiritual aspects
of   the preadolescent self-concept is:
    a. counselling
    b. praying
    c. debating
    d. story-telling

21. Harter suggests that self-esteem is influenced by the _____.
    a. discrepancy between who a child feels he ought to be and who he thinks he is
    b. sum total of the assessments the child makes about her skills
    c. addition of all the positive assessments minus the negative ones
    d. relationship between physical abilities and cultural expectations

22. Self-care children who are monitored closely are _____.
    a. more likely to be involved in criminal behaviour
    b. more likely to make poor grades
    c. less likely to experience the negative effects of self-care
    d. less likely to complete their homework

23. Which one of the following is the most important factor in managing self-care?
    a. sibling monitoring
    b. after-school programs
    c. neighbour monitoring
    d. parental monitoring

24. What are the effects of television viewing on children?
    a. Television has nothing but harmful effects.
    b. Television can have both positive and negative effects.
    c. There is no consistent evidence of television's effects.
    d. The evidence suggests that the effects of television are mostly positive.

25. Which one of the following strategies is the best to enable parents to control what
    their children view on television?
    a. plan family viewing time
    b. monitor what their children watch on television
    c. restrict television viewing during the week
    d. allow children to watch self-selected programs three times per week.

RESEARCH PROJECT

Student Project 18: Understanding of Friendship

For this project, based on Selman (1980, pp. 321–333), you will need to locate a child between the ages of 6 and 12. After obtaining the appropriate permission(s), arrange with the parents to spend some time with the child, explaining that you want to talk to the child for a school project, and that this is not a test of any kind. Try to find a time and a place to be alone with your subject; it will not work as well if siblings or parents are present. You may want to tape the child's answers, to give a more accurate account of his or her comments.

Procedure

After chatting for a while to establish rapport, say to the child something like:

> *I'd like to talk to you about friends. Let me tell you a story about some children who were friends.*

Then read the following story:

> Kathy and Becky have been best friends since they were 5 years old. They went to the same kindergarten and have been in the same class ever since. Every Saturday they would try to do something special together, such as go to the park or the store, or play something special at home. They always had a good time with each other.
>
> One day a new girl, Jeanette, moved into their neighbourhood, and soon introduced herself to Kathy and Becky. Right away, Jeanette and Kathy seemed to hit it off very well. They talked about where Jeanette was from and the things she could do in her new town. Becky, on the other hand, didn't seem to like Jeanette very well. She thought Jeanette was a show-off, but was also jealous of all the attention Kathy was giving Jeanette.
>
> When Jeanette left the other two alone, Becky told Kathy how she felt about Jeanette. "What did you think of her, Kathy? I thought she was kind of pushy, butting in on us like that."
>
> "Come on, Becky. She's new in town and just trying to make friends. The least we can do is be nice to her."
>
> "Yeah, but that doesn't mean we have to be friends with her," replied Becky. "Anyway, what would you like to do this Saturday? You know those old puppets of mine? I thought we could fix them up and make our own puppet show."
>
> "Sure, Becky, that sounds great," said Kathy. "I'll be over after lunch. I'd better go home now. See you tomorrow."
>
> Later that evening, Jeanette called Kathy and surprised her with an invitation to the circus, the last show before it left town. The only problem was that the show happened to be at the same time Kathy had promised to go to Becky's. Kathy didn't know what to do: go to the circus and leave her best friend alone, or stick with her best friend and miss a good time.

After reading the child the story, ask the following open-ended questions to probe the child's understanding of friendship:

1. What do you think the problem is in this story?

2. What do you think Kathy will do: choose to be with her old friend Becky, or go with the new girl, Jeanette? Why? Which do you think is more important: to be with an old friend or to make new friends? Why?

3. Do you have a best friend? What kind of friendship do you have with that person? What makes that person your best friend?

You may then want to ask one or more of the following questions, depending on the child's comments:

1. What kind of friendship do you think Kathy and Becky have? Do you think it is a good, close relationship? What is a really good, close relation? Does it take something special to have a very good friendship? What kinds of things do friends know about each other?

2. What does being friends for a long time, like Kathy and Becky have been, do for a friendship?

3. What makes good, close friendships last?

4. What kinds of things can good friends talk about that other friends sometimes can't? What kinds of problems can they talk over?

5. What makes two friends feel really close to each other?

6. What is the difference between the kind of friendship Becky and Kathy have, and Kathy and Jeanette's friendship? Are there different kinds of friendship? What is the difference between "regular" and "best" friendships?

7. Is it better when close friends are like each other or different from each other? Why? In what ways should good friends be the same? In what ways should they be different?

8. Which is better to have (be with), one close friend or a group of regular friends? Why?

Analysis and Report

Transcribe your child's answers as close to verbatim as you can. Describe the child's understanding of friendship and compare it to the description of friendships in the text.

Reference

Selman, R.L. (1980). *The Growth of Interpersonal Understanding*. New York: Academic Press.

AT-HOME PROJECT

Student Project 19: Television Aggression

You may want to combine this project with the next one, which involves observing sex-role presentations on TV. If so, you or your instructor may wish to modify the following instructions somewhat. But if you are doing this in isolation, proceed as follows:

Procedure

Using the definition of violence offered by George Gerbner ("the overt expression of physical forces against others or self, or the compelling of action against one's will on pain of being hurt or killed"), select a minimum of four half-hour television programs normally watched by children and count the number of aggressive or violent episodes in each. Extend Gerbner's definition somewhat, however, to count verbal aggression as well as physical aggression.

You may select any four (or more) programs, but consider distributing them in the following way:

- At least one "educational" television program, such as *Sesame Street* or *Mr. Rogers' Neighborhood*.

- At least one Saturday morning cartoon.

- At least one early evening adult program that is watched by young children: a family comedy, a western, a crime film, or one of each.

For each program that you watch, record the number of violent episodes, separating the instances of verbal and physical violence.

Analysis and Report

In thinking of writing about the details of your observations, consider the following questions:

1. What kind of variation in the number of violent episodes is there among the programs that you watched?

2. Are some programs more verbally aggressive, some more physically aggressive?

3. Do the numbers of violent episodes per program correspond to the numbers found by Gerbner?

4. What about the consequences of aggression in the television films? Are those who act violently rewarded or punished? How often do reward and punishment occur?

5. What behaviours other than aggression might a child learn from watching the programs you viewed? This question is particularly relevant for *Sesame Street* or *Mr. Rogers' Neighborhood*, but applies to more traditional entertainment as well.

6. In view of the material in this chapter and your own observations for this project, what rules or limits (if any) would you place on television viewing for your own child?" Why?

AT-HOME PROJECT

Student Project 20: Sex Roles on TV

If you combine this project with the preceding one, recording both aggressive episodes and sex-role behaviour on TV programs, you will gain a very good sense of the portrayals of "real life" given on TV.

Procedure

You can gain some experience designing your own research by selecting among the following options:

Option 1. Watch at least 5 hours of TV, spread over several time periods, and record the number of male and female characters and whether they are the central character or a minor character.

Option 2. Watch 4 to 6 hours of TV, selecting among several different types of programs, and note the activities of each male and female character in the following categories: aggression, nurturance, problem-solving, conformity, and physical exertion.

Option 3. Watch and analyze the commercials on at least 10 programs, making sure that the programs cover the full range of types, from sports to soap operas. You might count the number of male and female participants in the commercials and the nature of their activity in each case, using some of the same categories listed in Option 2.

Analysis and Report

In preparing your report, you need to specify clearly which of these options (or some other) you chose, which programs you watched, how often you defined your terms, and what results you obtained. What do you think these results mean for the average TV viewer?

CHAPTER 10 ANSWER KEY

Guided Study Questions

32. Canadian researchers have found that social competence is closely related to <u>a reduction in both internalizing and externalizing behaviour problems in children.</u>

42. Tremblay et al. (1996) <u>found that there were social class and family differences</u> in rates of aggression in children.

47. Not all aggressive children are rejected. Among girls, <u>aggression, whether physical or relational, seems to lead to peer rejection consistently. Among boys, however, aggression may result in either popularity or rejection.</u>

57. As a child moves through the concrete operational period, her psychological self becomes <u>more complex, more comparative, less tied to external features, and more centred on feelings and ideas.</u>

60. Over the years of elementary school and high school, children's evaluations of their own abilities <u>become increasingly differentiated, with quite separate judgements about academic and athletic skills, physical appearance, social acceptance, friendships, romantic appeal, and relationships with parents.</u>

Practice Questions

1.d	6. a	11. d	16. c	21. a
2. b	7. c	12. a	17. c	22. c
3. a	8. a	13. c	18. b	23. d
4. d	9. b	14. c	19. d	24. b
5. b	10. b	15. d	20. d	25. b

PHYSICAL AND COGNITIVE DEVELOPMENT IN ADOLESCENCE

OVERVIEW OF CHAPTER

Development in adolescence is marked by strides as well as challenges. Along with physical maturity come new health risks. Advances in cognitive functioning enable teenagers to function almost as well as adults. School experiences are critical to adolescent development.

Physical Changes

- Puberty is triggered by a complex set of hormones, beginning at about age 7 or 8. Menarche, a girl's first menstrual period, typically occurs 2 years after the beginning of other visible changes. In boys, the peak of the growth spurt typically comes fairly late in the sequence of physical development.

- Each teenager has an internal model or mental image of the "normal" or "right" timing for puberty. Gender differences exist regarding early development. Maturing girls seem to seek inclusion in groups of older peers who display antisocial behaviour. Meanwhile, the earlier the development in boys, the more positive their self image.

- Many changes occur in the brain during adolescence and up to adulthood. An inverted U-shaped trajectory in gray matter volume from early childhood to adolescence occurs as synaptogenesis is followed by synaptic pruning. Puberty is accompanied by a rapid growth spurt in height and an increase in muscle mass and fat. Boys add more muscles, and girls add more fat.

Adolescent Health

- Teenagers get sick less frequently than children and infants. In general, teenagers show heightened levels of sensation-seeking, including unprotected sex, drug use, and fast driving.

- Sexual activity among teens has increased in recent decades in Canada. Many do not use condoms consistently. The most common sexually transmitted infection (STI) reported in Canada is chlamydia. A more serious viral STI is genital warts caused by the human papillomavirus (HPV). A HPV vaccination is available in Canada for females between ages 9 and 26. Health Canada's (1997) *Canadian Guidelines for Sexual Health Education* focuses on promoting behaviours of teenagers to make informed and responsible sexual decisions.

- In Canada, the rate of teenage pregnancy has declined for females aged 15 to 19. However, the rate of abortion is higher among women aged 18 and 19, reflecting a higher pregnancy rate among older teenagers.

- Long-term consequences for teenaged mothers are generally negative, although some girls are able to overcome the challenges.

Substance Abuse and Mental Health Problems

- Alcohol and marijuana are commonly used by Canadian youth. The average age of first-time drug use is 13 to 14 years. Sensation-seeking behaviour promotes peer associations with similar interests and interacts with parenting style to increase the likelihood of drug use. Cigarette smoking is less prevalent for Canadian youth than for the general population. For those who do smoke, peer influences appear to outweigh perceptions of future health risks.

- Eating disorders such as bulimia and anorexia are among the most significant mental health problems and are more common among teenaged girls than boys.

- A Canadian study found that more young females than males have experienced one major depressive episode. Suicide is the second leading cause of death for Canadian young people aged 15–19. The likelihood of completing a suicide is higher for adolescent boys. The suicide rate is much higher for First Nations people than for non-Aboriginal people. Contributing factors in completed suicides include depression, aggression, and a family history of psychiatric disorders or suicide, or a pattern of drug or alcohol abuse.

Changes in Thinking and Memory

- Piaget's fourth stage of cognitive development—the formal operational period—is characterized by the ability to apply basic operations to ideas and possibilities, that is, to engage in systematic problem solving, in addition to actual objects.

- There is clear evidence of some advanced forms of thinking in at least some adolescents, but formal operational thinking is not universal, nor is it consistently used even by those who possess the ability.

- Memory functions improve in adolescence when teens become more proficient in the uses of metacognition, metamemory, and memory strategy.

Schooling

- The transition to junior high/middle school may be accompanied by changes in the child's goal orientation that result in declines in achievement and self-esteem.

- Canadian girls not only obtain higher marks but out-perform boys on some standard achievement measures. Currently, more Canadian women than men pursue post-secondary education.

- Adolescents who succeed academically in secondary school are typically from authoritative families. Early leavers from secondary school are shaped by complex interactions of academic and social variables

- Adolescents who work beyond 15 to 20 hours per week experience more chronic stress and a decline in their academic achievement, and they may engage in risky behaviour. Work can be beneficial for students who have positive work experiences.

LEARNING GOALS

After completing Chapter 11, students should be able to:
1. Trace the physical changes during adolescence.
2. Identify the health issues affecting teenagers.
3. Discuss the risks of substance abuse for adolescents, and describe the potential mental health problems.
4. Summarize the cognitive changes in formal operational thinking and information-processing skills during adolescence.
5. Describe the issues surrounding the schooling of teenagers.

GUIDED STUDY QUESTIONS

PHYSICAL CHANGES

The Endocrine and Reproductive Systems (pp. 333–336)

Objective 11.1: Identify the changes in the endocrine system and the reproductive system that occur during adolescence.

1. Define the following terms:
    a. endocrine glands
    b. pituitary gland
    c. gonadotrophic hormones
    d. sex hormones
    e. primary sex characteristics
    f. secondary sex characteristics
    g. menarche
    h. secular trend

2. List the major hormones that contribute to physical growth and development.

3. Differentiate between the sexual development of girls and that of boys.

4. Describe the results of a Canadian study based on NLSCY data on girls who are early developers.

5. What is the effect of early development on boys?

Other Body Systems (pp. 336–339)

Objective 11.2: Describe the changes in other body systems that allow adolescents to acquire new cognitive and motor skills.

6   Explain brain changes regarding grey matter volume.

7.   Explain the brain changes that are due to increases in white matter volume.

8.   Give examples of how the cephalocaudal and proximodistal patterns of development are reversed in adolescence.

9.   Distinguish between the development of joints in girls and in boys.

10.   Compare the gains in muscles between boys and girls.

11.   What have been the results in Canadian youth, over the past few decades, due to pattern changes in eating and physical activity?

12.   What are the findings of Canadian researchers regarding the hearts and lungs of boys versus girls in terms of endurance, size, strength, and speed, following puberty?

ADOLESCENT HEALTH

Health Care Issues (pp. 339–341)

Objective 11.3: Describe the health care issues affecting teenagers.

13.   Define the term "sensation-seeking." Give examples of adolescent sensation-seeking behaviour.

14.   State reasons why risky behaviours are more common during adolescence than other periods.

15.   Give examples of how television and other forms of the popular media may influence teens' risky behaviour.

Sexual Behaviour (pp. 341–342)

Objective 11.4: Identify the issues involved with the sexual behaviour of adolescents.

16.   What is the percentage difference in the use of condoms among females and males in their recent sexual encounters?

17.   State the findings in the Canadian Contraceptive Study.

18.   List the social factors that predict teenagers' sexual activity.

19.   Left untreated, chlamydia can lead to _____.

20.   A more serious viral sexually transmitted infection (STI) is _____ caused by _____.

21. With which type of cancer is the human papillomavirus virus (HPV) associated? What do the Canadian public health experts recommend for females between the ages of 9 and 26?

22. What do the Canadian Guidelines for Sexual Health Education emphasize? What is the belief of Canadian parents and teens regarding sex education?

Teenaged Pregnancy (pp. 343–344)

Objective 11.5: Summarize the issues involved in teenaged pregnancy.

23. What is the present rate of teenage pregnancy in Canada?

24. List the factors that predict sexual activity in general.

25. How are the children of teenaged mothers at risk?

SUBSTANCE ABUSE AND MENTAL HEALTH PROBLEMS

Drugs, Alcohol, and Tobacco (pp. 344–346)

Objective 11.6: Describe the use of drugs, alcohol, and tobacco among adolescents.

26. What is the substance-use of choice for Canadian students?

27. What substances follow in preference?

28. Teenagers who express the most interest in _____ are those who are most likely to _____.

29. How does sensation-seeking interact with parenting style?

30. What may be the two main reasons for teenagers to begin smoking?

Eating Disorders (pp. 346–348)

Objective 11.7: Identify the issues involved with eating disorders among teenagers.

31. What is the Canadian data on eating disorders among youth?

32. Define and distinguish between the following two eating disorders:
    a. bulimia, or bulimia nervosa
    b. anorexia nervosa

33. Some developmentalists suggest that an _____ as a characteristic of attractive women, which is common in Western cultures, contributes to _____ of eating disorders.

34. Give an example of how a general tendency toward mental illness may be a factor in eating disorders.

35. Define obsessive-compulsive disorder.

Depression and Suicide (pp. 348–350)

Objective 11.8: Identify the issues involved in adolescent depression and suicide.

36. What are the research findings, from the University of Alberta, regarding major depressive episodes (MDE)?

37. The search for developmental pathways leading to adolescent depression begins with the clear finding that

_____

_____

_____

38. Give examples of family stresses that might affect adolescent depression.

39. Give examples of how depression can hinder academic achievement.

40. What is the second leading cause of death for Canadian youth aged 15 to 19?

41. State the controversy of using newer antidepressant drugs in treating depression associated with suicidal behaviour.

42. List and describe the factors that contribute to completed suicides.

43. Describe suicide prevention programs.

No Easy Answers: First Nations Youth Suicide Crisis (p. 349)

Objective 11.9: Discuss the issues surrounding First Nations youth suicide crisis

44. Compare the suicide rates of First Nations people to non-Aboriginal people in Canada.

45. List factors that promote cultural continuity which are related to suicide reduction.

CHANGES IN THINKING AND MEMORY

Piaget's Formal Operational Stage (pp. 351–353)

Objective 11.10: Describe Piaget's stage of formal operational thought.

46. Define the following terms:
    a. formal operational stage
    b. hypothetico-deductive reasoning
    c. systematic problem-solving

47. Describe the methods Piaget used to test for systematic problem-solving skills. Include the pendulum problem.

48. How would an adolescent using a formal operational approach differ from a concrete-operational thinker in attempting to solve the pendulum problem?

49. Give examples of deductive reasoning. Explain how deductive reasoning is related to the scientific process.

Research Report: Elkind's Adolescent Egocentrism (p. 353)

Objective 11.11: Summarize Elkind's research on egocentrism

50. What is adolescent egocentrism?

51. Give examples of the two components of adolescent egocentrism.

Component   Example

_____   _____

_____   _____

52. Describe the new look theory. Explain how projection is involved.

Direct Tests of Piaget's View (pp. 353–355)

Objective 11.12: Describe the direct tests of Piaget's view of formal operational thinking.

53. Give examples of how adolescents gain formal operational skills in the pendulum problem and in understanding figurative language.

54. Give examples of how formal operational thinking alters the ways teenagers make decisions.

Advances in Information-Processing (pp. 355–357)

Objective 11.13: Summarize the advances in information-processing skills during the teenage years.

55. List the gains in information-processing skills of adolescents as compared to elementary school children.

56. Give examples of how the metacognitive and metamemory skills of adolescents far exceed those of younger children.

57. Give examples to illustrate the difference between younger children's and adolescents' processing of a memory for text. Include the four rules that participants used in writing summaries.

SCHOOLING

Transition to Secondary School (pp. 357–359)

Objective 11.14: Describe the issues involved in adolescents' transition to secondary school.

58. Describe two models of transitional schools from elementary school to secondary school.

59. Define and distinguish between task goals and ability goals, and give examples of how a student's goal (task or ability) influences his or her behaviour.

60. Describe two strategies to address the shift in goal structure.

Strategy	Description	Examples of Strategy
_____	_____	_____
_____	_____	_____

61. How can electives and extracurricular activities in secondary school make the transition more positive?

Gender and Academic Achievement (p. 359)

Objective 11.15: Identify the gender issues involved in academic achievement among adolescents.

62. Compare the academic achievement of Canadian girls to boys.

63. What is the likelihood that elementary school girls will complete a university degree?

64. List several factors associated with school achievement of high achievers and low achievers.

Early School Leavers (pp. 359–361)

Objective 11.16: Summarize the research on teenagers who drop out of school.

65. In Canada, what is considered to be the minimum requirement for access into the labour market and life long learning?

66. Describe the profile of adolescents who are early leavers from secondary school. What are the results regarding drop rates from the School-Leavers Follow-Up Survey?

67. Describe the complex interaction of academic and social variables that contribute in dropping out of secondary school.

68. List results of the longitudinal studies regarding predictors influencing dropping-out behaviours.

69. Describe the findings from Canadian studies in regards to characteristics of students who drop out of school.

70. List the long-term consequences of dropping out of high school.

Working Teens (p. 361)

Objective 11.17: Discuss the issues that arise for teenagers who are employed.

71. Describe the findings from Canadian studies regarding working teens.

72. List the positive effects of teenage employment.

CRITICAL REFLECTION EXERCISE

Puberty and Adolescence

Using information from the text, provide answers to the following questions. Be sure and provide specific examples and evidence from the chapters to support your answers.

1. What effect does the timing of the onset of puberty have on the developing adolescent? Name and discuss three factors that influence the type of effects an early or later onset of puberty will have.

2. Why are physical and cognitive changes so closely linked during adolescent development? Provide at least three possible reasons.

3. You are conducting a parents-as-teachers session. You have been asked to explain some of the factors that influence why teens might turn to drugs and alcohol. Provide four reasons that adolescents might start drinking or using other drugs. In addition, provide four pieces of advice to these parents on how to approach the concept with their children.

PRACTICE QUESTIONS

1. The pituitary gland _____.
   a. regulates bodily systems such as temperature and hunger
   b. provides the trigger for the release of hormones from other glands
   c. produces and releases thyroxin, which regulates sexual growth
   d. triggers the development of primary and secondary sex characteristics

2. Menarche refers to the _____.
   a. occurrence of first menstruation in girls
   b. cracking of a boy's voice as he experiences pubertal changes
   c. first spontaneous ejaculation in boys
   d. changes in breast development in girls

3. In the adolescent brain a decreasing amount of grey matter reflects which one of the following processes?
    a. neuron growth
    b. synaptogenesis
    c. pruning
    d. dendrite myelinization

4. Canadian researchers found that dramatic changes in the eating and physical activity patterns during adolescence have led to _____.
    a. undereating
    b. obesity
    c. depression
    d. hypertension

5. Teenagers who indicate high rates of reckless behaviours are most likely to experience all of the following except _____.
    a. early rejection by peers
    b. lack of success at school
    c. neglect at home
    d. popularity with older girls

6. In the Canadian Contraceptive Study, the contraceptive method favoured by sexually active unmarried women aged 15 to 17 was _____.
    a. contraceptive foam
    b. diaphragms
    c. oral contraceptives
    d. condoms

7. Elaine, age 17, is contemplating being vaccinated for the human papillomavirus (HPV). This virus is strongly associated with _____.
    a. leukemia
    b. cervical cancer
    c. lymphodema
    d. uterine cancer

8. A large majority of Canadian parents and teens believe that sex education provides information on all of the following topics except _____.
    a. sexual techniques
    b. birth control
    c. sexual orientation
    d. STD/AIDS prevention

9. Ashley is a pregnant teenager. Which one of the following is a predictive factor regarding her pregnancy?
    a. She comes from a family in a high socioeconomic bracket.
    b. She became sexually active at a young age.
    c. Both of her parents are professionals.
    d. She is popular with her peers.

10. Which one of the following substances is the top choice of use for Canadian students?
    a. marijuana
    b. cigarettes
    c. alcohol
    d. hallucinogens

11. Which of the following is true about anorexia nervosa?
    a. It is less common than bulimia.
    b. It is more common in underdeveloped countries than industrialized ones.
    c. It is fatal in about 5% of cases.
    d. It involves bingeing but not purging.

12. A condition associated with eating disorders that is characterized by an excessive need for control of the environment is called _____.
    a. obsessive-compulsive disorder
    b. schizophrenia
    c. borderline personality disorder
    d. panic disorder

13. For the treatment of depression associated with suicidal behaviour, one of the outcomes of the newer antidepressant drugs known as SSRIs/SNRIs is:
    a. hallucinations and tremors
    b. increased involuntary movements of the face
    c. increased suicidal ideation
    d. cogwheel motion of the arms

14. According to the text, suicide prevention efforts have focused on _____ .
    a. rehabilitation
    b. emotive strategies
    c. education
    d. cognitive strategies

15. According to Piaget, the adolescent is in the formal operational cognitive stage and _____.
    a. engages in more sophisticated concrete logic than ever before
    b. is able to consider possible occurrences more than before
    c. still cannot demonstrate adult-like logic
    d. still shows irregularities in approaches to problem solving

16. The logical outcome following a consideration of the hypotheses, "If all people are equal, then you and I must be equal" involves _____.
    a. hypothetico-deductive reasoning
    b. formal deductive reasoning
    c. inductive reasoning
    d. abstract thinking

17. A process in which a problem-solver searches for a solution by testing hypotheses about single factors is called _____.
    a. the period of the pendulum
    b. systematic problem-solving
    c. abstract thinking
    d. inductive reasoning

18. Which of the following statements about formal operational reasoning is true?
    a. Piaget was overly pessimistic about adolescents' thinking abilities.
    b. People develop formal operational thinking even if their life situations or cultures do not require it.
    c. In adulthood, rates of formal operational thinking decrease with education.
    d. Piaget was overly optimistic about adolescents' thinking abilities.

19. John, age 16, studies for his science test of wild animals. For memorizing the names of wild animals, he associates them with different towns. For example, polar bears are from Churchill. This suggests that he uses a/an _____.
    a. figurative skill
    b. executive process
    c. memory strategy
    d. inductive process

20. Goals based on personal standards and on a desire to become more competent at something are called _____.
    a. metacognition
    b. ability goals
    c. task goals
    d. metamemory

21. Which of the following statements is true about the transition from elementary school to secondary school?
    a. Teenagers who fail one or more courses in the first year of secondary school are far less likely than their peers to graduate.
    b. Junior high/middle schools solve the transition.
    c. The extracurricular approach is useful only in elementary school.
    d. An emphasis on ability grouping in middle school is essential in assisting young teenagers in making the transition to secondary school.

22. Factors associated with high achievers are all of the following except _____.
    a. accurate perception of oneself
    b. risk-taking behaviours
    c. good relationships with school and parents
    d. satisfaction with school

23. Which one of the following is the most representative of reasons that teenagers become early school leavers?
    a. growing up in a blended family
    b. finding an attractive job out of province.
    c. dealing with extended family issues.
    d. receiving negative feedback from peers on achievement.

24. According to Canadian researchers, which one of the following is the most accurate characteristics of a secondary school student who is at risk to be an early school leaver?
    a. well adjusted
    b. loud
    c. moderate-achieving
    d. disengaged

25. Which one of the following factors is associated with Canadian male students who seem to benefit from work?
    a. They employ a tutor to assist them in their schoolwork.
    b. They cut back on their leisure activities.
    c. They reduce their sleeping time.
    d. They have a more positive temperament.

CASE STUDY

Jan, age 15, is sexually active. She is afraid to discuss condom use with her boyfriend because he might leave her. Her girlfriends are pressuring her to get a HPV vaccination. She thinks she is not old enough. She doesn't quite know how to approach her family. Both of her parents are working and Jan's dating rules have been lax. She feels she should be responsible for her actions.

Based on your understanding of sexually transmitted disease which one is preventable through condom use? What are some of the side effects of this infection if left untreated?

What is your understanding of HPV vaccination?

What would you say to Jan if she approached you with her issues?

RESEARCH PROJECT

Student Project 20: The Pendulum

This is a simplified version of the Inhelder and Piaget pendulum problem. To complete this project, you should locate a child between roughly age 8 and 16, obtaining the parents' permission for the testing in the prescribed way.

Equipment

Because the physical objects are so important for this problem, you will need to collect your equipment carefully and test it before you start. You will need three pieces of strong, flexible string (one about 25 cm, one about 37 cm, and one 50 cm long). You will also need three similar objects of varying weights. Fishing sinkers work well, as do keys, but the lightest one should be heavy enough so that it will weigh down the string and allow it to swing.

It would be best if you could complete the testing in some location where you have the opportunity to tie all three strings to an overhead rod or other object. Doing so would leave you free to write down what your subject does. Otherwise, you will have to hold the top of each string when your subject wishes to use that string in the test.

Procedure

Tell your subject:

> *I am doing a class project about how different people go about solving a problem. The problem I would like you to solve is to find out what makes a pendulum swing faster or slower.*

Pause at this point and demonstrate how you can attach a weight to the string, then push the weight to start the pendulum swinging. Demonstrate this with more than one weight/string combination so that it is clear that there is variability in the speed of the pendulum swing. Then say:

> *You need to figure out what makes the pendulum swing faster or slower. You can use any of these strings and these three weights to help you figure this out. I'll be taking notes about what you do and say while you are working on the problem.*

Record each combination the subject tries, in the order of the attempts. If you can, you should also record any comments the subject makes in the process. Allow the subject to continue until he or she gives you an answer. If no answer is forthcoming after a period of time, you may ask some question like:

> *Can you figure out what makes the pendulum move fast or slow?*

If that does not elicit an answer, or if the subject seems very frustrated or bored, you may terminate the procedure and thank the subject for his or her help. If the subject has not solved the problem, you will want to reassure him or her by pointing out that this is a really hard problem and that lots of kids have a hard time figuring it out.

Analysis and Report

In reporting on your project, make sure to discuss the following points:

- Did your subject solve the problem? (That is, did he or she figure out that it is the length of the string and not the weight that determines the speed of the pendulum?)

- How many separate swing/weight combination tests did it take to reach some conclusion, whether the conclusion was correct or not?

- Did the subject try various string/weight combinations in any systematic order? Or were the various attempts more random?

- Did the subject talk to him or herself while working on the problem? Was this self-talk directed at keeping track of things that had been tried, or at thinking through the problem?

- Did your subject's performance fit the findings from Piaget's and others' studies on the age at which formal operations develop?

AT-HOME PROJECT

Student Project 21: Plotting Your Own Growth

This project will work best if your parents are among those who routinely stood you up against a convenient doorjamb and measured you—and if you still live in the house with the marked-up doorjamb. Alternatively, you may have a friend or an acquaintance who has access to doorjamb data you could use. Assuming you can locate such a set of measurements, you should plot your own (or your friend's) rate of growth over the years of childhood. Calculate the centimetres you grew each year (estimating when needed), plot the ages and the height, and draw a curve.

When was your maximum height spurt (the year in which you grew the most centimetres)? During elementary school, did you grow about the same number of centimetres per year? If you are female, add to the graph a point that represents your first menstruation (to the best of your recollection). Where did menarche fall on the curve; that is, did menarche occur after your major growth spurt?

CHAPTER 11 ANSWER KEY

Guided Study Questions

19. Left untreated, chlamydia can lead to <u>pelvic inflammatory disease (PID), ectopic pregnancy, and infertility in females, and to a number of genital and urinary tract disorders in males.</u>

20. A more serious viral sexually transmitted infection (STI) is <u>genital warts</u> caused by the <u>human papillomavirus.</u>

28. Teenagers who express the most interest in <u>sensation-seeking</u> are those who are most likely to <u>use drugs and consume alcohol.</u>

33. Some developmentalists suggest that an <u>emphasis on thinness</u> as a characteristic of attractive women, which is common in Western cultures, contributes to <u>the prevalence</u> of eating disorders.

37. The search for developmental pathways leading to adolescent depression begins with the clear finding that <u>children growing up with depressed parents are much more likely to develop depression than are those growing up with non-depressed parents.</u>

Practice Questions

1. b	6. c	11. a	16. a	21. a
2. a	7. b	12. a	17. b	22. b
3. c	8. a	13. c	18. d	23. d
4. b	9. b	14. c	19. c	24. d
5. d	10. c	15. b	20. c	25. b

Case Study

Chapter 11 (p. 342). Chlamydia, the most reported STI in Canada, is preventable though condom use. Left untreated, chlamydia can lead to pelvic inflammatory disease (PID), ectopic pregnancy, and infertility in women, and a number of genital and urinary tract disorders in men. Canadian public health experts recommend nation-wide HPV vaccination of females between the ages of 9 and 26, as well as continued Pap tests for cervical cancer. It may be good to listen to Jan, offer her support, and refer her to counselling services.

SOCIAL AND PERSONALITY DEVELOPMENT IN ADOLESCENCE

OVERVIEW OF CHAPTER

The social and personality development of adolescents is strongly influenced by the process of identity development. Other factors influencing development include changes in adolescents' self-concept and social relationships. Moral reasoning also develops during adolescence.

Theories of Social and Personality Development

- For Freud, the primary developmental task of the genital stage is to channel the libido into a healthy sexual relationship. Erikson, on the other hand, emphasizes the development of the identity.

- James Marcia, a psychology professor from Simon Fraser University, bases his descriptions of identity statuses on Erikson's ideas. They include two key parts: crisis and commitment. Combining the two elements leads to four possible identity statuses.

Self-Concept and Personality

- In adolescence, the teen's self-concept becomes more abstract and differentiated. More emphasis is placed on enduring traits, internal qualities, and ideology. A Canadian longitudinal study on teens found that a strong self-concept is important to the development of good mental and physical health.

- Gender-related aspects of the psychological self are termed sex-role identity.

- Self-esteem undergoes interesting shifts during the teenage years. The overall trend is towards a rise in self-esteem during the adolescent years. But for Canadian adolescents, findings reveal that self-esteem is lower than for other age groups.

- Minority teenagers, especially recent immigrant youth, face the task of creating two identities in adolescence: a sense of individual identity that sets them apart from others, and an ethnic identity that includes self-identification as a member of their specific group. Over the course of 10 years, immigrant youth adopt patterns of lifestyle behaviours similar to those of Canadian-born youth.

- Teens who are introverted, neurotic, and pessimistic and who blame their problems on forces outside themselves encounter more difficulties than peers with a more positive outlook.

Social Relationships

- Adolescents have two apparently contradictory tasks: to establish autonomy while maintaining a sense of relatedness with their parents.

- Peer relationships become far more significant in adolescence than they have been at any earlier period, and perhaps than they will be at any time later in life. Perhaps the most profound change in social relationships is the shift toward the inclusion of heterosexual relationships that prepare teens for assuming a full adult sexual identity.

- Teens who are homosexual, or who are unsure about their sexual orientation, face many obstacles in the formation of an identity. Statistics Canada (2004) revealed that a slightly higher number of young Canadians considered themselves either homosexual or bisexual, compared to older Canadians.

- Canada's present youth are the first generation to be accustomed to electronic communication. The social factors of using the Internet are valuable for secondary school students. However, for younger teenagers, primary risks are involved.

Moral Development

- Kohlberg proposed six stages of moral reasoning, organized into three levels. Research findings suggest that these stages and levels correlate loosely with age, develop in a specified order, and appear in the same sequence in all cultures studied so far.

- The acquisition of cognitive role-taking skills is important to moral development, but the social environment is important as well. Specifically, to encourage moral reasoning, adults must provide children with opportunities for the discussion of moral issues.

- Kohlberg's theory has been criticized by theorists who place more emphasis on learning moral behaviour and others who believe that moral reasoning may be based more on emotional factors than on ideas about justice and fairness.

- The developmental pathway for early-onset youth criminality seems to be directed by internal factors such as temperament and personality. Socializing factors that predict youth crime rates are parenting style, peer influences, and other relationship variables.

- In Canada, a young person who commits an offence is distinguished from other youth who engage in other forms of antisocial behaviour on the basis of actual law-breaking (criminality). Canada's new *Youth Criminal Justice Act* contains three main objectives: to prevent crime, to rehabilitate and reintegrate offenders into society, and to ensure meaningful consequences for offences committed by young people. Youth who commit offences are usually found to be far behind their peers in both role-taking and moral reasoning.

LEARNING GOALS

After completing Chapter 12, students should be able to:
1. Explain the theories of social and personality development in the teenage years.
2. Summarize the development of self-concept and personality in adolescence.
3. Identify the changes in social relationships during the teenage years.
4. Describe Kohlberg's theory of moral development, and explain its impact on antisocial behaviour.
5. Discuss youth criminality and Canada's new *Youth Criminal Justice Act.*

GUIDED STUDY QUESTIONS

THEORIES OF SOCIAL AND PERSONALITY DEVELOPMENT

Psychoanalytic Perspectives (pp. 367–369)

Objective 12.1: Describe the key points in the psychoanalytic perspective that are relevant to adolescence.

1. Define the following terms:
   a. genital stage
   b. identity versus role confusion
   c. identity crisis

2. For Freud, what is the primary developmental task of the genital stage?

3. According to Erikson, what is the central crisis of adolescence?

4. Explain why Erikson states that an identity crisis is inevitable during adolescence.

5. What, according to Erikson, is the function of the peer group?

Marcia's Theory of Identity Achievement (pp. 368–369)

Objective 12.2: Explain Marcia's theory of identity achievement.

6. Define the following terms:
   a. crisis
   b. identity achievement
   c.. moratorium
   d.. foreclosure
   e. identity diffusion

7. Most identity theorists agree that _____.

8. What makes the formation of an identity special during adolescence?

9.   What are two key reasons suggested by Marcia why adolescence is so important in the lifecycle?

SELF-CONCEPT AND PERSONALITY

Self-Understanding (pp. 370–371)

Objective 12.3: Describe the changes in self-understanding during the teenage years.

10.   Compare the school-aged child's self-understanding with that of an adolescent.

11.   Give a few examples of how an adolescent's self-concept becomes differentiated as they begin to see themselves somewhat differently in each of several roles.

12.   A longitudinal study of Canadian teens found that _____.

13.   Describe the essence of adolescents' academic concepts. How do these concepts come to develop?

14.   Give examples of how social self-concepts predict behaviour.

15.   Compare and contrast the different ways that boys and girls construct various components of the self-concept differently.

Sex-Role Identity (pp. 371–372)

Objective 12.4: Summarize the development of sex-role identity.

16.   Define sex-role identity.

17.   List and define the four basic sex-role types.

Self-Esteem (pp. 372–374)

Objective 12.5: Describe the development of self-esteem during adolescence.

18.   Either an androgynous or a masculine sex-role identity is associated with higher self-esteem in both boys and girls. Why might this be explained by the existence of a masculine bias?

19.   Give an example of how the adoption of an androgynous or masculine orientation by a girl can lead to lower self-esteem in some cultures.

20.   What is the overall trend of self-esteem during the years of adolescence? What were the findings from the National Population Survey of self-esteem for Canadian adolescence?

21.   List and describe the four groups based on the stability of their self-esteem rating across adolescence.

Ethnic Identity (pp. 374–375)

Objective 12.6: Discuss the issues involved in ethnic identity.

22. How many distinct ethnic identities are there in Canada?

23. Define ethnic identity.

24. What may be some issues in developing an ethnic identity?

25. Describe three phases of ethnic identity development.

26. State the findings of the Canadian Council of Social Development.

27. Identify the ways that immigrant youth seek social support.

28. What occurs to immigrant youth who live in Canada over the course of 10 years?

Locus of Control and Other Traits (pp. 375–377)

Objective 12.7: Discuss the issues involved with locus of control.

29. Define locus of control.

30. Differentiate between external and internal locus of control by giving examples of each.

External Locus of Control	*Internal Locus of Control*

31. Give examples of correlations between locus of control and behaviour.

32. List the cluster of personality variables associated with external locus of control and describe their characteristics. What is the outlook for teens with these characteristics?

The Real World/Empowered Youth: The Students Commission (p. 376)

Objective 12.8: Summarize the purpose of, and the issues involved in, The Students Commission.

33. What is a topic discussed by youth in The Students Commission? Comment on some excerpts of responses by youth that illustrate what Canadian life looked like from their point of view.

SOCIAL RELATIONSHIPS

Relationships with Parents (pp. 377–380)

Objective 12.9: Describe the changing relationships of adolescents with their parents.

34. Teenagers have two apparently contradictory tasks in their relationships with their parents: _____ and to _____.

35. State some of the issues of disagreement between teens and their parents, as indicated by a Canadian researcher.

36. Give examples of research on teenagers' emotional attachment to their parents.

37. What is the relationship between close attachment between teens and their parents and:
     a. academic success
     b. antisocial behaviour
     c. drug use in later adolescence and early adulthood?

38. Give examples of why the authoritative parenting style is associated with more positive outcomes during adolescence.

39. In what ways does family structure affect teenagers?

Relationships with Peers (pp. 380–383)

Objective 12.10: Discuss the issues involved in adolescents' relationships with peers.

40. Give examples of how the similarity of psychological characteristics and attitudes take on new significance in adolescence.

41. Give examples of how adolescent friendships are more stable than are those of younger children.

42. Trace the pattern of peer-group conformity across adolescence.

43. Describe how the structure of the peer group changes over the years of adolescence.

44. Distinguish between a clique and a crowd, according to Dunphy. Give examples of each.

45. Give examples, in both Canadian and North American schools, of how the term "crowd" is used to refer to the reputation-based group with which a young person is identified, either by choice or by peer designation.

46. Define identity prototype and give examples.

47. What is the most profound change in social relationships to occur during adolescence?

48. Why is the sense of being in love an important factor in adolescent dating patterns?

Homosexuality (pp. 383, 385–386)

Objective 12.11: Discuss the issues involved in homosexuality among adolescents.

49. What is the difference between younger and older Canadians in reporting their homosexuality or bisexuality?

50. State the concordant rates of homosexuality for the following groups:

Group	Concordant Rate
Identical twins	
Fraternal twins	
Biologically unrelated boys	

51. What hypothesis is strengthened by family studies that suggest that male homosexuality is programmed in at birth?

52. Give examples of commonly held concerns that are common to both homosexual adolescents and heterosexual adolescents.

Development in the Information Age: The Social Aspects of Electronic Communication (pp. 384–385)

Objective 12.12: Summarize the issues regarding the social aspects of electronic communication.

53. What is significant about Canadian youth and electronic communication?

54. State the benefits of cell phones.

55. What is the perception of today's generation of youth regarding computers and the Internet?

56. Describe several uses that the Internet has for youth according to the MNet surveys (2001a–2004).

57 State four primary risks of Internet use, particularly by boys.

MORAL DEVELOPMENT

Kohlberg's Theory of Moral Reasoning (pp. 386–390)

Objective 12.13: Explain Kohlberg's theory of moral reasoning.

58. Define the following terms:
    a. preconventional morality
    b. conventional morality
    c. postconventional morality

59. Describe Kohlberg's research method.

60. What is the relationship between age and the stages in Kohlberg's theory?

61. List and describe the three levels and six stages of Kohlberg's theory by completing the following table.

Level	*Stages*	*Description*

Causes and Consequences of Moral Development (p. 391)

Objective 12.14: Identify the causes and consequences of moral development.

62. Describe how cognitive development affects Kohlberg's stages and chronological age.

63. Define role-taking, and explain why it is related to cognitive development and Kohlberg's stages.

64. How is the social environment involved in the development of moral reasoning?

65. How do parenting style and family climate relate to the levels of moral reasoning?

66. Give examples of how teenagers' levels of moral reasoning appear to be positively correlated with prosocial behaviour and negatively related to antisocial behaviour.

Criticisms of Kohlberg's Theory (pp. 391–393)

Objective 12.15: Identify the criticisms of Kohlberg's theory.

67. Give an example of an aspect of moral reasoning found in non-Western cultures that does not fit well with Kohlberg's approach.

68. Define empathy and explain how Nancy Eisenberg uses it to connect moral reasoning and moral emotions.

69. Carol Gilligan claims that an ethic based on _____ _____ may be as important to moral reasoning as _____.

70. Explain how justice and care are involved in moral reasoning.

71. What are the sex differences in moral reasoning, according to Gilligan?

72. To explain inconsistencies between reasoning and behaviour, learning theorists suggest that moral reasoning is situational rather than developmental. List two examples of research that learning theorists state to support this assertion.

Moral Development and Antisocial Behaviour (pp. 393–395)

Objective 12.16: Describe the relationship between moral development and antisocial behaviour.

73. State the focus of Canada's new *Youth Criminal Justice Act*.

74. Youth who commit offences appear to be behind their peers in moral reasoning because of _____.

75. State the two sub-varieties of youth who commit offences. Describe the developmental pathway for each.

No Easy Answers: Youth Criminal Justice (p. 394)

Objective 12.17: Discuss the issues involved with youth criminal justice.

76. Describe the uneven trends in the incidence of youth crimes.

77. What are the variations of youth crime in Canada?

78. What are socializing factors that predict youth crime?

79. Describe the new approach to youth crime that has resulted in a major restructuring of Canada's youth justice system.

CRITICAL REFLECTION EXERCISE

Sense of Self

Using information from the text, provide detailed answers to the following questions:

1. You are a teacher at an inner-city school. You firmly believe that one of the most important things you can provide for youth is a sense of self-worth and purpose. Develop a program that you could use to help adolescents develop a positive image of themselves. Why did you design the program this way? What impact(s) will this program have on these youth as they mature into adulthood?

2. What does self-concept look like? Draw a diagram or picture that illustrates self-concept and how it develops. It does not matter what you draw as long as you would be able to explain to someone else how the drawing illustrates the major factors that determine self-concept and feelings of self-worth. Write out an explanation of how your drawing illustrates these factors.

3. Choose any characteristic of your self. Consider how this characteristic has developed in the fashion that it has. Are you pleased with this development? Why or why not? If you are not pleased, what would you do to change it? Why would you change it?

PRACTICE QUESTIONS

1. According to Freud, what is the stage during which psychosexual maturity is reached?
   a. anal
   b. phallic
   c. latency
   d. genital

2. A period during which an adolescent is troubled by his or her lack of identity is called the _____.
   a. identity crisis
   b. identity shift
   c. identity commitment
   d. identity status

3. Jane, age 16, is re-examining old values and old choices. According to Marcia, this period of decision-making is called a _____.
   a. conviction
   b. crisis
   c. curiosity-seeking experience
   d. commitment

4.   A foreclosed identity means that an individual _____.
     a.   has resolved the identity crisis and is self-satisfied
     b.   is in the midst of crisis
     c.   has resolved all crises and is committed to an identity
     d.   has simply adopted an identity prescribed by others

5.   One reason why identity formation is special in adolescence is because
     _____.
     a.   a stage of rigid identity acceptance exists.
     b.   youth continue to seek self-related feedback
     c.   a separation from parental guidance occurs.
     d.   all essential elements are present for the first time.

6.   In comparison to younger children, the adolescent's self-concept may be described as
     _____.
     a.   centring more on ideology than in childhood
     b.   less differentiated than in childhood
     c.   centring more on external characteristics than in childhood
     d.   centring more on physical characteristics than in childhood

7.   Gender-related aspects of the psychological self are referred to as _____.
     a.   gender characteristics
     b.   sex-role identity
     c.   the genital stage
     d.   sexually active behaviour

8.   An androgynous individual is likely to _____.
     a.   be homosexual
     b.   have more feminine than masculine personality traits
     c.   have both masculine and feminine personality traits
     d.   have neither masculine nor feminine personality traits

9.   The National Population Survey found that in Canada adolescent self-esteem was
     _____.
     a.   high
     b.   relatively unimportant
     c.   low
     d.   wellness-related

10. Several studies have found that high self-esteem is correlated with _____.
     a.   positive developmental outcomes.
     b.   popularity with peers
     c.   attaining high grades in secondary school
     d.   being president of the school council

11. What is one of the best benefits to the immigrant adolescent who forms a strong and favourable ethnic identity?
    a. higher level of self-esteem
    b. higher level of success in the prevailing culture
    c. lower inclusion in fraternity/sorority groups
    d. freedom to date in cross-cultural groups

12. Important correlations exist between locus of control and behaviour. If John, age 16, has an external locus of control, which of the following behaviours would he display?
    a. excellent study habits
    b. optimistic attitude about school
    c. favouritism about certain school tasks
    d. delay in doing his nightly homework

13. According to a Canadian source, parents and teens disagree most as a result of _____.
    a. clothing and hairstyle
    b. chores around the house
    c. attendance at church
    d. money matters

14. Which of the following is an appropriate summary of what adolescents need from their parents?
    a. to be left alone to figure out who they are
    b. money, money, and more money
    c. a psychological safe base
    d. a firm, consistent set of rules and discipline

15. Who is more likely to be affected by parental divorce or remarriage?
    a. boys and girls are affected equally.
    b. girls in middle childhood
    c. teenage boys
    d. adolescent girls

16. Gina, age 15, has found that her group of friends is engaging in behaviours of which she disapproves. Gina will most likely _____.
    a. inform her parents of their behaviour
    b. switch to a more compatible group
    c. make an appointment with her school counsellor
    d. adapt to their behaviour

17. What is a clique?
    a. a group of ten to 12 persons who really are not attached to each other
    b. four to six young people strongly attached to one another
    c. a group of adolescents who are together because there is power in numbers
    d. a street gang that terrorizes the neighbourhood

18. Homosexual teenagers comprise a minority that faces high levels of _____.
    a. acceptance and support
    b. racial and cultural discrimination
    c. prejudice and stereotyping
    d. well-being and health

19. Secondary school students report that the most valuable aspect of using the Internet is _____.
    a. spiritual
    b. social
    c. sensual
    d. sexual

20. Which of the following illustrates Stage 4 moral development, according to Kohlberg's theory?
    a. Moral actions are defined by expectations from a significant group.
    b. Moral actions are defined by a larger social group, such as society.
    c. Moral actions are defined by whether or not the outcome is positive or negative.
    d. Moral actions are defined by universal ethical principles.

21. The term _____ is used to refer to the ability to look at a situation from another person's perspective.
    a. role-taking
    b. sympathy
    c. empathy
    d. civil disobedience

22. According to Gilligan, the two distinct moral orientations involved in moral reasoning are _____.
    a. justice and empathy
    b. justice and care
    c. honesty and sincerity
    d. right and wrong

23. Which one of the following statements best describes the relationship between moral reasoning and moral behaviour?
    a. There is no correlation.
    b. There is a perfect negative correlation.
    c. There is a perfect positive correlation.
    d. They are correlated, but the relationship is far from perfect.

24. Canada's *Youth Criminal Justice Act* focuses on_____.
    a. delinquents in reform school
    b. rehabilitation and reintegration of a young person into society.
    c. adolescent defensive behaviours
    d. antisocial behaviour in young adulthood

25.   Two socializing factors that predict youth crime rates are: _____.
      a.   drug use and parenting style
      b.   isolation and peer rejection
      c.   peer influences and parenting style.
      d.   low achievement and peer influences

CASE STUDY

Jean, age 14, and Bill, age 16, have begun to date each other. Jean has had many conflicts with her parents and is afraid to inform them about Bill. Yesterday, Jean had a disagreement about Bill with Sue, who is the same age as Jean. Sue thinks that Bill is "a real geek." Jean is somewhat hurt and would like to share her feelings with Bill. She is, however, not sure whether or not Bill is ready to listen to her.

From you understanding of this chapter, what are some of the findings about teen conflicts with parents as reported by a Canadian researcher?

1.   How do 14-year-olds solve disagreements between friends?
2.   Do you think that Bill is ready to listen to Jean's hurt feelings?

RESEARCH PROJECT

Student Project 22: Who Am I?

The purpose of this project is to replicate, on a small scale, the research by Montemayor and Eisen (1977). For the project you will need to find three or four teenagers, preferably one or two who are in early adolescence (ages 12 to 14), and several who are near the end of high school (ages 16 to 18). Obtain the appropriate informed consent from each of these young people, following whatever guidelines your instructor specifies.

Procedure

For each student, prepare a sheet of paper with 20 numbered spaces on it. At the top, write the instructions:

In the spaces below, write 20 different answers to the question, "Who am I?"

Each subject should be interviewed alone. Hand the teenager the sheet, and ask him or her to fill out all 20 blanks, each listing one answer to the "Who am I" question.

Analysis and Report

Analyze the answers your subjects give using the categories of physical appearance and ideology (or any other categories you may identify). Do your subjects' answers match the pattern reported in the text? Are there any other differences in the responses given by your younger and older subjects?

Reference

Montemayor, R., & Eisen, M. (1977). The development of self-conceptions from childhood to adolescence. *Developmental psychology*, *13*, 314–319.

CHAPTER 12 ANSWER KEY

Guided Study Questions

7.　Most identity theorists agree that <u>the quest for personal identity continues throughout the lifespan, with alternating periods of instability and stability.</u>

12.　A longitudinal study of Canadian teens found that <u>a strong concept is important to the development of good mental and physical health.</u>

34.　Teenagers have two, apparently contradictory, tasks in their relationships with their parents: <u>to establish autonomy from them and to maintain a sense of relatedness with them.</u>

69.　Carol Gilligan claims that an ethic based on <u>caring for others and on maintaining social relationships</u> may be as important to moral reasoning as <u>ideas about justice</u>.

74.　Youth who commit offences appear to be behind their peers in moral reasoning because of <u>deficits in role-taking skills</u>.

Practice Questions

1. d	6. a	11. a	16. b	21. a
2. a	7. b	12. d	17. b	22. b
3. b	8. c	13. b	18. c	23. d
4. d	9. c	14. c	19. b	24. b
5. d	10. a	15. d	20. b	25. c

Case Study

Chapter 12 (p. 378). University of Lethbridge sociologist Reginald Beeby found that Canadian teens disagree with their parents most when it comes to issues such as chores around the house, school, their parents' reactions to the way they talk to them, and their parents' concern about their safety. It is interesting that there was less parent-teen conflict over issues such as dating, drugs, their apperarance (clothing and hairstyle), and sex. Chapter 12 (378). Table 12-1. "Children's and Adolescents' Comments about How to Solve Disagreements between Friends", gives a range of comments for various ages. In the 14-year-old category, the main thrust of the comments is for two adolescents to try to work it out together and be happy about the outcome.

Chapter 12 (p. 383). Girls, more than boys, see romantic relationships as a context for self-disclosures. Girls seem to want to have more psychological intimacy from those early relationships than their partners want them to.

POLICY QUESTION IV

WHAT CAN BE DONE ABOUT GAMBLING AMONG CANADIAN YOUTH?

Learning Objective: Summarize the issues regarding gambling among Canadian youth (pp. 399-400).

1. Today's youth are the first generation of Canadians to live within a culture that views gambling as _____.

2. State some of the startling facts that Canadian researchers have discovered about the depth of the gambling problem in Canadian youth.

3. What is the data reported in the survey conducted by the researchers from Laval University, which supports the premise that gambling and wagering are popular and on the rise among children and adolescents?

4. Gambling, like many high-risk behaviours, is more prevalent in _____ than _____; _____ are two to four times as likely as _____ to have _____.

5. Differentiate among types of wagers set by adolescents, adults, underage youth, and by children.

6. In what reasonable ways can parents inform their children and adolescents about the inherent dangers of gambling? What guidelines might you offer parents?

7. Cognitively, children and young adolescents are at a _____ because _____.

8. Like other addictive behaviours, gambling_____.

9. List several effects associated with gambling that have been experienced by young problem gamblers? What other effects/behaviours have you personally seen in young gamblers?

10. Describe some preventative strategies provided by researchers.

11. To what extent do you think that problem gamblers attend your own post-secondary institution? What resources are available at that institution for problem gamblers?

12. What are your realistic options regarding speaking to an adolescent whom you are reasonably convinced has a problem with gambling?

POLICY QUESTION IV ANSWER KEY

1. Today's youth are the first generation of Canadians to live within a culture that views <u>gambling as an everyday and acceptable form of entertainment</u>.

4. Gambling, like many high-risk behaviours, is more prevalent in <u>males</u> than <u>females</u>: <u>boys</u> are two to four times as likely as <u>girls</u> to have <u>a serious gambling problem</u>.

7. Cognitively, children and young adolescents are at a <u>disadvantage because they lack an appreciation of what the odds of winning are, and they have an overly optimistic view of the probability of winning</u>.

8. Like other addictive behaviours, gambling <u>offers ways to temporarily escape problems, boredom, and stress</u>.

PHYSICAL AND COGNITIVE DEVELOPMENT IN EARLY ADULTHOOD

OVERVIEW OF CHAPTER

Young adulthood, the period from 20 to 40, is the time in life when individuals' developmental pathways begin to diverge significantly.

Physical Functioning

- Primary aging is an inevitable aging process. Secondary aging is the result of illness and lifestyle choices. Developed nations with an equitable distribution of wealth have the healthiest populations.

- MRI studies show that the human brain continues to mature throughout early adulthood. Strong evidence exists that the frontal lobes of the brain do not fully mature until young adulthood. This neural development is strongly connected to the increases in the capacity of cognitive abilities, such as abstract reasoning, logic, planning, and emotional control.

- Young adults are at their peak functioning. During these years, an individual has more muscle tissue, more bone calcium, better sensory acuity, greater aerobic capacity, and a more efficient immune system.

Health Promotion and Wellness

- Sexually transmitted infections are relatively more common among young adults.

- Individual differences in health habits, social support networks, and personality variables begin to affect physical functioning in early adulthood. Adults with good health habits have lower risk of death and disease at any age. Social support and a sense of personal control affect rates of disease and death.

- Intimate partner abuse is another health risk of early adulthood; women are at greater risk than men. Causal factors include cultural beliefs about gender roles, as well as personal variables such as alcohol and drug use.

- Many young adults, especially women, are victimized by sexual assault. Canadian law proscribes three levels of sexual assault. Date rape is non-consensual sex that takes place in the context of a date. One of the effects of sexual assault is low self-esteem.

- Mental health problems are more prevalent in early adulthood than in later periods. The most likely reason is that early adulthood is the time during which adults have both the highest expectations and the highest levels of role conflict and role strain. Next to anxiety disorders, problems associated with moods are the most common type of mental difficulty in early adulthood.

Cognitive Changes

• Young adults more often exhibit more formal operational thinking than do adolescents, and many psychologists believe there are even more advanced levels of thought than Piaget's final stage of cognitive development.

• Some studies of measures of intelligence show a decline with age. Adults maintain crystallized intelligence throughout early and middle adulthood, but fluid intelligence declines fairly steadily over adulthood. Memory differences between younger and older adults are usually restricted to tasks involving speed of processing.

Post-Secondary Education

• Post-secondary education has become a necessity virtually for everyone. Post-secondary education has beneficial effects on both cognitive and social development. In addition, post-secondary education is associated with better career opportunities and benefits.

LEARNING GOALS

After completing Chapter 13, students should be able to:
1. Describe how physical functioning changes in the years from 20 to 40.
2. Identify the major health issues during early adulthood.
3. Summarize how thinking and problem-solving improve in early adulthood.
4. Discuss how post-secondary education helps shape young adults' development.

GUIDED STUDY QUESTIONS

PHYSICAL FUNCTIONING

Primary and Secondary Aging (p. 403)

Objective 13.1: Distinguish between primary and secondary aging.

1. Define the following terms, and give examples of each to distinguish between them:
   a. primary aging
   b. secondary aging

2. List common indicators of the population health approach.

3. List three aggregate health indicators that measure quality of life.

The Brain and Nervous System (pp. 403, 405)

Objective 13.2: Summarize the changes in the brain and nervous system in early adulthood.

4. Define the following terms:
    a. response inhibition
    b. limbic system

5. What evidence about the brain function have neuroscientists obtained based on MRI studies?

6. Explain the apparent function of the development of response inhibition in the brain.

Research Report: The Distribution of Wealth and Health (pp. 404–405)

Objective 13.3: Summarize the relationships among socioeconomic status, income distribution, and health outcomes.

7. Give examples of how social class differences and income distribution may influence secondary aging.

8. State the findings of the Joint Canada/United States Survey of Health 2002–03.

Other Body Systems (pp. 405, 407–410)

Objective 13.4: Identify the physical changes that take place in early adulthood.

9. Compared to older adults, adults in their 20s and 30s have _____
    _____.
    The young adult is _____.

10. List the bodily functions that show a gradual decline in physical functioning through the years of adulthood (from Table 13.1).

11. Define the following terms, and give examples of changes as a person ages:
    a. maximum oxygen uptake (VO_2 max)
    b. cardiac output

12. Give examples of changes in strength and speed with age.

13. Compare the reproductive capacity of women and men.

14. List the two key organs in the immune system, and explain how they are involved in immune system functioning.

15. Differentiate between B cells and T cells.

16. State the role of the thymus gland during adulthood.

17. Give examples of how life experiences that demand high levels of change or adaptation can affect the functioning of the immune system.

Research Report: The Brain Matures into Adulthood (pp. 406–407)

Objective 13.5: Describe the changes that occur in the brain.

18. Explain the difference between the grey matter and white matter in the brain.

19. Outline the normal development and the maturing process of the brain.

HEALTH PROMOTION AND WELLNESS

Sexually Transmitted Infections (pp. 411–412)

Objective 13.6: Describe the risk of acquiring sexually transmitted infections during early adulthood.

20. In contrast to other types of disease, most sexually transmitted infections (STIs), including _____, are more common among _____.

21. Describe the historical occurrence of HIV infection in Canada.

22. What particular segments of the Canadian population has the HIV epidemic invaded?

23. List the possible high-risk behaviours linked to STIs that young adults may engage in.

Health Habits and Personal Factors (pp. 412–414)

Objective 13.7: Identify health habits and personal factors that have long-term effects.

24. List the five good health habits that researchers identified from the Alameda County Study.

25. Describe the findings of the Nurses' Health Study.

26. Give examples of how a person's perception of the adequacy of social contacts and emotional support is more strongly related to physical and emotional health than is the actual number of such contacts.

27. Complete the following table. Describe each of the following terms, identify the researcher associated with each, and explain how it is related to a sense of control in a person's life.

Term	Theorist	Relationship to a Sense of Control
Perceived control		
Self-efficacy		
Optimism		
Helplessness		

Intimate Partner Abuse (pp. 414–416)

Objective 13.8: Identify the issues involved in intimate partner abuse.

28. Define intimate partner abuse.

29. Briefly summarize the prevalence of intimate partner abuse in Canada.

30. Give examples of how each of the following can contribute to the rates of intimate partner abuse:
    a. cultural attitudes
    b. gender-role prescriptions

31. List the characteristics of intimate partner abusers.

32. List the characteristics of intimate partner abuse victims.

33. Describe the effects of intimate partner abuse on women.

34. Outline ways to prevent intimate partner abuse.

Sexual Assault (pp. 416–418)

Objective 13.9: Summarize the issues involved in sexual violence.

35. Define the following terms:
    a. sexual assault
    b. date rape

36. Describe the three levels of sexual assault proscribed by Canadian law.

37. Briefly summarize the prevalence of sexual assault in Canada.

38. How do the rates of sexual assaults compare across cultures?

39. List the possible effects of sexual assault.

40. How can sexual assault be prevented?

Mental Health Problems (pp. 418–420)

Objective 13.10: Identify the risks to mental health in young adulthood.

41. State the possible causes of mental disorders in young adulthood.

42. What are the most common mental disorders?

43. What may be the outcome, in normal daily functioning of severe anxiety disorders?

44. Explain why the rates of depression are higher in early adulthood than in either adolescence or middle age.

45. Define binge drinking, and describe the problem behaviours associated with it.

46. Define personality disorder, and list the five most common personality disorders.

47. What behaviours need to occur before a young adult is diagnosed with a personality disorder?

48. Define schizophrenia.

49. Differentiate between delusions and hallucinations.

COGNITIVE CHANGES

Formal Operations and Beyond (pp. 421–422)

Objective 13.11: Summarize the theories of cognitive change in adulthood.

50. Like most aspects of physical functioning, intellectual processes are _____ _____. Indeed, it now seems clear that the intellectual peak _____.

51. Using the following table, describe three concepts of new structures of thinking that occur in adulthood.

Theorist	Concept	Description
Gisela Labouvie-Vief	Contextual validity	
Michael Basseches	Dialectical thought	
Patricia Arlin	Problem finding/ creativity	

Intelligence and Memory (pp. 422–424)

Objective 13.12: Summarize the research on the course of intelligence and memory in early adulthood.

52. Give examples of how IQ scores remain stable across middle childhood, adolescence, and early adulthood. Include the survey of Canadian army veterans conducted by Gold et al. and Werner Schaie's Seattle Longitudinal Study in your examples.

53. Define the following terms, and give examples to distinguish them:
    a. crystallized intelligence
    b. fluid intelligence

54. Summarize the conclusions about intellectual maintenance or decline over adulthood.

55. Describe the pattern of results from studies of memory ability, including the encoding and retrieval of long-term memories.

POST-SECONDARY EDUCATION

Developmental Impact (pp. 425–426)

Objective 13.13: Describe the developmental impact of post-secondary education.

56. Define post-secondary education and describe its economic impact.

57. State the reason why post-secondary education has been on the rise in Canada.

58. How does post-secondary education provide socialization opportunities? What other opportunities does post-secondary education provide?

CRITICAL REFLECTION EXERCISES

Crystallized Intelligence and Fluid Intelligence

Give three examples of crystallized intelligence and three examples of fluid intelligence. What profession are you pursuing and which of these intelligences will you rely on more in that profession? Why?

Social Stress

Describe the concept of social stress. Why is this type of stress so potentially damaging? Discuss three things a person could do to minimize the negative effects of social stress.

PRACTICE QUESTIONS

1. Inevitable aging could also be called _____.
    a. primary aging
    b. auxiliary aging
    c. a rotten crying shame
    d. maturation

2. Which one of the following is a common indicator of the population health approach?
   a. dietary habits
   b. economic levels
   c. stress levels
   d. hospitalization rates

3. The part of the brain that regulates emotional responses is the _____.
   a. pituitary gland
   b. thymus
   c. limbic system
   d. grey matter

4. VO$_2$ max, measured in a person at rest, _____.
   a. begins to decline gradually at about age 35
   b. does not change as we get older
   c. increases gradually starting at age 40
   d. declines for women and goes up for men as a function of aging

5. Which gland appears to be central to the aging process?
   a. pituitary
   b. thyroid
   c. thymus
   d. adrenal

6. In contrast to other types of disease, most _____ is (are) more common among young adults than in any other age group.
   a. sexually transmitted infections
   b. colds and the flu
   c. coronary heart disease
   d. osteoporosis

7. Which one of the following segments of the population has the HIV epidemic recently invaded to a disproportionately high level?
   a. homosexuals
   b. Aboriginals
   c. males
   d. Asians

8. Which one of the following factors is specifically linked to sexually transmitted infections?
   a. adequate sex protection
   b. multiple sexual partners
   c. poor health habits
   d. blood-borne infections

9. Nina, age 21, believes in her own capacity to cause an intended event to occur or to perform. According to Bandura this belief is called _____.
    a. hardiness
    b. pessimism
    c. helplessness
    d. self-efficacy

10. Physical acts or other behaviours intended to intimidate or harm an intimate partner are called _____.
    a. pessimism
    b. intimate partner abuse
    c. helplessness
    d. depression

11. Sexual activity with another person without his or her consent is called
    _____.
    a. intimate partner abuse
    b. sexual violence
    c. sexual assault
    d. date rape

12. Which of the following is called level 2 of sexual assault according to Canadian law?
    a. sexual assault with a weapon resulting in bodily harm
    b. kissing and touching over all bodily parts
    c. endangering the life of the victim
    d. intercourse or other form of penetration

13. Steve, age 24 has an anxiety disorder. This disorder may contribute most readily to his
    _____.
    a. punctuality at work
    b. aggressive states
    c. lost productivity
    d. delusional states

14. A person with _____ personality disorder is suspicious of others' behaviour and is emotionally guarded and highly sensitive to minor violations of personal space or perceived rights.
    a. paranoid
    b. antisocial
    c. borderline
    d. narcissistic

15. False sensory experiences are called _____.
    a. personality disorders
    b. narcissistic responses
    c. delusions
    d. hallucinations

16. A couple who is thinking of adopting a baby would use dialectical thinking. This type of thinking is characterized by _____.
    a. fact
    b. declarative memories
    c. uncertainty
    d. hypothetical reasoning

17. Choosing the type of refrigerator to buy might be aided by which of the following thought process?
    a. postformal thought
    b. contextual validity
    c. dialectical thought
    d. problem finding

18. Which of the following statements about IQ is true?
    a. It is fairly stable as we age.
    b. It will inevitably decline in old age.
    c. It increases throughout adulthood unless we experience disease.
    d. There are consistent age- and culture-related declines in old age.

19. Which of the following is an example of fluid intelligence?
    a. a reaction time test
    b. technical job skills
    c. knowledge about your culture
    d. the ability to read

20. John, age 25, has an intellectually more taxing job than his friend Henry has. Compared to Henry, John will experience some _____ in intellectual skills.
    a. subtle decline
    b. increase
    c. dramatic change
    d. decrease

21. Lisa's older sister forgets a phone number as soon as she looks it up. This example is indicative that as one gets older short-term memory generally_____.
    a. remains the same.
    b. drops with age
    c. is gender specific
    d. erodes substantially

22. The process of getting memories into long-term storage is called _____.
    a. event processing
    b. encoding
    c. seriation
    d. semantic encryption

23. Any formal educational experience that follows high school is called _____.
    a. formal operational thinking
    b. dialectical learning
    c. post-secondary education
    d. the virtual college

24. Longitudinal evidence suggests that the longer a person remains in college, the better his or her performance on _____.
    a. Piaget's formal operational tasks
    b. memory tests
    c. reaction time tests
    d. knowledge about her culture

25. Which of the following is associated with college or university attendance?
    a. getting married faster
    b. advancing in moral reasoning
    c. travelling abroad
    d. being able to sympathize with others

AT-HOME PROJECT

Student Project 23: Estimating Your Own Longevity

Given the importance of health habits in longevity (the length of expected life), you may be interested in estimating your own longevity, based on your own habits and other factors that we know affect the length of life. Respond to each of the following items honestly and sum the various negative and positive factors. The average 20-year-old male in Canada can expect to live to age 76.58; the average 20-year-old female can expect to live to age 81.67, so add or subtract your total number from this expectation to find your estimated length of life. (Remember, please, that this will provide only a very rough estimate. We are not offering a guarantee here that you will live as long or as short a time as the formula suggests.)

Health Habits

1. *Weight*: Using the following table, determine the number of years to subtract (if any):

	10%–30% Heavier than Standard Weight Tables		*More than 30% Above Standard Weight Tables*	
	Women	Men	Women	Men
Age 20–29	-5	-10	-6.5	-13
Age 30–49	–4	–4	-5	-6
Age 50 +	-2	-2	–4	–4

2. *Diet*: If your diet is truly low in fat and sugar, and you never eat to the point past fullness, +1

3. *Smoking*: If you smoke less than a pack a day, -2; between 1 and 2 packs a day, -7; more than 2 packs a day, -12.

4. *Drinking*: Heavy drinkers, -8; moderate drinkers, +2; light or abstainer, +1 1/2.

5. *Exercise*: If you do some aerobic exercise for 20 to 30 minutes at least 3 times a week, + 3.

6. *Sleep*: If you sleep more than 10 or less than 7 hours a night, -2

Health History

1. If you have any chronic health condition, such as high blood pressure, diabetes, cancer, or ulcers, or are frequently ill, -5.

2. If your mother was older than 35 or younger than 18 at your birth, -1.

3. If you are the oldest child in your family. +1.

4. If you have an annual physical examination, +2.

5. Women only: If you have no children (or plan to have none), -1/2.

Heredity

1. For each of your grandparents who has lived past age 80, +1. (If your grandparents have not yet reached this age, simply ignore the item).

2. For each grandparent who have lived past 70, but not 80, +1/2.

3. If your mother lived past 80, +4.

4. If your father lived past 80, +2.

5. For each sibling, parent, or grandparent who died of heart disease before age 50, –4.

6. For each sibling, parent, or grandparent who died of heart disease between age 50 and 60, -2

7. Women only: For each mother or sister who died of breast cancer before age 60, -1.

Social Class, Personality, and Other Characteristics

1. If your intelligence is superior, +2.

2. If you have only an Grade 8 education or less, -2; if you have completed high school but no further, +1; if you have completed 1 to 3 years of university or college, +2; if you have completed 4 or more years of university or college, +3.

3. If your occupation is professional, technical, or managerial, +1; if it is unskilled, –4.

4. If your income is above average for your education and occupation, +1; if it is below average, -1.

5. If your job is sedentary, -2; if it is physically active, +2.

6. If you have lived in urban areas most of your life, -1; if you have lived mostly in a rural area, +1.

7. If you are married and living with your spouse, +1.

8. If you are separated or divorced, –4 if you are a women, -9 if you are a man.

9. If you are widowed, –4 if you are a women, -7 if you are a man.

10. Women: If you have never been married, and whether you are living with your family or alone, -1 for each decade unmarried past the age of 25.

11. Men: if you have never married and are living with your family, -1 for each decade unmarried past age 25; if you live alone, -2 for each decade unmarried past age 25.

12. If you have at least two close confidants, +1.

13. If your personality is noticeably hostile and aggressive, and you regularly feel under time pressure, subtract between 2 and 5 years, depending on how well the description fits.

14. If you are easy-going, relaxed, and calm, and adapt easily to changing circumstances, add between 1 and 3 years, depending on how well the description fits.

15. If you have a lot of fun in life and are basically happy, +2.

16. If you have had at least one period of a year or more in your life when you were depressed, very tense, very worried, or guilty, subtract between 1 and 3, depending on how severe the depression was.

17. If you live in a high crime neighbourhood, or take physical risk regularly, -2.

18. If you generally avoid risk and wear seatbelts regularly, +1.

When you have calculated the score, think about the result. How many of the factors that affect longevity do you have control over? Make a list of specific steps you could take today that might increase your longevity.

Reference

Adapted from D. S. Woodruff-Pak (1988), *Psychology and aging*. Englewood Cliffs, NJ: Prentice-Hall, pp. 145–154.

CHAPTER 13 ANSWER KEY

Guided Study Questions

9. Compared to older adults, adults in their 20s and 30s have <u>more muscle tissue;</u> <u>maximum bone calcium; more brain mass; better eyesight, hearing, and sense of smell;</u> <u>greater oxygen capacity; and a more efficient immune system</u>.

   The younger adult is <u>stronger, faster, and better able to recover from exercise or to</u> <u>adapt to changing conditions, such as alterations in temperature or light levels</u>.

20. In contrast to other types of disease, most sexually transmitted infections (STIs), including <u>chlamydia, gonorrhea, and syphilis,</u> are more common among <u>young adults</u> <u>than in any other age group</u>.

50. Like most aspects of physical functioning, intellectual processes are <u>at their peak in</u> <u>early adulthood</u>. Indeed, it now seems clear that the intellectual peak <u>lasts longer than</u> <u>many early researchers had thought, and that the rate of decline is quite slow</u>.

Practice Questions

1. a	6. a	11. c	16. c	21. b
2. d	7. b	12. a	17. a	22. b
3. c	8. b	13. c	18. a	23. c
4. b	9. d	14. a	19. a	24. a
5. c	10. b	15. d	20. a	25. b

SOCIAL AND PERSONALITY DEVELOPMENT IN EARLY ADULTHOOD

OVERVIEW OF CHAPTER

In early adulthood, individuals turn away from the preoccupation with self that is characteristic of social relationships in adolescence. For most, the formation of an intimate relationship with a long-term partner is a theme that dominates this period of development.

Theories of Social and Personality Development

- Erikson proposed that the crisis of intimacy versus isolation is the defining theme of early adulthood.

- Levinson's theory suggests that adult development is characterized by alternating periods of stability and instability, such as the young adult's moving away from home. Through these periods of instability, adults redefine what Levinson calls their *life structures*.

- Evolutionary theories of mate selection suggest that sex differences in mate preferences and mating behaviour are the result of natural selection.

- Social role theory emphasizes factors such as gender roles, similarity, and economic exchange in explaining sex differences in mating.

Intimate Relationships

- Many young Canadian adults use the Internet. The appeal of Internet dating is growing, as is the field of advice on cyber-dating. However, major drawbacks exist, such as the possibility of being deceived.

- Internal working models of attachment are related to relationship success in early adulthood. Sternberg's theory of love suggests that romantic attachment has three dimensions: intimacy, passion, and commitment.

- The management of conflict is an important predictor of relationship quality. Those who create positive interactive systems are more likely to enjoy enduring relationships and avoid divorce or separation.

- Married adults are generally healthier and more satisfied with their lives than those who are single. However, it appears to be relationship quality, not just being married, that is responsible for the correlation between marriage and well-being. Singles who do not have intimate partners rely on family and friends for intimacy. After many years of singlehood, single adults tend to incorporate "singleness" into their sense of identity.

- Many young adults go through divorce. The statistical likelihood is that 38% of marriages in Canada will end in divorce within 30 years of marriage. For many adults, divorce brings on a new set of roles involving family and work.

Parenthood and Other Relationships

- In Canada, the vast majority of young people, both men and women, expect to have at least one child.

- The transition to parenthood is stressful and is made more so by perceived inequities in the division of labour between mother and father and by several other factors, including sleep deprivation and (potentially) post-partum depression.

- Marital satisfaction peaks before the birth of the first child, drops thereafter, and remains at a lower level until the last child leaves home.

- Canadians are more likely to remain child-free if they assign a lower value to the importance of marriage or to being part of a couple.

- Young adults' relationships with their own parents are less central to their lives but continue to be important. Proximity is a factor that influences contact with kin. Cultural differences also play a role in young adults' involvement with their families.

- Young adults' social networks are important sources of support. These networks include friends as well as an intimate partner and other family members.

The Role of Worker

- Career choice is influenced by family history, intelligence, resources, personality, gender, and other variables.

- Job satisfaction rises during early adulthood. The work role appears to have two stages: a trial stage in which an individual explores different types of work, and an establishment stage, in which the career path becomes stable.

- Women's work patterns and attitudes are changing rapidly. In Canada, more women are holding down formerly male-dominated jobs.

- The more continuous a woman's work history, the more successful she is likely to be at her job. Women struggle between focusing on family responsibilities and employment.

LEARNING GOALS

After completing Chapter 14, students should be able to:
1. Explain the theories of social and personality development in the early adulthood years.
2. Summarize the issues involved in establishing intimate relationships as a young adult.
3. Discuss the effects of parenthood and other relationships on development in early adulthood.
4. Describe the changing trends of women's work patterns and attitudes.

5.   Identify the issues young adults face in assuming the role of worker.

GUIDED STUDY QUESTIONS

THEORIES OF SOCIAL AND PERSONALITY DEVELOPMENT

Erikson's Stages of Intimacy versus Isolation (pp. 430–431)

Objective 14.1: Describe the key points in Erickson's theory that are relevant to early adulthood.

1.   Define the following terms:
   a.   intimacy versus isolation
   b.   intimacy

2.   According to Erikson, what does the successful resolution of intimacy versus isolation depend upon? Why?

3.   How accurate is Erikson's theory for young adults who do not have intimate relationships? Give examples of the problems that they experience.

Levinson's Life Structures (pp. 431–432)

Objective 14.2: Summarize Levinson's theory of life structures.

4.   Define life structure, and explain how it changes over the course of adulthood.

5.   List and describe the three phases of each life structure. Give an example to support the definitions.

Evolutionary Theory and Mate Selection (pp. 432–434)

Objective 14.3: Explain the evolutionary theory of mate selection.

6.   How do evolutionary explanations of behaviour explain mate selection?

7.   Define parental investment theory, and give examples of how it explains mate selection.

No Easy Answers: Does Cohabitation Help Couples Construct a Life Structure for Marriage? (p. 433)

Objective 14.4: Identify the relationship between cohabitation and subsequent success in marriage.

8.   What are the results of research on the relationship between cohabitation and satisfaction in a subsequent marriage? Give two reasons to explain the results.

Social Role Theory and Mate Selection (pp. 434–435)

Objective 14.5: Explain the social role theory of mate selection.

9.   Define the following terms:
     a.   social role theory
     b.   assortative mating, or homogamy

10. Distinguish social role theory from evolutionary theory as they address mate selection.

INTIMATE RELATIONSHIPS

Development in the Information Age: Internet Relationships (p. 436)

Objective 14.6: Summarize the issues involved in Internet relationships

11. State the name of the book available for individuals who wish to increase their knowledge about cyber-dating.

12. State the reasons people use Internet dating.

13. Describe the drawbacks of Internet dating.

Psychological Aspects of Marriage (pp. 436–440)

Objective 14.7: Identify the factors involved in marital success.

14. Give an example of each of the following influences on marital success.

Factor	*Example*
Personality characteristics	
Attachment to family of origin	
Emotional affection	
Conflict management	

15. List and define the three components of Robert Sternberg's theory of love.

16. List and describe all the combinations of the components of Sternberg's theory.

17. Describe Gottman's theory of the three types of stable or enduring marriages and two types of unsuccessful marriages by completing the following tables.

Type of Stable or Enduring Marriage	Description
Validating couples	
Volatile couples	
Avoidant couples	

Type of Unsuccessful Marriage	Description
Hostile/engaged couples	
Hostile/detached couples	

18. Married young adults are _____
and they _____ than do young adults without committed partners.

19. How do self-selection and health practices explain the pattern of marital satisfaction described in the previous question?

20. Give examples of how levels of cortisol explain the quality of a person's marriage.

Research Report: Comparing Heterosexual and Homosexual Partnerships (pp. 438–439)

Objective 14.8: Summarize the research comparing heterosexual and homosexual partnerships.

21. List the differences and the similarities between heterosexual and homosexual relationships.

Singlehood (440–441)

Objective 14.9: Describe how singlehood affects intimacy

22. Describe the findings of a Canadian study on mature singles and their views on marriage.

23. How does singleness affect a person's relationship with family and friends?

24. Trace the development of singleness as a positive component of the individual's identity.

Divorce (pp. 441–442)

Objective 14.10: Discuss the impact of divorce on adults.

25. Give examples of how different ways of computing the divorce rate distort our ideas about how frequently divorce happens. Cite Statistics Canada figures regarding the likelihood of the occurrence of divorce.

26. At a psychological level, divorce is clearly a _____. It is associated with increases in both _____.

27. Describe the long-term psychological effects of divorce.

28. Explain how the economic effects of divorce may be worse for women than for men.

29. How might divorce affect the sequence and timing of family and work roles?

PARENTHOOD AND OTHER RELATIONSHIPS

Parenthood (pp. 443–446)

Objective 14.11: Identify the changes brought about by becoming a parent.

30. Summarize the Canadian statistics about the desire to become a parent.

31. Examine postpartum depression (PPD).

32. Describe the transition experience for new parents.

33. What is the positive impact of the transition to parenthood?

34. List the variables that may affect marital satisfaction as a result of the transition to parenthood.

35. How does being child-free affect the shape of an adult's life?

Social Networks (pp. 446–447)

Objective 14.12: Identify the role of social networks in early adulthood.

36. Summarize young adults' relationships with their parents.

37. How does proximity affect a young adult's contact with his or her family?

38. Give examples of how cultural differences affect young adults' involvement with their families.

Friends (p. 447)

Objective 14.13: Identify the role of friends in early adulthood.

39. We choose our friends as we choose our partners, from among those who are similar to us in _____.

40. Describe the sex differences in both the number and quality of friendships in the social networks of young adults.

41. Define the kin-keeper role, and give examples of the behaviour of a person who is a kin-keeper.

THE ROLE OF WORKER

Choosing an Occupation (pp. 448–450)

Objective 14.14: List the influences that affect a young person's choice of job or career.

42. List the factors that influence a young person's choice of job or career.

43. Give examples of how families influence a young person's choice of job or career.

44. Give brief examples of how the following areas can influence a young person's choice of job of career.

Areas	*Examples*
Education and intelligence	
Gender	
Personality	

45. List the six personality types, according to John Holland. Describe the characteristics of each and identify the work preferences of each by completing the following table.

Type	Description of Personality	Work Preferences
Realistic		
Investigative		
Artistic		
Social		
Enterprising		
Conventional		

Jobs over Time (pp. 450–451)

Objective 14.15: Trace the issues in keeping jobs over time.

46. List the reasons why job satisfaction is at its lowest in early adulthood, and why it rises steadily until retirement.

47. What are the variables that contribute to job satisfaction in young adults?

48. What are the workplace variables that influence job satisfaction?

49. Describe the stages of work sequence proposed by Donald Super.

Sex Differences in Work Patterns (pp. 451–453)

Objective 14.16: Discuss the sex differences in work patterns.

50. Describe the transition from school to work for the Canadian youth.

51. What are the most striking differences between women's work experiences and men's work experiences in early adulthood? What repercussions does this pattern have for women's work roles?

52. State the findings of a Canadian study regarding women's work patterns and attitudes.

53. What was Daly's research finding regarding time-related stress for young Canadian single mothers and married parents?

54. List the reasons that women feel more role conflict than men feel among their roles as a worker, a parent, and a spouse.

The Real World/Working: Strategies for Coping with Conflict Between Work and Family Life (p. 454)

Objective 14.17: List strategies for coping with conflict between work and family life.

55. List five strategies for coping with the conflict between work and family life.

CRITICAL REFLECTION EXERCISES

Relationships in Early Adulthood

Using the information in the text, provide detailed responses to the following questions:
1. What is the percentage of marriages in Canada that will end in divorce within 30 years of marriage?
2. What are the effects of divorce?
3. If you are married, name and discuss three things you can do to maximize the success of your marriage. If you are not currently married, name and discuss three things that you can do with a potential partner prior to getting married to increase the likelihood that an eventual marriage will succeed.

Parenting an Adolescent

You are the parent of a 14-year-old. Based on the information in the text, discuss at least three things that you could do to enhance the likelihood that your adolescent will make a smooth and successful transition into young adulthood.

PRACTICE QUESTIONS

1. For Erikson, the central crisis of early adulthood is _____.
   a. industry versus inferiority
   b. identity versus role confusion
   c. intimacy versus isolation
   d. integrity versus despair

2. The ability to fuse your identity with someone else's without fear that you are going to lose something yourself, is the definition of _____.
   a. selflessness
   b. intimacy
   c. generativity
   d. role confusion

3. All the roles an individual occupies, all his or her relationships, and the conflicts and balance that exist among them is called _____.
    a. a life structure
    b. intimacy
    c. homogamy
    d. a kin-keeper

4. According to Levinson, the first phase of a period of adjustment is called the _____.
    a. culmination phase
    b. beginning phase
    c. mid-era phase
    d. novice phase

5. What effect does cohabiting have on the subsequent marriage?
    a. It tends to stabilize the marriage, and the couple is less likely to divorce.
    b. The couples report being less satisfied and are more likely to divorce.
    c. It tends to result in less marital satisfaction, but only in the U.S.
    d. It depends on the age of the cohabiting couple.

6. The theory that contrasts men's and women's differing amounts of investment in bearing children is called _____.
    a. mate-switching
    b. the parental investment theory
    c. assortative mating
    d. social role theory

7. According to the social role theory on average, what are women concerned with in a potential mate?
    a. economic prospects
    b. education level
    c. physical attractiveness
    d. personality similarity

8. Jane and Bill wish to marry. They are similar in age, religion and interests. Sociologists refer to this tendency to mate with someone who has traits similar to one's own as

    _____.
    a. romantic infatuation
    b. homogamy
    c. companionate love
    d. partnership

9. A major drawback to Internet dating is the possibility of _____.
    a. developing enabling relationships
    b. losing one's identity
    c. being deceived
    d. engaging in sexual intimacy

10. Sternberg suggests that love has the following three key components:
    a. intimacy, passion, and commitment
    b. sincerity, consistency, and convenience
    c. significance, maintenance, and playfulness
    d. lust, compatibility, and persistence

11. Which of the following marriages represents volatile couples?
    a. The couple has no humour or affection.
    b. The couple agrees to disagree.
    c. The couple does not listen to each other well during arguments.
    d. The couple expresses mutual respect for each other.

12. Nellie, age 24, is single. Although she has an intimate partner who she enjoys being with, which one of the following best acts as an important source of emotional intimacy for her?
    a. family of creation
    b. co-workers
    c. hairdresser
    d. family of origin

13. Which of the following statements about homosexual relationships is true? Homosexual couples _____.
    a. report being less satisfied than heterosexual couples
    b. tend to be more monogamous than heterosexual couples
    c. are more egalitarian than heterosexual couples
    d. tend to experience more physical abuse than heterosexual couples

14. Which one of the following facts is true regarding separated or divorced adults?
    a. They are more likely to exhibit depression.
    b. They display more stability in other relationships.
    c. They have fewer automobile accidents.
    d. They report an increase in self-esteem.

15. Which of the following groups generally experience an improvement in their economic status after a divorce?
    a. men
    b. women
    c. both men and women
    d. neither men nor women

16. Which one of the following statements is indicative of postpartum depression in women?
    a. when the pregnancy is planned for a length of time
    b. when the women is relaxed and carefree during her pregnancy
    c. when the women's partner is unsupportive
    d. when the women drinks alcohol on occasion during her pregnancy

17. Which of the following best fits regarding the couple that remaining child-free?
    a. They more likely to divorce after one year
    b. They may be the envy of many couples.
    c. They more likely to be shunned by their families
    d. The woman in the marriage is more likely to have a continuous career.

18. The amount and kind of contact an adult has with his/her family is strongly influenced by _____.
    a. personality traits.
    b. work habits.
    c. proximity to family.
    d. quality of relationship

19. Which of the following statements about adult friendships appears to be true?
    a. Men are generally less satisfied with their friendships than women.
    b. Men's friendships involve a lot more social support than women's friendships.
    c. Women have fewer friends, but they are very close to them.
    d. There tends to be no real significant differences in men's and women's friendships.

20. According to John Holland, which of the following personality types tends to choose a career such as nursing or education?
    a. social
    b. conventional
    c. artistic
    d. enterprising

21. Which one of the following may influence young women to choose a traditionally masculine career?
    a. less likely to be a high achiever in high school.
    b. more likely to have a mother who had a long-term career.
    c. less likely to be successful in interacting with other women.
    d. more likely to be influenced by her father in career choice..

22. Jill is searching for a fit between her interests and personality and the jobs available. According to Donald Super in which one of the following stages of work is Jill?
    a. trial stage.
    b. establishment stage.
    c. stabilization stage.
    d. endurance stage.

23. Which one of the following statements best describes Canadian women today regarding career and family goals?
    a. All women believe that they can be continuously employed
    b. Women feel an essential conflict between work and family
    c. All women believe that family goals are not so important as career goals
    d. Women do not feel any conflict between work and family

24. Which of the following accurately describes family roles?
    a. Men feel more conflict between the roles of spouse, worker, and parent than women.
    b. Work and family roles tend to be sequential for women.
    c. Work and family roles tend to be simultaneous for men.
    d. Women view themselves as mother and wives all day.

25. A strategy by which one can recast or reframe a situation in a way that identifies the positive elements is called _____.
    a. conflict management
    b. depression
    c. homogamy
    d. cognitive restructuring

CASE STUDY

Sophie and Fred are a young working couple who were close to one another for several years. Sophie is a waitress and Fred a painter. They have been married for four years and have a child aged 2. They increased their hours of work to save and buy a home. However, for the past year, they have been in frequent conflict over finances. Both have been stressed and they have decided to seek a divorce.

1. From you understanding of Sternberg's theory, what key component of love did Sophie and Fred initially demonstrate?
2. During their conflict, what could have been happening to their cortisol levels in their bodies?
3. After the divorce, who may be the one more affected economically? Discuss your answer.

INVESTIGATIVE PROJECT

Student Project 26: Social Networks Among Young Adults

For this project, which is based on the work of Antonucci and Akiyama (1987), collect some data from young adults. You should locate at least four adults, one each in the following age ranges: 20–24, 25–29, 30–34, and 35–40. It would be simpler if they were all the same sex, but that may not be practical. If you can, find eight willing subjects; try for one woman and one man in each group. (If all the students in your class complete this project, each with a minimum of four subjects, you could end up with quite a large sample, allowing you to look at sex differences and age trends.) You will need to obtain the appropriate informed consent from each subject, following the procedure as specified by your instructor.

Procedure

For each subject prepare an 8½″ x 11″ sheet of paper on which you have drawn a bull's-eye. In the centre should be a very small circle (about the size of a dime) labelled "you." Around this circle draw three concentric circles, spaced equally apart. This will give you three areas, each further from the centred "you."

Tell your subject that you are interested in knowing something about the people who are important in his or her life. Present the sheet with the concentric circles on it and say:

> *Think of the three circles as including people who are important in your life right now, but to whom you are not equally close. The innermost circle (point to the circle immediately next to "you") includes people to whom you feel so close that it is hard to imagine life without them. Please put the names of anyone who fits that description into this innermost circle, along with some indication of how they are related to you—friend, parent, spouse, or whoever.*

When the subject has entered names in the innermost circle, point to the next circle and say:

> *Please put in this circle the names of people to whom you may not feel quite that close but who are still very important to you, and indicate your relationship to each one.*

Finally, point to the outermost circle and say:

> *Finally, put here the names of the people you haven't already mentioned but who are close enough and important enough in your life that they should be placed in your personal network. As usual, indicate how you are related to each one.*

In addition, you will need to ask each subject a set of questions to amplify your analysis:

> *Are you married?*
>
> *How old are you?*
>
> *How many years of education have you completed?*

Write the answers on the back of the subject's concentric circle sheet. Also note the gender of the subject on the back of the sheet. Your subject's name should NOT appear anywhere on the sheet.

Analysis and Report

For each circle, count the total number of names, the number of males and females listed, and the relationship listed (family member, friend, or spouse). Is there any noticeable difference in these characteristics as a function of age, sex,, or education among your subjects?

Some other questions you might consider:

- Do all married subjects put their spouse in the centre circle?

- How many put either or both parents in the centre circle?

- Is there any married subject who put both the spouse and one or both parents in the centre circle? If so, what does this say about the issue of the relative strength of a person's attachment to partner and parent?

- Is there a friend in the centre circle, or do friends only begin to be listed in the second circle? Does this vary as a function of marital status? That is, do unmarried adults put more friends in the centre circle?

Consider all these results in light of what is said in the text about networks and relationships in early life. What else might you want to know about your subjects to help you interpret their answers?

Reference

Antonucci, T. C., & Akiyama, H. (1987). Social networks in adult life and a preliminary examination of the convoy model. *Journal of Gerontology*, *42*, 519–527.

CHAPTER 14 ANSWER KEY

Guided Study Questions

18. Married young adults are <u>happier and healthier,</u> and they <u>live longer, and have lower rates of a variety of psychiatric problems</u> than do young adults without committed partners.

26. At a psychological level, divorce is clearly a <u>major stressor</u>. It is associated with increases in both <u>physical and emotional illness</u>.

39. We choose our friends as we choose our partners, from among those who are similar to us in <u>education, social class, interests, family background, or family life-cycle stage</u>.

Practice Questions

1. c	6. b	11. c	16. c	21. b
2. b	7. a	12. d	17. d	22. a
3. a	8. b	13. c	18. c	23. b
4. d	9. c	14. a	19. a	24. d
5. b	10. a	15. a	20. a	25. d

Case Study

1. Chapter 14 (p. 437). The most compelling theory of romantic love comes from Robert Sternberg, who argues that love has three key components. The love that is being demonstrated in the case study between Sophie and Fred is intimacy, which includes feelings that promote closeness and connectedness.

2. Chapter 14 (p. 440). Researchers have found that cortisol is known to increase when individuals experience negative emotions. It is one of the many stress hormones that are thought to impair immune functioning.

3. Chapter 14 (p. 441). The psychological effects of divorce are often significantly worsened by serious economic effects, particularly for women. Several longitudinal studies have shown that divorced men slightly improve their economic position while divorced women are adversely affected.

CHAPTER 15

PHYSICAL AND COGNITIVE DEVELOPMENT IN MIDDLE ADULTHOOD

OVERVIEW OF CHAPTER

In middle adulthood, the period from 40 to 60, the story of human development in the physical and cognitive domains becomes more an account of differences than a description of universals. This happens because there are so many factors—behavioural choices, poor health, and so on—that determine the developmental pathway that an individual adult follows.

Physical Changes

- During middle adulthood white matter crests and grey matter volume continues its decline. When middle-aged adults and young adults are compared regarding driving tasks, middle-aged adults often outperform younger adults.

- Both males and females experience changes in reproductive hormones—the climacteric—in these years. In women, reproductive capacity declines slightly and then ceases altogether at menopause. In men, the process is more gradual, and most continue to be capable of fathering children into late adulthood.

- The Society of Obstetricians and Gynaecologists of Canada (SOGC) provides accurate information and tips for coping with perimenopause and menopause. Regarding hormone replacement therapy, Canadian experts advise that women should discuss their concerns with health care professionals in order to make an informed choice based on one's own unique medical history.

- At about age 30, bone mass begins to decline. This process, called osteoporosis, is accelerated in women at menopause. Lifestyle choices, such as diet and exercise, can help prevent osteoporosis.

- Both visual and auditory acuity decline in most middle-aged adults. Men experience greater losses than women do.

Health Promotion and Wellness

- The rates of illness and death increase dramatically by the end of the middle adult years. Heart disease and cancer are the leading causes of death among middle-aged adults.

- Cardiovascular disease (CVD) results from the build-up of a fatty substance in the arteries—atherosclerosis. Smoking, high blood pressure, high cholesterol, obesity, and a high-fat diet increase the likelihood that a middle-aged adult will suffer from cardiovascular disease. Men are more likely than women to have this disease.

- In Canada, lung cancer remains the number one cause of death, followed by prostate cancer in men and breast cancer in women. Smoking, obesity, and an inactive lifestyle may also contribute to cancer. Scientists debate the role of dietary fat as a potential risk factor.

- On average, women live longer than men, but they are more likely to suffer from chronic conditions such as arthritis.

- Canadian men and women report improved mental health with increasing age. However, some disorders, such as alcoholism, may go undiagnosed until middle adulthood, when their effects begin to interact with those of primary aging. Some mental health professionals claim to have discovered a new disorder they call Internet Addictive Disorder (IAD).

Cognitive Functioning

- Denney's model of aging hypothesizes that exercising physical and cognitive abilities slows down the rate of decline in the middle and later adulthood years. According to this model, such exercise may also improve the level of functioning. However, Denney's model does emphasize that an underlying decay curve exists.

- Research suggests that variations in health are associated with variations in cognitive functioning in middle-aged and older adults. Physical exercise clearly affects health, but its effects on cognitive function are less conclusive.

- Some memory skills decline, but middle-aged adults maintain high levels of functioning in areas of expertise. Verbal abilities increase in middle age. Meanwhile, performance on more complex tasks declines with age. Research has indicated that there are age differences in working memory.

- In adults who have challenging professions, creative productivity appears to be at its peak in middle adulthood.

LEARNING GOALS

After completing Chapter 15, students should be able to:
1. Trace the physical changes that occur during middle age.
2. Summarize the issues relevant to health promotion and wellness during middle adulthood.
3. Describe the changes in cognitive functioning during middle adulthood.

GUIDED STUDY QUESTIONS

PHYSICAL CHANGES

The Brain and Nervous System (pp. 459–461)

Objective 15.1: Summarize the research on the brain and nervous system in middle adulthood.

1. State the findings of a research study, based at UCLA Dept. of Neurology, which compared brain development in a cross-section of people ranging in age from first to ninth decade of life.

2. The general rule of brain maturation is_____.

3. Give examples of how cognitive tasks activate a larger area of brain tissue in middle-aged adults than they do in younger adults.

4. Give examples of how the brains of middle-aged and younger adults respond differently to sensory stimuli.

The Reproductive System (pp. 461–465)

Objective 15.2: Describe the changes in the reproductive system in middle age.

5. Define the following terms:
    a. climacteric
    b. menopause

6. Describe the male climacteric, including the causal factor.

7. How is the production of testosterone implicated in the incidence of impotence?

8. What are contributing factors to erectile dysfunction?

9. Which Society in Canada sponsors the annual National Menopause Awareness Month? When does this month occur in the yearly calendar?

10. List the hormones involved in menopause.

11. Describe the results of research on the psychological effects of menopause.

12. Describe patterns of sexual activity for middle-aged adults.

13.   Describe the phases of menopause by completing the following table.

Phase	Description
Premenopausal phase	
Perimenopausal phase	
Postmenopausal phase	

No Easy Answers: The Pros and Cons of Hormone Replacement Therapy (pp. 463–464)

Objective 15.3: Summarize the pros and cons of hormone replacement therapy.

14.   Describe the benefits and risks of hormone replacement therapy by completing the following table.

Benefits	Risks

15.   What do Canadian experts advise women regarding menopause and hormonal replacement therapy?

The Skeletal System (pp. 465–466)

Objective 15.4: Describe the change in the skeletal system in middle adulthood.

16. Define osteoporosis and explain how it is linked to levels of estrogen and progesterone.

17. List the risks that may lead to osteoporosis and the health promotion strategies to prevent this disease.

Vision and Hearing (p. 467)

Objective 15.5: Identify the changes in vision and hearing in middle adulthood.

18. Define the following terms:
    a. presbyopia
    b. presbycusis

HEALTH PROMOTION AND WELLNESS

Health Trends at Mid-Life (pp. 468–469)

Objective 15.6: Describe the health trends at mid-life.

19. What is the life expectancy of a 40-year-old, according to Statistics Canada?

20. What are the two leading causes of death in middle age?

Cardiovascular Disease (pp. 469–471)

Objective 15.7: Summarize the risks of coronary heart disease in middle-aged adults.

21. Define the following terms:
    a. cardiovascular disease (CVD)
    b. plaque
    c. atherosclerosis
    d. type A personality factor

22.   Describe the risk factors of heart disease by completing the following table:

Risk	*Description of Risk for Heart Disease*
Alcohol	
Blood pressure	
Cholesterol	
Diet	
Heredity	
Inactivity	
Smoking	
Weight	

23.   State an important point to be made regarding CVD in Canadians.

Cancer (pp. 471—473)

Objective 15.8: Discuss the risk factors involved in cancer in middle adulthood.

24.   State the number one cause of cancer deaths in Canada.

25.   The second leading cause of cancer death for Canadians is_____in men, and _____in women.

26.   What warning does the Canadian Cancer Society (2004) sound regarding cancer?

27.   By completing the following table, describe the risk factors of cancer:

Risk	*Description of Risk for Cancer*
Dietary fat	
Infectious agents	
Viral infections	
Bacterial infections	
Alcohol	
Smoking	
Heredity	
Inactivity	

28.   State several health promotion strategies to prevent the occurrence of cancer.

Gender and Health (pp. 473–474)

Objective 15.9: Describe the relationship between gender and health in middle adulthood.

29.   State the paradox involving the life expectancy of women and men.

30.   Give examples of the sex differences in potentially fatal diseases such as cardiovascular disease and in non-fatal diseases such as arthritis.

Mental Health (pp. 474–475)

Objective 15.10: Summarize the issues surrounding mental health during the mid-life years.

31.   What do Canadian men and women report regarding mental health with increasing age?

32.   Compare the mental health problems of middle-aged adults to those of young adults.

33.   Define alcoholism. State the findings of the Statistical Report on the Health of Canadians regarding drinking patterns.

34.   List several consequences of alcoholism..

Development in the Information Age: Is the Internet Addictive? (p. 475)

Objective 15.11: Discuss the issues involved in Internet addiction.

35.   Define Internet Addictive Disorder (IAD). List the criteria for the diagnosis of IAD.

36.   What are the arguments proposed by mental health professions who oppose the idea of Internet addiction?

COGNITIVE FUNCTIONING

A Model of Physical and Cognitive Aging (pp. 476–477)

Objective 15.12: Explain Nancy Denney's model of physical and cognitive aging.

37.   Explain Nancy Denney's model of physical and cognitive changes in adulthood.

38.   Define "exercise" as Denney uses it in her model.

Health and Cognitive Functioning (pp. 477–479)

Objective 15.13: Describe the relationship between health and cognitive functioning.

39.   How does Nancy Denney's model help illuminate the links between primary aging and cognitive functioning?

40.   Describe the findings of Walter Schaie's Seattle Longitudinal Study.

41.   Describe the longitudinal study of physical activity of Harvard alumni.

42. What is the connection between physical exercise and cognitive abilities in middle-adulthood?

Changes in Memory and Cognition (pp. 479–481)

Objective 15.14: Describe the changes in memory and cognition in middle adulthood.

43. Why do researchers often infer the memory performance of middle-aged adults?

44. How can middle-aged adults overcome perceived memory limitations?

45. Compare memory for visual and auditory stimuli in middle age.

46. State the evidence for age differences in working memory.

47. Define the following terms:
    a. episodic memory
    b. semantic memory
    c. flashbulb memories

48. How do semantic memories and episodic memories differ in young adults and middle-aged adults?

49. How does the dictum "use it or lose it" hold true for cognitive abilities? Give examples.

50. Give examples of how expertise in a particular field helps to compensate for age-related deficits in cognitive functioning.

51. How do middle-aged adults compare with younger adults in their ability to acquire new knowledge?

52. Describe Labouvie-Vief's view of memory change with age.

53. Define schematic processing, and describe how it is involved in solving everyday problems.

Creativity (pp. 481–483)

Objective 15.15: Discuss creative productivity at mid-life.

54. Describe Simonton's research on the lifetime creativity and productivity of notable scientists from the 19th century and earlier. Compare the results to the lifetime creative output of modern-day scientists.

55. Give examples on how age is related to creativity or professional effectiveness.

The Real World/Working: Maintaining the Creative "Edge" in Mid-Life and Beyond (p. 482)

Objective 15.16: Summarize the research on maintaining the creative "edge" in mid-life and beyond.

56.   List the two conclusions of Streufert et al. research on maintaining creativity and productivity in the middle and late adult years.

CRITICAL REFLECTION EXERCISE

Mid-Life Development

Utilizing information from the text, provide complete answers to the following questions:

1.   What is type A personality pattern? Suggest three things that an individual could do to minimize the likelihood of type A characteristics influencing his or her health.

2.   Do you believe in the concept of a mid-life crisis? Why or why not?

3.   Discuss how identity development in the early phases of development may be related to life satisfaction in middle adulthood.

PRACTICE QUESTIONS

1.   Which of the following statements is true about brain development according to a study based at UCLA Department of Neurology?
   a.   There is no difference in the distribution of electrical activity in the brains of alcoholics and non-alcoholics.
   b.   White matter volume crests during middle aged adults.
   c.   The volume of cerebral spinal fluid decreases steadily during the life span.
   d.   Synaptic density continues to increase across adulthood.

2.   What reproductive event in middle adulthood is included in the term climacteric?
   a.   a gradual loss of interest in sexual activity
   b.   a steady increase in the number of miscarriages
   c.   the occurrence of menopause in women
   d.   decreased incidence of impotence in men

3.   What seems to be one of the contributing factors to the increase in erectile dysfunction in middle-aged men?
   a.   less sexual activity, which results in decreased sperm production
   b.   increased exposure to teratogens from the environment
   c.   there is no drop in viable sperm production.
   d.   gradual decline in testosterone levels beginning in early adulthood

4. What hormonal activity occurs during the premenopausal phase?
   a. decreasing estrogen levels
   b. increasing testosterone levels
   c. decreasing levels of the thyroid stimulating hormone
   d. increased estrogen levels and decreased estradiol levels

5. Susan, aged 48, complains of hot flashes. In which one of the following phases would hot flashes most likely occur?
   a. premenopausal phase
   b. perimenopausal phase
   c. postmenopausal phase
   d. anovulatory cycle

6. What do we know about the psychological effects of menopause on women?
   a. It inevitably causes decreased self-esteem and increased depression.
   b. It depends on when menopause starts.
   c. There are no consistent negative effects.
   d. There are effects, but they appear to be ethnic and not biological.

7. Molly has osteoporosis. Which one of the following health promotion strategies should she include in her daily life?
   a. taking herbal remedies.
   b. engaging in weight-bearing exercise.
   c. playing tennis or racquet ball
   d. avoiding dairy products.

8. Presbyopia is _____.
   a. a process by which muscle mass is lost
   b. the thickening of the lens that causes the eye muscles to have difficulty changing the shape of the lens for focusing
   c. the hardening of the arteries accompanied by a slight, but steady, decline in blood pressure during middle adulthood
   d. a sharp decline in taste sensitivity

9. What are the two leading causes of death in middle age?
   a. heart disease and cancer
   b. arthritis and hip fractures
   c. viral infections and gout
   d. diabetes and dementia

10. What is atherosclerosis?
    a. hardening of the arteries due to age
    b. clogging of the arteries with fibrous or fatty tissue
    c. a neuromuscular disorder often diagnosed in middle adulthood
    d. a normal part of aging that can be slowed but not avoided

11. In recent years, the rate of cardiovascular disease (CVD) in Canada and most other industrialized countries has been _____.
    a. increasing rapidly
    b. dropping slightly
    c. increasing slightly
    d. dropping rapidly

12. Which of the following statements about risk factors for heart disease is true?
    a. The risk factors are cumulative.
    b. All risk factors are completely controllable with the right effort.
    c. The only consistently controllable cause is smoking.
    d. Men are at a higher risk because they strain their hearts more than women.

13. Type A personality is _____.
    a. a personality characteristic involving an easy-going mood
    b. a combination of low self-esteem and hopelessness
    c. an extremely organized and punctual person
    d. an individual who is competitive, urgent, and hostile or aggressive

14. In Canada, what is the number one cause of cancer death in middle age?
    a. breast cancer
    b. prostate cancer
    c. lung cancer
    d. colorectal cancer

15. Which of the following statements is true concerning gender and health?
    a. Men are more likely to live longer than women.
    b. Women have fewer diseases and disabilities than men.
    c. Men live longer once they contract a disease than women do.
    d. Women live longer, but they have more diseases and disabilities than men.

16. Women are more likely than men to suffer from non-fatal chronic ailments such as

    _____.
    a. arthritis
    b. high blood pressure
    c. low blood sugar
    d. glaucoma

17. According to some health professionals, which one of the following may be a criterion for individuals to be diagnosed with Internet Addictive Disorder (IAD)?
    a. demonstrating a pattern of high cognitive functioning on intelligence and achievement tests
    b. indulging in a variety of dysfunctional behaviours within the family system and work situation

c.   demonstrating a pattern that interferes with normal educational, occupational, and social functioning

d.   displaying personality characteristics such as neuroticism and openness to experience

18.   The strongest risk factor for alcoholism in both men and women is _____ .
a.   cardiovascular disease
b.   a family history of problem drinking
c.   undiagnosed diabetes
d.   divorced parents

19.   Which one of the following self-help groups do you think most mental health professionals recommend for the individual who is an alcoholic?
a.   Let's Live Again.
b.   Al-Anon.
c.   Partners without Drugs.
d.   Alcoholics Anonymous.

20.   Which of the following statements describes Nancy Denney's model of physical and cognitive aging?
a.   Denney uses the word "exercise" to refer to physical exercise.
b.   Unexercised abilities generally have a lower peak of performance; exercised abilities generally have a higher peak.
c.   Only crystallized intelligence, not fluid intelligence, is affected by exercise.
d.   Skills that are not exercised by age 30 can never be improved.

21.   Which of the following statements accurately reflects the results of the longitudinal study of the physical activity of Harvard alumni?
a.   The more exercise a man reported in his 30s, 40s, and 50s, the lower his mortality risk over the next 25 years.
b.   Physical activity and cognitive functioning are not related.
c.   Physical activity and cognitive functioning are negatively correlated.
d.   Cardiovascular disease is linked to the presence of lead in drinking water.

22.   Middle aged adults become proficient at overcoming perceived memory limitations by using:
a.   a recording device
b.   the Internet periodically
c.   cues and reminders
d.   friends and acquaintances

23.   Recollection of personal events is called _____ .
a.   semantic memory
b.   short-term memory
c.   procedural memory
d.   episodic memory

24. What happens to creativity and productivity as we age?
    a. It peaks at around age 65, and then declines gradually.
    b. It peaks at different ages for women and men.
    c. It peaks at around age 40.
    d. Creativity is so individual that consistent results have not been found.

25. According to Streufert et al., how do younger and middle-aged groups differ on their professional effectiveness?
    a. Younger groups asked for less information about the task.
    b. Middle-aged groups used the information they obtained most effectively.
    c. The oldest groups performed the best on all measures because of wisdom.
    d. The all-women groups performed better than the all-men groups.

AT-HOME PROJECT

Student Project 25: Assessing Your Own Diet

Since both dietary fat and fibre intake are increasingly implicated as potential causal factors in cancer, heart disease, or both, it may be useful and informative for you to analyze your own diet.

For 3 days, write down everything you eat. Keep a record of the nutrition facts on the food labels. Do not change your normal eating pattern just to make a good impression and feel less guilty. If you normally eat candy bars, go ahead and eat them, but write it down—and keep the food label from the wrapper so that you can do a food analysis later.

You will need some source of detailed information about the total calories, fat, sodium, carbohydrate, and protein content. In Canada, mandatory nutrition labelling is now required on most prepackaged food. The Nutrition Facts Table provides you with the information needed to make informed food choices and compare products. Check *Eating Well with Canada Food Guide.* In addition, to help you learn more about the label, Health Canada provides an interactive tool called *Interactive Nutrition Label: Get the Facts.* You can obtain this information from the Health Canada web page http://www.hc-sc.gc.ca/.

Examine the food labels from the foods you ate in the past three days. Calculate the following totals:

- calories
- grams of fat
- milligrams of sodium
- grams of carbohydrates (fibre and sugars)
- grams of proteins

Average these figures over the three days, and then compare the averages with the recommendations from the new Canada Food Guide.

How does your diet measure up to the servings recommended in the Food Guide? What changes do you think you need to make in your diet?

CHAPTER 15 ANSWER KEY

Guided Study Questions

2.   The general rule of brain maturation is that the areas of the brain <u>that develop last begin to decline first, namely areas located within the frontal and parietal lobes.</u>

25.   The second leading cause of cancer death for Canadians is <u>prostate cancer</u> in men and <u>breast cancer</u> in women.

Practice Questions

1. b	6. c	11. d	16. a	21. a
2. c	7. b	12. a	17. c	22. c
3. d	8. b	13. d	18. b	23. d
4. a	9. a	14. c	19. d	24. c
5. b	10. b	15. d	20. b	25. b

SOCIAL AND PERSONALITY DEVELOPMENT IN MIDDLE ADULTHOOD

OVERVIEW OF CHAPTER

In Western culture, middle-aged adults are viewed as highly competent and capable of assuming important family and occupational roles. Consequently, in most families, the middle-aged cohort provides some degree of both material and emotional support for both younger and older family members. Still, most middle-aged adults feel much less constricted by social roles than in earlier periods, and, for most, these roles shift considerably between the ages of 40 and 60.

Theories of Social and Personality Development

- For Erikson, the primary task of middle adulthood is the development of generativity through mentoring younger individuals.

- Although changes may occur in mid-life, researchers who have conducted longitudinal studies do not find much support for the notion of mid-life crisis. A more appropriate term may be "mid-life transition," with a focus on growth rather than on stress.

- Sociologists have proposed that the role transitions of middle age occur in a life-stage pattern. However, research suggests that such life-stage models don't fully explain middle adulthood development.

Changes in Relationships

- Marital conflict declines in middle age, leading to higher levels of relationship satisfaction. This higher level of satisfaction appears to be due to a decline in problems and conflicts.

- Middle-aged adults are "sandwiched" between younger and older cohorts. They provide assistance and advice both up and down the generational chain. This pattern was confirmed within the Canadian population by gerontological researchers.

- When adult children leave home, most middle-aged adults experience a decrease in the role demands that accompany parenthood. Canadian men who parent experience the "empty nest" in a positive way.

- The "revolving door" is the pattern in which adult children who have been living independently return to live in their parents' home. There are mixed reactions on the parents' part regarding this pattern. Some experience a decline in life satisfaction, but others enjoy the companionship provided by their adult children.

- More than half of Canadian adults become grandparents by the end of middle adulthood. For most, the role is a very rewarding one. In Canada, grandparents are an important source of stability in the lives of children of divorced parents.

- In Canada, about one-quarter of Canadians aged 45 to 54 provide the greatest proportion of unpaid care for elderly parents. Some caregivers, who are highly involved in assisting with daily needs, report feeling depressed and have lower marital satisfaction. The culmination of untoward effects surrounding caregiving is termed *caregiver burden*. For a majority of mid-life adults, the relationship with aging parents is positive. Canadian women are more likely than men to become primary caretakers for elders. One factor that increases daughters' involvement in parental care is proximity.

- The number of friendships that an individual adult has declines in middle age, perhaps narrowing the social network to include only those friends to whom an adult feels particularly close.

- The Big Five personality traits are stable across middle adulthood. However, evidence exists for personality change in middle age as well. There are some signs of "mellowing" of negative traits. Middle-aged adults vary more in personality traits than do younger adults.

Mid-Life Career Issues

- Job satisfaction peaks in middle age; however, work takes on a less important role in an adult's overall sense of well-being during these years.

- Most middle-aged adults continue to be highly productive in their careers except in those occupations in which physical strength or speedy reaction time is a critical element.

- Anxiety and depression sometimes accompany both involuntary and voluntary mid-life career changes.

- Preparation for retirement includes financial planning as well as a decline in the number of hours a middle-aged adult works each week. For Baby Boomers, who are currently middle-aged, retirement preparations will be quite different compared to those of their parents.

LEARNING GOALS

After completing Chapter 16, students should be able to:
1. Explain the theories of social and personality development in middle adulthood.
2. Trace the changes in relationships and personality across middle adulthood.
3. Discuss the impact of continuity and change on adults in mid-life.
4. Identify the changes in the importance of work in middle adulthood.

GUIDED STUDY QUESTIONS

THEORIES OF SOCIAL AND PERSONALITY DEVELOPMENT

Erikson's Generativity versus Stagnation Stage (pp. 487–488)

Objective 16.1: Describe the key points in Erikson's theory relevant to middle adulthood.

1. Define the following terms:
   a. generativity versus stagnation stage
   b. generativity

2. Give examples of ways that generativity can be expressed, in addition to bearing and rearing one's own children.

3. Describe Erikson's view of those who do not express generativity.

Mid-Life Crisis: Fact or Fiction? (p. 489)

Objective 16.2: Examine the evidence of the possible existence of a mid-life crisis.

4. Who popularized the term 'mid-life' crisis?

5. Outline the historical perspective of the term 'mid-life crisis'.

6. State the evidence to discount the existence of a mid-life crisis.

Role Transitions (pp. 489–491)

Objective 16.3: Summarize the effects of the overall changes in roles in middle adulthood.

7. Define the following terms:
   a. role conflict
   b. role strain

8. Give examples of statuses in a social system.

9. List two aspects of the concept of a role that are important for an understanding of development.

10. Describe Evelyn Duvall's stages of the family life cycle by completing the following table:

Stage	Description
1	
2	
3	
4	
5	
6	
7	
8	

11. List two major flaws in Duvall's theory.

12. Define life course markers, and give examples in middle adulthood.

CHANGES IN RELATIONSHIPS AND PERSONALITY

Partnerships (p. 492)

Objective 16.4: Trace the pattern of partnerships in middle adulthood.

13. Why do marital stability and marital satisfaction, on average, increase in middle adulthood?

14. Define skilled diplomacy, and describe how it is helpful in solving problems in a partnership.

Children and Parents (pp. 492–495)

Objective 16.5: Summarize the research on the relationships of middle-aged adults with their children and their parents.

15. When looking at family relationships from the perspective of middle age, we have to look in both directions: _____

_____.

16. Define the following terms, and give examples of how they affect middle-aged adults:
    a. mid-life squeeze
    b. sandwich generation

17. What have the Canadian gerontology researchers confirmed regarding the sandwich generation?

18. Describe the results of Hagestad's research on attempts to influence other generations in the family.

19. How do men and women differ in the patterns of family conflict?

Emptying the Nest (pp. 495–496)

Objective 16.6: Describe the results of the empty nest.

20. Define the following terms:
    a. empty nest
    b. post-parental phase

21. Describe the findings obtained by Canadian researchers regarding the empty nest experience of women and men.

22. Describe the folklore in Western cultures about the empty nest and the evidence to support or dismiss it.

The Revolving Door (pp. 496–497)

Objective 16.7: Describe the relationship between parents and their adult children who live with them.

23. Define boomerang generation.

24. Describe the possible conflicts between parents and their adult children living with them.

Grandparenting (pp. 497–499)

Objective 16.8: Describe the impact of grandparenting on middle-aged adults.

25. State the number of grandparents in Canada. What is the proportion of grandchildren for each grandparent?

26. Describe the legal basis for issues of visitation or access to grandchildren by their grandparents. Which three provinces in Canada have such legislation?

27. Define the following terms:
    a. remote relationships
    b. companionate relationships
    c. involved relationships

28. What have the Canadian gerontologists found regarding grandparent care to their adult children and grandchildren?

Caring for Aging Parents (pp. 499–501)

Objective 16.9: Describe the issues involved in caring for aging parents during middle adulthood.

29. What factual evidence exists regarding the provision of elder care in Canada by middle-aged adults?

30. Describe the impact of the caregiver role on the middle aged.

31. Describe the research findings concerning caregiver burden, and list factors that can significantly lessen the burden.

32. Describe the relationship for the majority of mid-life adults with their aging parents. Why are parents symbolically important to middle-aged adults?

No Easy Answers: Who Cares for Aging Parents in Canada? (pp. 499–501)

Objective 16.10: Summarize the evidence of who cares for aging parents.

33. What are the options in Canada for the care of aging parents?

34. Within a group of siblings, who is most likely to take on the task of caregiver of an aging parent? What is the finding of a Canadian gerontologist regarding Canadian women in a caregiving role?

35. Describe how daughters and sons typically are involved in the caregiver role.

Friends (pp. 501–502)

Objective 16.11: Describe the friendships of adults in middle adulthood.

36. What does research suggest about the total number of friendships of middle-aged adults? What does research suggest about the quality of the friendships of middle-aged adults?

37. Friendship depends less on _____ than on a sense that _____.

Continuity and Change in Personality (502–503)

Objective 16.12: Identify the areas of continuity and of change in personality in middle adulthood.

38. Describe the difference between the evidence for continuity of personality across adulthood and the perception of most people.

39. State the evidence of real change in personality in adulthood.

40.   What are the cohort differences in continuity and stability?

41.   Define the following terms:
a.   tenacious goal pursuit
b.   flexible goal pursuit.

MID-LIFE CAREER ISSUES

Work Satisfaction (pp. 504–505)

Objective 16.13: Describe the satisfaction with work of men and women in middle adulthood.

42.   List the two paradoxes that characterize work in mid-life.

43.   Give examples of how the patterns of work satisfaction among women may be more complex than those of men.

44.   Differentiate between the differences in coping styles of men and women at work.

45.   List some reasons why both men and women in mid-life have a greater sense of control over their work lives than younger adults do.

Job Performance (pp. 505–506)

Objective 16.14: Identify the processes in optimizing job performance in middle adulthood.

46.   Give examples of occupations in which physical strength or speedy reaction time is a factor in job performance.

47.   List and describe the three sub-processes of selective optimization with compensation by completing the following table:

Subprocess	*Description*

48.   What is the relationship between increasing age and the use of selection, optimization, and compensation?

Unemployment and Career Transitions (pp. 506–508)

Objective 16.15: Describe the effects of unemployment on middle-aged adults.

49.   Why might career transitions be more difficult in middle age than earlier in adulthood?

50. Describe involuntary career changers.

51. Describe the direct and the indirect links between job loss and emotional or physical distress.

52. How might the stages of men's work lives increase the negative effects of unemployment?

53. Which of the Big Five personality dimensions contribute to mental health during involuntary career transitions?

54. What suggestions do career counsellors offer to assist a person who is an involuntary career changer?

55. Describe voluntary career changers.

56. How do voluntary career changers differ from involuntary career changers? How are they similar?

Preparing for Retirement (pp. 508–509)

Objective 16.16: Describe the preparations for retirement made by middle-aged adults.

57. Give examples of the gradual reduction in workload in mid-life.

58. List ways that middle-aged adults prepare for retirement.

59. Describe several ways that the Baby Boom cohort's retirement plans may differ dramatically from their parents' plans.

CRITICAL REFLECTION EXERCISE

Mid-life Transitions

Using information from the text, provide complete responses to the following issues. Whenever possible, cite specific information from the readings to support your responses.

1. What are three major life transitions that may be experienced during middle adulthood? Be sure to discuss the positive and negative effects of these life transitions. What advice would you give someone about how he or she can respond successfully to these life transitions?

Generativity Versus Stagnation

2. Discuss the concepts of generativity and stagnation. What effects might divorce have on these life crises?

3. How would you define mentoring? What kind of a program could you develop to use the knowledge and experience of those in late middle adulthood? Be sure that the program you develop uses Erikson's concepts of generativity versus stagnation, and integrity versus despair. Why would you design the program in these ways?

PRACTICE QUESTIONS

1. Which of the following individuals is exhibiting generativity?
   a. She believes that having children is important for one's identity
   b. He is doing volunteer work training youth
   c. She has come to terms with what she has done with her life
   d. He feels that his life has had little meaning

2. Which of the following statements about the mid-life crisis is true?
   a. There is little evidence that the stresses in mid-life are more likely to overwhelm an adult's coping resources at this age than at any other.
   b. The scores on the mid-life crisis scale are significantly higher at age 45 than at any other age.
   c. There is a dramatic increase in divorce, depression, and alcoholism in men and women during mid-life.
   d. Serious mid-life crises occur in 50% of middle-aged men.

3. Georgina has a full-time job, but she wants to attend university classes at 10 a.m. every morning for a few hours. This situation in which two roles are at least partially incompatible is called _____.
   a. role status
   b. role strain
   c. role conflict
   d. role incompatibility

4. Transitions that are highly predictable and widely shared in any given culture or cohort are called _____.
   a. life structures
   b. life course markers
   c. life statuses
   d. life transitions

5. Bob and Shelley are middle-aged adults who have been married for over 25 years. For them, which one of the following best describes what happens during mid-life?
   a. marital satisfaction tends to increase
   b. depression begins to increase gradually
   c. role overload begins to set in
   d. self-esteem increases, but boredom also sets in

6. Middle-aged adults are sometimes referred to as the sandwich generation because
    _____.
    a. financial burdens of retirement begin to squeeze these persons
    b. these individuals are trying to help both their children and their own parents
    c. time begins to seem as if it were passing faster than ever before
    d. the changes in role status cause these individuals to feel less needed

7. What do we know about multigenerational family conflicts?
    a. They are predominantly about parenting choices.
    b. They are always about money.
    c. The type of conflict differs based on the sex of the family members.
    d. Multigenerational family conflict is rare.

8. In Canada, when children leave home, the male parent sees this event as
    _____.
    a. positive
    b. a depressive event
    c. negative
    d. a financial relief

9. Which one of the following statements about the revolving door is true?
    a. Stress decreases for parents and their adult children when they share a home
    b. Parents feel that their privacy is maintained
    c. Few parents with adult children manage to work out a system for handling stress
    d. Some parents enjoy social support from their adult children

10. Laura and Tom see their grandchildren infrequently and have little influence over their lives. This type of relationship belongs to which one of the following categories?
    a. involved relationships
    b. companionate relationship
    c. limited privilege relationship
    d. remote relationships

11. Which of the following is a sign of having a positive caregiving experience for the middle aged?
    a. fearing death less
    b. having a spiritual experience
    c. understanding one's self better
    d. feeling affectionate

12. What effect does a high level of assistance for a disabled elderly parent have on the middle-aged adult?
    a. It tends to increase some aspects of depression and to lower marital satisfaction.
    b. It tends to give the individual a sense of direction and purpose.
    c. It creates a sense of conflict and hostility.
    d. It creates a jaded sense of futility about the future.

13. Which of the following is likely to be a factor in determining who cares for an aging parent?
    a. proximity of the grown child to the parent
    b. completion of post-secondary education
    c. birth order (first-born)
    d. decision of a health care professional

14. What happens to friendships in middle adulthood?
    a. They become more numerous but less satisfying.
    b. They become more same-sexed again, just as in childhood.
    c. The total number remains the same but the degree of intimacy is lessened.
    d. The total number decreases.

15. Which of the following research findings is true about the change of personality?
    a. Masculinity and femininity are correlated with self-esteem in adults of all ages.
    b. More change occurs in personality over time than was expected.
    c. Personality consistently changes with age.
    d. Traits are gained across adulthood, but traits are not lost.

16. Which of the following statements is true?
    a. Tenacious goal pursuit tends to decrease in middle adulthood.
    b. Flexible goal pursuit tends to decrease in middle adulthood.
    c. Mellowing happens only in late adulthood.
    d. Both tenacious goal pursuit and flexible goal pursuit decrease in middle adulthood.

17. Which of the following, found on the Big Five personality traits, decreases for both men and women in middle adulthood?
    a. neuroticism.
    b. extraversion
    c. contentiousness.
    d. openness

18. Work satisfaction is _____.
    a. only minimally linked to self-esteem
    b. on the increase in middle age
    c. at a plateau in young adulthood, and increasingly lower after that
    d. closely related to marital satisfaction in middle adulthood

19. Overall life satisfaction and work satisfaction for men _____.
    a. are positively correlated in young adulthood, but not in middle adulthood
    b. are positively related, and this correlation increases with age
    c. are negatively correlated in all age ranges
    d. cannot clearly be linked based on the current literature

20. For which of the following jobs would we expect performance to drop throughout middle adulthood?
    a. truck driver
    b. book editor
    c. salesperson
    d. musician

21. The Baltes suggest that _____.
    a. men experience more work-related declines in aging than women
    b. ethnic differences in work-related declines are striking
    c. cognitive decline and its associated work-related deficits are inevitable
    d. adults engage in selective optimization with compensation

22. What is optimization?
    a. pragmatic strategies for overcoming specific obstacles
    b. increases in job skills as a function of age
    c. deliberate practice of crucial abilities
    d. seeking jobs that most closely match our abilities

23. Voluntary career changers _____.
    a. are people who are in transition because of external reasons
    b. leave one career to pursue another for a variety of internal reasons
    c. are young adults in the trial stage of employment
    d. are older adults who retire

24. Which of the following people would probably plan the least for retirement?
    a. She is dissatisfied with her work.
    b. He believes that retirement will be unsatisfying.
    c. She has a retired friend.
    d. He is looking forward to retirement.

25. Which of the following is a difference between Baby Boomers and their parents?
    a. Baby Boomers expect to die in their mid-70s or later; their parents expect to die long after age 80.
    b. Baby Boomers saved for their retirement funds; their parents borrowed for their retirement investments.
    c. Baby Boomers put their nest eggs into the stock market; their parents put their funds for retirement in very safe investments.
    d. Baby Boomers expect to retire in their mid-60s; their parents expect to retire before age 60.

CASE STUDY

Mary has returned with her child to live with her parents in a small town in Saskatchewan. Her parents are not happy about her coming home because they have just retired and had planned a vacation they had dreamed about for a long time. Mary thinks that her parents have changed a lot and decides to move out. She calls them and clearly states that they are not allowed to see their granddaughter. The parents are visibly upset and decide to consult their neighbour, who is a parish nurse.

1. From your understanding of the "revolving door" pattern, what are some of the reactions of middle-aged parents when their adult children come home?

2. What are some changes that her parents might be experiencing?

3. What does the provincial legislation say in Saskatchewan regarding grandparents' rights to have access to their grandchildren?

4. If you were the parish nurse, how would you handle this situation?

RESEARCH PROJECT
Student Project 26: Social Networks Among Middle-Aged Adults

It would be extremely interesting to repeat Project 17, except this time with middle-aged subjects. You should locate at least six adults between the ages of 40 and 65. They could be all men, all women, or three of each, and should cover the age range as much as possible. Obtain the appropriate informed consent from each, and follow the identical procedure as for Project 17. If a group of students in your class all completes this project, you will have a fascinating cross-sectional study.

If you have completed both Projects 17 and 26, compare the responses of the two age groups. Do your middle-aged subjects include fewer people in their three circles? Do they list fewer friends? Are their friends more likely to be in the first or second circle, rather than in the outermost circle? Are there any differences you can detect?

CHAPTER 16 ANSWER KEY

Guided Study Questions

15. When looking at family relationships from the perspective of middle age, we have to look in both directions: <u>down the generational chain to relationships with grown children, and up the chain to relationships with aging parents</u>.

37. Friendship depends less on <u>frequent contact</u> than on a sense that <u>friends are there to provide support as needed</u>.

Practice Questions

1. b	6. b	11. d	16. a	21. d
2. a	7. c	12. a	17. d	22. c
3. c	8. a	13. a	18. b	23. b
4. b	9. d	14. d	19. a	24. b
5. a	10. b	15. b	20. a	25. c

Case Study

1. Chapter 16 (p. 496). The revolving door pattern is when adult children come back home. Middle aged parents' sense of obligation to their children may cause them to feel that they can't pursue their own goals. Some parents with the adult resident child manage to work out good systems for handling the potential stresses and say they are satisfied with their arrangement. Some parents even enjoy the greater social support the adult children bring. However, the new set of tasks and roles do bring on higher stress levels in families.

2. Chapter 16 (p. 502). There is some evidence of real change in personality in adulthood. Some of theses changes are positive but there is increased individual variability. Regarding the Big Five personality traits, both men and women decreased in openness after age 30 but increased in agreeableness.

3. Chapter 16 (p. 498). Only in Quebec, Alberta, and B.C. does provincial legislation provide grandparents with a legal basis for matters such as visitation or access to their grandchildren. The best thing to do with Mary's parents is to listen to them and be empathetic.

POLICY QUESTION V

WHAT IS CANADA'S POSITION ON STEM CELL RESEARCH?

Learning Objective: Summarize the issues on stem cell research (pp. 513–515).

1. What are stem cells?

2. What potential do stem cells have according to scientists? List three or four such potentials.

3. The Stem cell Oversight Committee (SCOC) has listed at least six requirements that must be undertaken in research. List four of the requirements.

4. What special characteristic differentiates an eight-cell zygote from a zygote containing more than eight cells?

5. Compare and contrast embryonic stem cells and somatic and adult stem cells.

6. Describe how adult stem cells are used for the treatment of injury, disease or the natural aging process.

7. Explain why stem cell research is controversial.

8. Discuss the significance of the study where neurons from embryonic stem cells were implanted in the spinal cord of laboratory animals.

9. Why do scientists believe that stem cells cannot, at this time, be used to treat diseases in humans?

10. What is the evidence to suggest that that the potential for using stem cells to treat disease is tremendous?

11. State the characteristics and importance of the oct4 gene.

12. Summarize the stem cell research policies in Canada.

13. Examine the Guidelines for Human Pluripotent Stem cell research found on the website http://www.cihr-irsc.gc.ca/e/28216.html. What is your opinion of the guidelines?

14. What are some of the ethical issues involved with stem cell research?

CHAPTER 17

PHYSICAL AND COGNITIVE DEVELOPMENT IN LATE ADULTHOOD

OVERVIEW OF CHAPTER

Most older adults experience some degree of physical and cognitive decline. Thus, the experience of aging often involves learning to offset weaknesses (such as increasing forgetfulness) with strengths (such as practicality and inventiveness).

Variability in Late Adulthood

In Canada, life expectancy increases as one gets older. The Canadian gender gap has been narrowing since 1981.

- The elderly are often classified as young-old (60–75), old-old (75–85), and oldest-old (85+). The oldest-old are the fastest-growing group of elderly, not only in Canada but also in every other industrialized country in the world. There are significant individual differences in aging within all three groups.

- Heredity, overall health, current and prior health habits (especially physical exercise) are important predictors in early, as well as late, adulthood.

Physical Changes

- Four main changes occur in the brain during the adult years: lower brain weight, a loss of grey matter, a decline in dendrite density, and slower synaptic speed. Loss of dendritic density results in slower reaction time to a variety of stimuli.

- Changes in vision and hearing affect the lives of most elderly adults. The senses of smell and touch become less sensitive in later years.

- Aging theorists suggest that there may be genetic limits on the human lifespan. Furthermore, the cumulative effects of cell malfunctions may be responsible for primary aging.

- Behaviour changes resulting from physical changes include general slowing, changing patterns of eating and sleeping, and an increased number of falls. The frequency of sexual activity decreases in late adulthood even though most older adults continue to be sexually active.

- ### *Mental Health*

- Dementia becomes steadily more common in the late adult years. In fact, dementia is the leading cause of institutionalization of the elderly in Canada, especially women. The most common type of dementia is Alzheimer's disease. It's difficult to diagnose definitely, and its causes are not fully understood.

- Although mild forms of depression occur in the later years, serious clinical depression is rare. Preventative measures can be taken to offset the effects of depression. In Canada, more elderly men than women are likely to commit suicide.

Cognitive Changes

- Cognitive changes result from the general slowing of the nervous system and perhaps from a loss of short-term memory capacity.

- Wisdom and creativity may be important aspects of cognitive functioning in old age.

LEARNING GOALS

After completing Chapter 17, students should be able to:
1. Describe the variability of characteristics of elderly adults.
2. Identify the physical changes in specific body systems in late adulthood.
3. Summarize the impact of mental health in the elderly.
4. Assess the cognitive changes in late adulthood.

GUIDED STUDY QUESTIONS

VARIABILITY IN LATE ADULTHOOD

Characteristics of the Elderly Population (pp. 517–520)

Objective 17.1: Identify the characteristics of the elderly population.

1. Define gerontology.

2. Give examples of how life expectancy increases as adults get older in Canada.

3. Define the following terms:
   a. young-old
   b. old-old
   c. oldest-old
   d. octogenarian
   e. centenarian
   f. frail elderly

4. How do the majority of older adults regard their health? How does the health of older adults compare to that of younger adults?

5. Describe the research findings, from McMaster University, on the cognitive functioning of the elderly.

6. How are sex hormones related to variations in cognitive performance?

7. Summarize the animal research by neurophysiologists on mental exercise.

8. Define the following terms, and give examples of each:
    a. functional status
    b. activities of daily living (ADLs)
    c. instrumental activities of daily living (IADLs)

9. List the two physical problems or diseases that are most likely to contribute to some functional disability in late adulthood.

10. What physical problem is common to both genders? How do women cope with this problem?

Longevity (pp. 520–524)

Objective 17.2: Describe the research findings on longevity.

11. List the three major factors that interact to affect longevity.

12. Define the following terms:
    a. Hayflick limit
    b. telomeres

13. What is the Hayflick limit for humans?

14. What evidence exists to support the idea that longevity is inherited?

15. Describe the results of the Canadian study which investigated the differences between smokers and non-smokers regarding longevity.

16. What is the importance of physical exercise on longevity?

17. Examine *Canada's Physical Activity Guide to Healthy Living for Older Adults*. What is the purpose of this exercise guide?

18. Examine *Eating Well with Canada's Food Guide*. What is the purpose of the food guide?

PHYSICAL CHANGES

The Brain and Nervous System (pp. 525–526)

Objective 17.3: Summarize the changes in the brain in late adulthood.

19. List the four main changes in the brain during the adult years.

20. How does education relate to dendritic density?

21. Define synaptic plasticity, and describe how it is related to dendritic loss.

The Senses and Other Body Systems (pp. 526–528)

Objective 17.4: Identify the changes in the senses of the elderly.

22. List three problems with vision in late adulthood, in addition to presbyopia.

23. State the gender difference in auditory problems of the elderly. How is the difference related to the work environment?

24. Describe the components of hearing difficulties in late adulthood by completing the following table:

Component	Description
Loss of ability to hear high-frequency sounds	
Difficulties with word discrimination	
Problems hearing under noisy conditions	
Tinnitus	

25. Describe the changes in the sense of taste associated with aging.

26. How does the sense of smell change in old age?

27. What sex difference accompanies the change in the sense of smell? What is the environmental component that accompanies it?

28. What changes in the sense of touch can occur in old age?

Theories of Biological Aging (pp. 528–529)

Objective 17.5: Describe the theories of biological aging.

29. Define the following terms:
    a. senescence
    b. programmed senescence theory
    c. cross-linking
    d. free radicals
    e. antioxidants
    f. lutein

30. Define and describe each of the following theories of biological aging.

Theory	*Definition*	*Explanation of Biological Aging*
Programmed senescence		
Repair of genetic material		
Cross-linking		
Free radicals		
Terminal drop		

Behavioural Effects of Physical Changes (pp. 529–531)

Objective 17.6: Describe the effect of general slowing on the elderly.

31. The biggest single behavioural effect of age-related physical changes is

    _____.

32. List several factors that explain the general slowing down in late adulthood, and explain how general slowing down affects functioning in late adulthood.

33. Describe the changes in sleeping patterns in late adulthood, and how it affects functioning.

34. Define satiety, and explain how it is involved in functioning in late adulthood.

35. The various physical changes associated with aging also combine to produce a reduction in _____, _____, and _____. How does each of these changes affect functioning in late adulthood?

36. How is sexual activity affected by the cumulative physical changes of aging?

MENTAL HEALTH

Alzheimer's Disease and Other Dementias (pp. 532–535)

Objective 17.7: Identify the symptoms and causes of Alzheimer's disease and other dementias.

37.   Define Alzheimer's disease, or dementia of the Alzheimer's type, and trace the symptoms as the disease progresses.

38.   How is Alzheimer's disease definitively diagnosed?

39.   Define neurofibrillary tangles.

40.   What is the effect of the drugs such as galantamine in individuals with Alzheimer's disease?

41.   What are a few research-based specific strategies that can help an individual with Alzheimer's disease?

42.   Describe the most common gene implicated in Alzheimer's disease.

43.   Define multi-infarct dementia, and describe how it is different from Alzheimer's disease.

44.   List other causes of dementia.

45.   What is the incidence of Alzheimer's disease in Canada?

The Real World/Caregiving: Institutionalization Among the Canadian Elderly (p. 533)

Objective 17.8: Summarize the data on the likelihood of the institutionalization of older adults in Canada.

46.   State factors that most strongly predict that a Canadian senior will live in an institution.

47.   Describe the concept of home care in Canada.

Development in the Information Age: Computers and Dementia (p. 535)

Objective 17.9: Summarize the information about computers and dementia.

48.   List several ways that computers are used in the treatment of various neurological disorders affecting the elderly.

Depression (pp. 535–538)

Objective 17.10: Describe the research on depression in late adulthood.

49. How can each of the following influence the diagnosis of depression in the elderly?

Factors	Influence
Ageism	
Confusion and memory loss	
Standard questionnaires used to assess depression	

50. Define geriatric dysthymia and distinguish it from a depressed mood and from full-fledged clinical depression.

51. Describe the risk factors for depression.

52. List the factors that predict suicide at all ages. Why is the suicide rate for elderly men higher?

53. Describe the therapies for depression in older adults. Why is the appropriate use of antidepressant medications among the elderly critical?

54. Give examples, by completing the following table, of how each of the following can help prevent depression in older adults:

Factor	Example
Improved health	
Regular exercise	
Social involvement	
Support of spiritual needs	

COGNITIVE CHANGES

Memory (pp. 539–542)

Objective 17.11: Describe the changes in memory in late adulthood.

55. What are the rules that apply to memory processes among both older and younger adults?

56. How is short-term memory affected in late adulthood?

57. Outline the evidence that the University of Victoria memory researchers found regarding memory function.

58. How can strategy-learning improve memory?

59. Describe how everyday memory is impacted in late adulthood.

60. Summarize Timothy Salthouse's research on the slower reaction times in older adults.

61. What is a key aspect of the process of memory decline?

Wisdom and Creativity (pp. 542–544)

Objective 17.12: Summarize the research on wisdom and creativity in late adulthood.

62. Define wisdom.

63. Describe Paul Baltes's research measuring wisdom, including the criteria that are central to wisdom.

64. Baltes's research has produced an important finding about wisdom and old age:

_____
_____. Moreover, _____
_____ remains constant across adulthood,
unlike the speed of _____ in other
domains.

65. By completing the following table, describe Gene Cohen's four-stage theory of mid- to late-life creativity.

Age	Stage	Description
50s		
60s		
70s		
80s		

CRITICAL REFLECTION EXERCISE

Longevity

Using information from the text, provide complete responses to the following issues. Whenever possible, cite specific information from the readings to support your responses.

1. Name and discuss three things that you do that you think will increase your chances of living a longer life. Why do you do these things? (I.e., were they taught to you by your parents? Did you learn them on your own?). How specifically do you think they will affect your longevity?

2. Name and discuss three things that you do that you think will decrease your chances of living a longer life. Why do you do these things (or where did these things come from—e.g. genetics)? How, specifically, do you think they will affect your longevity?

3. What four pieces of advice would you give a person on how to slow the effects of aging? What are these effects and what specific things can be done to slow them?

4. Imagine that you are being hired by a senior citizens' agency like Age and Opportunity to develop an activity program for the adults. Describe two activities that you would develop, and explain why you would develop them in the way you propose. What specific goals do you have for each of these activities? How would you recruit the older adults to attend these activities? How would you explain these goals to the individuals living in the community?

PRACTICE QUESTIONS

1. The scientific study of aging is called _____.
    a. senescence
    b. the Hayflick limit
    c. life expectancy
    d. gerontology

2. Which one of the following is the fastest growing segment of the population in Canada?
    a. early-old
    b. old-old
    c. oldest-old
    d. young-old

3. Which one of the following defines functional status?
    a. a measure of a person's ability to perform self-help tasks
    b. an event that interferes with the ability to continue to work
    c. persistent deficits in cognitive efficiency
    d. age-related hearing loss

4. Which of the following is consistent with the Hayflick limit?
    a. Cells can only divide a certain number of times before they begin to degenerate.
    b. Human beings have a set maximum age limit.
    c. Life expectancy is limited more by environment than by genetics.
    d. Cognitive changes lead to physical changes, which lead to death.

5. Which of the following appears to be true about physical exercise?
    a. It is more important in young adulthood than at any other age.
    b. It may be more important in older adulthood than at other ages.
    c. Even with moderate exercising, genetics influences overall health more.
    d. Men benefit more from physical exercise than women do.

6. What is the purpose for the development of *Canada's Physical Activity Guide to Healthy Active Living for Older Adults*?
    a. It allows all seniors to participate in exercise.
    b. It urges seniors to join recreational centres.
    c. It increases the fitness levels of inactive seniors.
    d. It promotes networking with other seniors in Canada.

7. What happens to dendritic density with aging?
    a. It continues to thicken.
    b. More redundant neural pathways are added.
    c. It begins to thin as dendrites are lost and not replaced.
    d. The loss of density is equally distributed throughout the brain.

8. An example of synaptic plasticity is _____.
    a. the expansion of dendritic tangling that leads to disorders such as Alzheimer's disease
    b. the elimination of redundant neural pathways
    c. the brain's ability to recall information memorized years ago
    d. the brain's ability to find the shortest routes between two neurons

9. Which of the following tends to happen to vision as we age?
    a. increased blood flow to the eyes, resulting in blurred peripheral vision
    b. an expanded field of vision, though with reduced lens focus
    c. an enlarged blind spot
    d. an increase in the density of the optic nerve

10. From which one of the following would a man, more than a woman, be likely to suffer in late adulthood?
    a. auditory problems
    b. cataracts
    c. Alzheimer's disease
    d. depression

11. At the clinic today, the doctor told Mr. Jones that he has tinnitus. What is tinnitus?
    a. a tendon problem associated with overexertion
    b. a recurring nasal problem that results in snoring
    c. a persistent ringing in the ears
    d. a gradual decline in taste sensitivity as a result of smoking

12. Which of the following appears to be true about the sense of taste?
    a. Older adults prefer salty foods because of a decline in taste discrimination.
    b. The ability to taste the four basic flavours does not decline over the years.
    c. Taste receptors are never replaced once they are lost.
    d. The sense of taste declines or increases depending on life experiences.

13. The gradual deterioration of body systems that happens as organisms age is called
    _____.
    a. life expectancy
    b. cross-linking
    c. terminal drop
    d. senescence

14. What is a free radical?
    a. an outspoken political deviant
    b. a derivative of beta carotene
    c. a molecule or atom that possesses an unpaired electron
    d. a toxin or carcinogen that floats in the body causing damage

15. The hypothesis that mental and physical functioning decline drastically only in the few years immediately preceding death is called the _____.
    a. repair of genetic material hypothesis
    b. terminal drop hypothesis
    c. programmed senescence hypothesis
    d. satiety hypothesis

16. Which of the following statements about automobile accidents is true?
    a. Older adults have more accidents than younger drivers because they drive too fast.
    b. Older adults have fewer accidents than any other age group.
    c. Older adults have more accidents than younger drivers, but the accidents are usually not fatal.
    d. Older adults have more accidents per mile than younger drivers but fewer accidents in total.

17. Older adults have noticed a shift in sleep patterns in old age.
    a. They become "night people" instead of "morning people."
    b. They wake up less frequently than younger adults but don't sleep as deeply.
    c. They take more naps because they need more sleep than younger adults.
    d. They show decreases in rapid eye movement (REM) sleep.

18. What is the definition of dementia?
    a. a sudden loss of memory
    b. a distortion of place or time
    c. any global deterioration of intellectual functions
    d. senility-induced paranoia

19. The gene most commonly implicated in Alzheimer's disease in on _____.
    a. chromosome 23
    b. chromosome 19
    c. chromosome 20
    d. chromosome 21

20. Mrs. Chapel has had a series of small strokes and shows signs of dementia. This condition is called _____.
    a. Alzheimer's disease
    b. multi-infarct dementia
    c. Parkinson's disease
    d. presenile disease

21. Chronic depressed mood in older adults is called _____.
    a. geriatric dysthymia
    b. insomnia
    c. grumpiness
    d. schizophrenia

22. Elderly men are more likely than women to commit suicide because they _____.
    a. lack the financial resources to travel around the world
    b. become indecisive regarding religious needs and practices
    c. have several risk factors, such as poor health and social isolation, in combination
    d. experience many physical losses at once at an early age, such as a loss of vision and hearing

23. Mr. Black, is taking longer to register new pieces of information like his daughter's new address. Which one of the following is a key aspect in the process of memory decline?
    a. decrease in axons
    b. iatrogenic factors
    c. loss of speed
    d. depression

24. Which of the following is *not* one of Paul Baltes's criteria of wisdom?
    a. understanding of relevance of context
    b. semantic knowledge
    c. factual knowledge
    d. procedural knowledge

25. Mr. Dunkirk is a creative individual. Which one of the following phases do creative individuals enter to reflect on past accomplishments and to formulate new goals?
    a. liberation
    b. summing-up
    c. encore
    d. re-evaluation

CASE STUDY

You are visiting your next door neighbour, Mr. Smith, age 75, who is a widower. He has not been eating well since his wife died. Since he thinks his wife died of Alzheimer's disease he worries that he may have it, mainly because at times he does not remember clearly. He also informs you that he has difficulties doing housework and managing money at times.
Today, he went to the clinic and informs you that he was told to follow the *Eating Well with Canada's Food Guide* in preparing his meals.

1. To what age group does Mr. Smith belong?

2. What are the activities called that include housework, cooking, and managing money?

3. What can you share with Mr. Smith about Alzheimer's disease and could help him stop worrying?

4. From your understanding of the food guide, what recommendations regarding their diet should men and women over 50 follow?

RESEARCH PROJECT

Student Project 27: Definitions of Wisdom

For this project, you will need to locate two adults in each of the three broad age-ranges of adulthood defined in the text: early adulthood, middle adulthood, and late adulthood.

Procedure

After obtaining suitable informed consent, following whatever procedure your instructor specifies, ask each subject the following four basic questions, with suitable probes:

1.   What is your definition of wisdom? (If the individual gives you a very brief answer, or one you do not understand, probe by asking him or her to tell you more about it. If that still doesn't elicit anything useful, ask "In what way would a wise person behave that would be different from the way a non-wise person would act?")

2.   Do you know people who are wise, according to your definition? How old are they? What gender? (Ask the subject to describe the wise individual(s), and say how they display their wisdom.)

3.   Do you think that wisdom is something that only comes with old age, or can a young person or a middle-aged person be wise?

4.   How do you think a person gets to be wise?

Analysis and Report

Compare the answers given by your six subjects in whatever way makes sense to you. Are there common themes in their definitions of wisdom, or in their ideas about origins of wisdom? What are the ages and genders of those named as wise?

If a number of students in your class complete this project, you can combine data, which will give you a cross-sectional comparison.

CHAPTER 17 ANSWER KEY

Guided Study Questions

31. The biggest single behavioural effect of age-related physical changes is a <u>general slowing down</u>.

35. The various physical changes associated with aging also combine to produce a reduction in <u>stamina</u>, <u>dexterity</u>, and <u>balance</u>.

65. Baltes's research has produced an important finding about wisdom and old age: <u>In contrast to performance on information-processing tasks such as memorizing nonsense words, performance on wisdom tasks does not decline with age</u>. Moreover, <u>the speed of accessing wisdom-related knowledge</u> remains constant across adulthood, unlike the speed of <u>information-processing</u> in other domains.

Practice Questions

1. d	6. c	11. c	16. d	21. a
2. c	7. c	12. b	17. d	22. c
3. a	8. d	13. d	18. c	23. c
4. a	9. c	14. c	19. b	24. b
5. b	10. a	15. b	20. b	25. d

Case Study

1. Chapter 17 (p. 517). The age group (75 to 85) fall into the old old subgroup.

2. Chapter 17 (p. 520). Instrumental activities of daily living (IADLs) include doing housework, cooking, and managing money.

3. Chapter 17 (p. 533). The difficulty in diagnosing Alzheimer's disease is magnified by the fact that nearly 80% of elderly complain of memory problems. A brief explanation of these facts may help Mr. Smith not to worry.

4. The food guide with various links can be obtained from the Health Canada website. One of the links is called "Men and Women over the Age of 50." Another link is "Food Guide Basics: Choosing Foods." Mr. Smith needs to know that everyone over the age of 50 needs a daily supplement of Vitamin D (400 IU).

SOCIAL AND PERSONALITY DEVELOPMENT IN LATE ADULTHOOD

OVERVIEW OF CHAPTER

Maintaining a sense of personal uniqueness can be especially challenging for older adults, who are often stereotyped by others as sick, disabled, or incompetent. Moreover, changes in social roles and relationships are just as important as the physical changes of late adulthood. Thus, late adulthood is perhaps the most socially and personally challenging period of life.

Theories of Social and Personality Development

- Erikson's ego integrity stage has been influential in studies of social and personality functioning in older adults; however, research does not support his view that ego integrity is essential to mental health in old age. The notion of reminiscence has been helpful in researchers' attempts to understand development in late adulthood.

- Most older adults are not disengaged from the social world and seem to benefit from social involvement as much as those who are younger.

Individual Differences

- The successful aging paradigm emphasizes the degree of control individuals have over how they experience the aging process. Productivity and life satisfaction are also elements of successful aging.

- Religious coping, defined both in social and psychological terms, appears to be important to health and well-being in late adulthood. This contention has been supported by research on Canadian adults.

Social Relationships

- Many of the social roles evident at younger ages are discarded in late adulthood. Occupying a smaller number of social roles may provide elders with more opportunities for the expression of individuality.

- Most unmarried Canadian elders live alone, and the majority prefer this living arrangement.

- Older adults who are married exhibit high levels of relationship satisfaction. Many elderly spouses are primary caretakers for a spouse who is ill or disabled. The benefits of marriage seem to be greater for men than for women.

- Canadian studies indicate that most older adults see their adult children at least once a week and enjoy satisfying relationships with them. Sibling relationships are often more positive in late adulthood than at younger ages.

- Contact with friends appears to be an important component of life satisfaction among the elderly.

- Women have larger social networks than men. Men's social networks provide them with the same kinds of emotional support as do women's networks.

Career Issues in Late Life

- The typical age of retirement in Canada is closer to 61 than to 65, as is the case in most Western countries.

- The timing of retirement is affected by an individual's health, economic circumstances, family responsibilities, and job satisfaction.

- Most of today's elders have adequate incomes. Older women and minorities are more likely to be poor in old age.

- Retirement is not stressful for most elders so long as the decision to retire is a voluntary one. For many, retirement brings an increase in choices as where to live. British Columbia is the province with the most seniors per capita.

- Some elders choose not to retire and continue to be productive in their occupations. Research suggests that older adults can learn new job skills just as well as younger adults. Some studies suggest that learning new skills sometimes takes longer for older adults.

LEARNING GOALS

After completing Chapter 18, students should be able to:
1. Explain the theories of social and personality development in late adulthood.
2. Examine the individual differences that impact successful aging.
3. Describe the social relationships of older adults.
4. Discuss the career issues in late life.

GUIDED STUDY QUESTIONS

THEORIES OF SOCIAL AND PERSONALITY DEVELOPMENT

Erikson's Stage of Ego Integrity versus Despair (pp. 548–549)

Objective 18.1: Describe Erikson's view of integrity.

1. Define the following terms:
   a. ego integrity versus despair stage
   b. ego integrity

2. Give examples of the behaviour of an elder who has achieved ego integrity.

3. Define reminiscence, and describe how it is a healthy part of achieving ego integrity.

Other Theories of Late-Life Psychosocial Functioning (pp. 549–550)

Objective 18.2: State the differences among other theories of late-life psychosocial functioning.

4. What is your understanding of selection, optimization, and compensation in the study of older adults?

5. Identify the differences between activity and disengagement theory.

6. List the three aspects of the disengagement theory. Discuss the controversy involved with the third aspect.

INDIVIDUAL DIFFERENCES

The Successful Aging Paradigm (pp. 551–554)

Objective 18.3: Identify the individual differences that impact successful aging.

7. Define the following terms:
   a. successful aging
   b. paradigm

8. List the five components of successful aging. Give examples of each.

Component	Description	Example

9. List the factors that predict health and physical functioning across the lifespan.

10. Give examples of aspects of staying healthy and able that most people never face until old age.

11. How is cognitive functioning linked to education?

12. Define and give examples of cognitive adventurousness.

13. Give examples of why older adults giving support (not just receiving it) is important to successful aging.

14. Define volunteerism, and explain why it is beneficial to older adults.

15. Define life satisfaction, and describe how it is related to a sense of control over one's life.

16. Why is a person's perception of his or her own situation more important than objective measures of life satisfaction?

17. List the criticisms of the successful aging paradigm.

Religious Coping (pp. 554–557)

Objective 18.4: Summarize the research on the use of religious coping in late adulthood.

18. Define religious coping.

19. List the benefits of religious coping found in later years.

20. Even though the frequency with which religious coping is used may differ according to race and gender, its effects seem to be similar in _____, and for _____.

21. State the benefits for Canadian adults of attending religious services.

22. Describe the alternative explanations of religious coping.

SOCIAL RELATIONSHIPS

Social Roles (pp. 557–558)

Objective 18.5: Summarize the effects of the changes in roles in late adulthood.

23. Describe the role changes in old age. How are some of these the result of ageism?

24. Give examples of how the roles of the elderly contain far fewer duties or expectations.

25. Define the term "license for eccentricity."

Living Arrangements (pp. 558–559)

Objective 18.6: Trace the pattern of the living arrangements of older adults.

26. What is the approximate percentage of Canadian elders over age 65 who resides in nursing homes? At what age does the percentage increase substantially? Where do most of the others live?

27. State and describe, by completing the following table, two factors that influence the older adult's decision to live with an adult child.

Factor	Description

Partnerships (pp. 559, 561)

Objective 18.7: Describe partner relationships in late adulthood.

28. Describe marital satisfaction in the late adult years.

29. State the gender differences in remarriage among the elderly.

30. List the advantages of being married in late adulthood.

The Real World/Caregiving: Elder Abuse in Canada (p. 560)

Objective 18.8: Summarize the research on elder abuse.

31. Describe the findings of recent surveys of elder abuse in Canada.

32. List the risk factors for elder abuse.

Family Relationships (pp. 561–563)

Objective 18.9: Describe family relationships in late adulthood.

33. What is the Canadian data regarding the contacts older adults have with adult children?

34. Identify the effects of older adults' relationships with adult children.

35. Describe the changes in the relationships of older adults with their adult children.

Friendships (p. 563–564)

Objective 18.10: Assess the importance of friends in late adulthood.

36.   Why are friends important to older adults? What impact do friends have on the lives of the elderly?

37.   What impact do friends have on the lives of the elderly?

Gender Differences in Social Networks (p. 564)

Objective 18.11: Identify the gender and racial differences in social networks.

38.   Compare the characteristics of women and men's social networks in late adulthood.

39.   What benefits do men derive from a men's social network?

CAREER ISSUES IN LATE LIFE

Timing of Retirement (p. 565)

Objective 18.12: Identify the changes involved in the timing of retirement.

40.   Describe the transition from work to retirement.

41.   Summarize how the age of retirement has changed in Canada in the last few decades.

Reasons for Retirement (pp. 565–566)

Objective 18.13: Examine the influences on a person's decision to retire.

42.   List six reasons for retirement, and describe how each may affect the decision to retire. Complete the following table.

Reason	Description

43.   The ranks of Canadian seniors who were employed _____, and the average age of these generally _____.

44.   What are the three occupations of the largest number of elder professions.

Effects of Retirement (pp. 566, 568–571)

Objective 18.14: Assess the effects of retirement.

45. There are a number of shifts that take place at retirement, some positive and some negative, but overall, _____.

46. How is income in Canada affected by retirement?

47. Identify the factors that influence the poverty rates among the elderly.

48. How does retirement affect the health and overall life satisfaction of older adults?

49. What is the best predictor of life satisfaction in late adulthood?

50. List the three types of moves that older adults make. Define each, and describe the elders who are likely to make that move. Complete the following table:

Type of Move	*Definition*	*Likely Characteristics of the Elder*

No Easy Answers: Deciding on Long-Term Care in Canada (p. 571–572)

Objective 18.15: Summarize the issues involved in deciding on nursing home care.

51. What are the typical perceptions of a long-term care home?

52. Explain how the economics of long-term institutional care in Canada make it unattractive for many older adults.

53. List the characteristics of a person who is a likely candidate for long-term institutional care.

Choosing Not to Retire (pp. 572–573)

Objective 18.16: Summarize the research on adults who choose not to retire.

54. List the two types of people who are likely to choose to continue working past the typical retirement age.

55. Describe the two categories of men who are most likely not to retire.

56. List the factors that predict learning success in older and younger adults.

57. How are supervisors likely to rate older adults with respect to job functioning?

CRITICAL REFLECTION EXERCISE

Elderly Adults

Using information from the text, provide complete responses to the following issues. Whenever possible, cite specific information from the readings to support your responses.

1. Think about the way your life has gone.

    • Discuss three things that you think will lead to feelings of integrity for you as you age. Why will these lead to feelings of integrity? Is there anything you would do to change these things? If so, how?

    • Discuss three things that you think might interfere with your developing feelings of integrity as you age. Why will these interfere with developing feelings of integrity? Is there anything you would do to change these things? If so, how?

2. Imagine that you have a 6-year-old child. She is asking you questions about why Grandma cannot do the things that other adults can do. How would you answer her questions? Suggest at least three things you would tell her.

3. You are working as a nurse and are approached by the son of one of your clients. His father has just been diagnosed with Alzheimer's, but he does not know anything about the disease. What initial explanation about the disease may benefit the son? Describe the suspected brain changes that may lead to Alzheimer's. What advice would you give this person about what effect these cognitive deficits will have on his father? What advice would you give this man on what can be done to help the family to adjust to these cognitive changes?

PRACTICE QUESTIONS

1. Which of the following illustrates what Erikson called integrity?
   a. accepting the imminence of death
   b. maintaining a strong relationship with one's spouse despite health problems
   c. wanting to give back to the community
   d. establishing identity

2. Mrs. Jones often reflects on her past experiences. This process is called _____.
   a. senility
   b. senescence
   c. reminiscence
   d. a waste of time

3. Older adults, who utilize selective optimization and compensation in their tasks, focus on which one of the following?
   a. metacognition
   b. strengths
   c. metamemory
   d. intelligence.

4. Mr. Fox, an elderly gentleman, is looking forward to getting married soon. Which one of the following components of successful aging does his upcoming marriage best demonstrate?
   a. productivity
   b. good physical health
   c. mental activity
   d. social engagement

5. A willingness to learn new things is called _____.
   a. cognitive adventurousness
   b. curiosity
   c. personal growth
   d. life perception

6. The performance of unpaid work for altruistic reasons is called _____.
   a. integrity
   b. volunteerism
   c. life satisfaction
   d. productivity

7. Research suggests that Canadian adults who regularly attend religious services experience all of the following except _____.
   a. being optimistic
   b. having more stress
   c. being physically healthier
   d. living longer lives

8. Which of the following statements about social roles is true?
   a. An older person's belief about his or her own competence does not affect his or her decisions about role transitions.
   b. Elderly adults are very unlikely to hold ageist stereotypes.
   c. Negative stereotypes of appearance are more often applied to men than to women.
   d. The older people look, the more negatively others stereotype them.

9. What is a licence of eccentricity?
   a. a loosening of role expectations that allows older adults to express their individuality
   b. a tendency to assume that all older adults are senile
   c. the loss of driving privileges due to poorer vision and memory
   d. the loss of ability to make strong cognitive associations

10. Which of the following statements about living arrangements for older adults is true?
    a. Men are more likely to be institutionalized than women.
    b. Women are significantly more likely to be widowed than men.
    c. Men are more likely to suffer homebound disabilities than women.
    d. Women are more likely to die in their own home than are men.

11. Which one of the following factors has an important impact on living arrangements?
    a. education
    b. religion
    c. age
    d. health

12. Marital satisfaction in late adulthood _____.
    a. increases for elder women, but decreases for elder men
    b. tends to drop as health becomes problematic
    c. is higher than when children were still at home
    d. drops initially, but then plateaus

13. Which of the following words best applies to long-term marriages in late adulthood?
    a. passionate
    b. committed
    c. intense
    d. romantic

14. The oldest old subgroup needs most assistance with which one of the following?
    a. transportation
    b. housework
    c. yard work
    d. baking

15. Which one of the following research findings sums up elder adults' feelings about their children?
    a. They have relatively little effect on seniors' health and happiness.
    b. They feel that their children are their only real friends.
    c. They describe generally their relationships with their children as mainly unhappy and unsatisfying.
    d. They tend to live life vicariously through their children.

16. Contact with friends in older adulthood _____.
    a. can decrease life satisfaction as the elders mourn the "good old days"
    b. can actually increase depression because these adults watch each other's health deteriorate
    c. is less important than contact with family in influencing life satisfaction
    d. has a positive impact on self-esteem and overall life satisfaction

17. Research findings indicate that men's social networks provide men with _____, as do women's social networks for women.
    a. financial support
    b. a list of travelling companions
    c. emotional support
    d. a list of good restaurants

18. Which of the following phrases accurately portrays the transition from work to retirement?
    a. Most elders demonstrate a robust capacity for adaptation.
    b. It is the beginning of the long downward slide into death.
    c. Women make this transition with much less difficulty than men.
    d. The age of the retiree affects how positive the transition is.

19. Which one of the following is a particularly strong push factor to retirement?
    a. poor health
    b. good financial plan
    c. restructuring at work
    d. family demands

20. The majority of working seniors are involved in which one of the following?
    a. caretaking
    b. farming
    c. teaching
    d. sportscasting

21. What effect does retirement have on health?
    a. It has a strong positive effect.
    b. It has a slight negative effect on blood pressure and heart rate.
    c. It depends on gender and physical condition at the time of retirement.
    d. It has no effect on health.

22. What is the most significant factor determining when a woman will retire?
    a. her health
    b. the characteristics of the job
    c. when her husband retires
    d. the lucrativeness of the retirement package

23. Who might respond to retirement the least positively?
    a. those who recently became married
    b. those who retire the earliest
    c. those who had the least control over the process
    d. those who value the work ethic

24. An elder's move to a warmer climate is called _____.
    a. an amenity move
    b. a compensatory migration
    c. a kinship migration
    d. institutional migration

25. Which of the following persons is most likely to continue working past the typical retirement age?
    a. a man who is highly educated and healthy
    b. a woman who is highly educated and healthy
    c. a man who has no family
    d. a woman with a limited education and poor retirement benefits

INVESTIGATIVE PROJECT

Student Project 28: Visiting and Assessing a Nursing Home

Procedure

In this visit, imagine that you are looking for a suitable nursing home for your aged parent, and you are evaluating several such institutions. You should spend at least an hour in each institution, preferably at a mealtime or activity time. You will also want to obtain brochures or other available literature about each institution.

During your visit, take notes if you wish, and chat with those you may fall into conversation with (although you should not harass the staff). At the end of your visit, rate the nursing home on each of the following 10 scales, where a rating of 5 always indicates "optimum" or "ideal" and a rating of 1 always means "unacceptable." If you find that you simply do not have the information you need for any scale, you may choose NA (not available), but try not to do that.

Rating Scales	*Circle One Number*
1. **Achievement fostering**: Does the environment provide opportunities for and encouragement to residents to engage in goal-directed activities, or reward them for doing so?	1 2 3 4 5 NA
2. **Individualism**: Are individuals encouraged to express individuality and treated as unique?	1 2 3 4 5 NA
3. **Dependency fostering**: Are residents "coddled" in ways that discourage or prevent the development of self-sufficiency or autonomy? (A rating of 5 in this case means that this was not done.)	1 2 3 4 5 NA
4. **Warmth**: Do the staff express warmth toward the residents, and did the residents express it toward each other?	1 2 3 4 5 NA
5. **Affiliation fostering**: Is social interaction encouraged, or is it occurring naturally in the environment?	1 2 3 4 5 NA
6. **Recognition**: Does the institution recognize, respond to, and reward the activities and accomplishments of the residents?	1 2 3 4 5 NA
7. **Stimulation**: Is there a variety of sights, sounds, and activities?	1 2 3 4 5 NA
8. **Physical attractiveness**: How aesthetically appealing is the physical setting?	1 2 3 4 5 NA
9. **Cue richness**: How clear and varied are the cues for orientation, such as signs, distinctive colours, odours, textures, sounds, and clutter?	1 2 3 4 5 NA
10. **Health care adequacy**: Is the institution equipped and well staffed to provide physical exams, physical therapy, and nursing care?	1 2 3 4 5 NA

Analysis and Report

In preparing your report, think about how confident you feel that you could make a decision about each individual nursing home based on your brief visit. What additional information would you need or like to have to do a better job of evaluating this or any other nursing home? Are there other items you would add to the checklist? Do some of the items seem more important than others? Why? If you really were making such a choice for your parent, would you use a checklist like this, or do you think you would use some other process?

Consider, also, whether your own attitudes and biases about nursing home care have been altered or strengthened by this visit. Were you impressed or depressed, if either? By what?

CHAPTER 18 ANSWER KEY

Guided Study Questions

20. Even though the frequency with which religious coping is used may differ according to race and gender, its effects seem to be similar in <u>all racial and ethnic groups</u> and for <u>both women and men</u>.

43. The ranks of Canadian seniors who were employed <u>have been on the rise since 1996</u>, and the average age of these generally <u>better-educated workers has also increased</u>.

45. There are a number of shifts that take place at retirement, some positive and some negative, but overall, <u>retirement seems to have positive effects on the lives of older adults</u>.

Practice Questions

1. a	6. b	11. d	16. d	21. d
2. c	7. b	12. c	17. c	22. c
3. b	8. d	13. b	18. a	23. c
4. d	9. a	14. a	19. a	24. a
5. a	10. b	15. a	20. b	25. a

DEATH, DYING, AND BEREAVEMENT

OVERVIEW OF CHAPTER

For most people, death occurs in late adulthood. However, many younger individuals contract fatal diseases or they may die in accidents. Thus, like most developmental events, the timing and mode of a particular individual's death affect its meaning and its effects on others.

The Experience of Death

- Medical personnel distinguish between clinical death, brain death, and social death.

- In Canada and in other parts of the industrialized world, death occurs most often in hospitals. Hospice care emphasizes patient and family control of the dying process and palliative care, rather than curative treatment.

The Meaning of Death Across the Lifespan

- By age 6 or 7 most children understand that death is permanent. Teens sometimes have distorted ideas about death and their own mortality.

- Many young adults believe they possess unique characteristics that protect them from death. For middle-aged adults, the death of a loved one—often a parent—signals a change in social roles.

- Among the middle-aged, fear of death is common. Older adults fear death less, especially those who are very religious.

- Preparation for death may include practical activities such as writing a will and making a living will. Reminiscence may also serve as a preparation. Some dying adults exhibit dramatic changes in functioning, both cognitive and personality-wise, just prior to death.

The Process of Dying

- Kübler-Ross's five stages of dying (denial, anger, bargaining, depression, and acceptance) have been widely studied.

- Critics of Kübler-Ross suggest that her stages may be culture-specific, or universal, and that the process of adjusting to impending death does not occur in stages.

- Reactions to the diagnoses and treatment appear to affect a terminally ill individual's longevity. Those who have a "fighting spirit" survive longer than do peers who are resigned to the inevitability of death.

The Experience of Grieving

- Funerals and other rituals redefine the roles of the bereaved, bring families together, and give meaning to the lives of both the deceased and the bereaved.

- Grief responses depend on the age and mode of death of the deceased as well as the characteristics of the bereaved.

- Losing a spouse appears to bring about the most intense grief response. The health of widows and widowers declines in the first year following spousal loss. The effects appear to be greater among widowers than widows.

Theoretical Perspectives on Grieving

- Psychoanalytic theory emphasizes the traumatic nature of grief and the defence mechanisms that often accompany the experience.

- Attachment theories suggest that grieving involves a series of stages across which the bereaved adjust to life without the deceased.

- Alternative approaches emphasize the individual nature of grieving, claiming that the experience is poorly explained by general theories.

LEARNING GOALS

After completing Chapter 19, students should be able to:
1. Define death and identify types of care available to the dying.
2. Trace the changes in attitude about death across the lifespan.
3. Discuss the issues involved in the process of dying.
4. Describe the experience of grieving.

GUIDED STUDY QUESTIONS

THE EXPERIENCE OF DEATH

Death Itself (pp. 578–579)

Objective 19.1: Define the three aspects of death.

1. Define the following terms:
   a. clinical death
   b. brain death
   c. social death

Where Death Occurs (pp. 579–581)

Objective 19.2: Compare death in hospitals to death in hospices.

2.   In Canada, where do the great majority of adults die?

3.   Define the following terms:
     a. hospice care
     b. palliative care

4.   List and describe the six aspects of the philosophy of the hospice care movement.

5.   List and describe the three general types of hospice care.

6.   Describe the ways in which traditional hospital care and hospice care compare in terms of patients' and caregivers' experiences.

7.   Assess the support measures for the caregivers and for the providers in a hospice setting.

8.   What is the purpose of the web-based Canadian Virtual Hospice?

THE MEANING OF DEATH ACROSS THE LIFESPAN

Children's and Adolescents' Understanding of Death (pp. 582–583)

Objective 19.3: Describe children's and adolescents' understanding of death.

9.   Compare the understanding of death for each of the following age groups:
     a. preschool-aged children
     b. school-aged children

10. Define a personal fable, and explain how it impacts teenagers' understanding of death.

11. How do unrealistic beliefs about personal death contribute to adolescent suicide?

The Meaning of Death for Adults (pp. 583–584)

Objective 19.4: Describe the meaning of death for adults.

12. Define unique invulnerability, and give examples of how it influences young adults.

13. Explain how the deaths of relatively young Canadians provide insight into young adults' ideas about death.

14. In middle and late adulthood, an understanding of death goes well beyond the simple acceptance of _____.

15. How does death change the roles and relationships within a family?

16. Give examples of how the prospect of death shapes one's view of time.

Fear of Death (pp. 585–587)

Objective 19.5: Discuss the issues involving fear of death.

17. List the six existential uncertainties as described by T. P. Wong, a Canadian existential researcher.

18. Give examples to explain why middle-aged adults are the most fearful of death.

19. The elderly think and talk more about death than do other age groups. How does this help them overcome their fear and anxiety of death?

20. How do religious beliefs affect a person's fear of death?

21. How are feelings about death linked to one's sense of personal worth?

Preparation for Death (pp. 588–589)

Objective 19.6: Describe people's preparations for death.

22. Describe how people prepare for death at a practical level.

23. Define a living will.

24. Describe the psychological changes associated with terminal drop.

No Easy Answers: Saying Goodbye (p. 588)

Objective 19.7: Summarize the research on dying persons saying goodbye to their family and friends.

25. Why is it important for dying persons to say goodbye to family and friends?

THE PROCESS OF DYING

Kübler-Ross's Stages of Dying (p. 590)

Objective 19.8: List Kübler-Ross's stages of dying.

26. List the five stages of grief proposed by Kübler-Ross, and give examples of each. Complete the following table:

Stage	Example

Criticisms and Alternative Views (pp. 590–592)

Objective 19.9: Summarize the criticisms and alternative views of Kübler-Ross's research.

27. Kübler-Ross's model has provided _____,
    and her highly compassionate descriptions have, without a doubt, _____
    _____.

28. Summarize the methodological problems of Kübler-Ross's research.

29. Give examples of how Kübler-Ross's research may not incorporate culture-specific behaviours.

30. State the most potent criticism of Kübler-Ross's model.

31. Of the five stages in Kübler-Ross's model, which one seems to be common among Western patients?

32. Classify the themes involved in the dying process that were suggested by Shneidman.

33. List and describe the four tasks that Corr suggests for the dying person.

Responses to Impending Death (pp. 592–594)

Objective 19.10: Discuss the issues impacting the responses to impending death.

34. Why do many of the research studies on individual adaptations to dying involve studies with terminal cancer?

35. List and describe the five types of responses to impending death, according to Greer.

36. What were the findings of Greer's research about the relationship between the patient's survival rate and the five groups of responses to impending death?

37. List two cautions that relate to Greer's findings.

38. How does social support relate to an individual's response to imminent death?

THE EXPERIENCE OF GRIEVING

Psychosocial Functions of Death Rituals (p. 595–596)

Objective 19.11: Identify some of the psychological functions of death rituals.

39. Define grieving.

40. Give examples of each of the following psychological functions that funerals, wakes, and other death rituals serve in helping family members cope with grief:
    a. giving a specific set of roles and rituals to play
    b. bringing family members together

    c.   understanding the meaning of death
    d.   giving a transcendent meaning to death

The Process of Grieving (pp. 596–597)

Objective 19.12: Discuss the issues involved in the process of grieving.

41.   How do each of the following age groups express their feelings of grief?
    a.   children
    b.   adolescents

42.   Give examples of how the mode of death affects the grief process.

Mode of Death	*Example of Impact*
Death of a spouse after a period of illness	
Death in the line of duty	
Sudden and violent death	
Death in a natural disaster	
Death in a politically motivated mass murder	
Death by suicide	

Widowhood (pp. 597–601)

Objective 19.13: Discuss the issues surrounding widowhood.

43.   Describe the long-term and short-term effects on the immune system of the experience of widowhood.

44.   In the year following bereavement, the incidence of depression among widows and widowers _____, though rates of death and disease _____.

45. List several factors that contribute to the variability of how long the effects of bereavement last.

46. Define pathological grief, and explain why some psychologists believe it should be thought of as a disorder separate from depression.

47. Give examples to explain why the death of a spouse appears to be a more negative experience for men than for women.

48. How can support groups help a person manage their grief?

The Real World/Caregiving: When an Infant Dies (p. 598)

Objective 19.14: Explain the issues involved when an infant dies.

49. How might the grief of parents be different when an older child dies than when an infant dies?

50. List the guidelines that can be useful to family members or friends in supporting parents   who have lost an infant.

CRITICAL REFLECTION EXERCISES

Death of a Loved One

Using information from the text, provide complete answers to the following questions:

1. What do you think would be the best way to describe a grandparent's death to a 4-year-old? Why would you describe it this way?

2. How does our society appear to approach the reality of death? Do you agree with this approach? Why or why not?

3. Why is mourning an important part of the grieving process? Briefly discuss at least three reasons why it is important.

Imminent Death

Imagine that you have just discovered that you have 4 months to live. Consider how you would address each of the following issues, knowing that the 4 months will be pain-free and that you will not be debilitated.

1. Describe what you think your initial reactions might be. Why do you think you would react this way? How do you think your family might react?

2. What are the five things you would do with your remaining time? Why did you pick each of these?

3.   Using Erikson's theory of human development as a model, write a eulogy of your life. What would you most like people to remember about you and the life that you have lived?

PRACTICE QUESTIONS

1.   Which of the following accurately describes clinical death?
   a.   The person can still breathe, but she is in a vegetative state.
   b.   There is no evident brain functioning.
   c.   The heart can still beat.
   d.   There is no activity in the brain.

2.   Social death _____.
   a.   occurs when older adults are treated as if they are already dead
   b.   involves the older adult making final plans for death
   c.   is a symbolic event occurring after the point of death, such as closing the dead person's eyelids
   d.   includes a major withdrawal from significant relationships prior to death

3.   In comparing patients' perceptions of hospital care to hospice care, the researchers found _____.
   a.   no major differences in length of survival or reports of pain were found
   b.   it was discovered that hospital care was rated as significantly more satisfying by the dying patients
   c.   hospital care was associated with the increased length of survival of chronic patients
   d.   significant differences in perceptions of the quality of care were found

4.   Rose is a hospice care provider. Which one of the following do you think she requires?
   a.   income bonuses
   b.   support services
   c.   rotation to another unit
   d.   additional personal benefits

5.   The Canadian Virtual Hospice enables physicians and other health care professionals to _____.
   a.   assist children cope with the death of their parents.
   b.   help families obtain unemployment insurance during bereavement.
   c.   bring medical care to urban areas.
   d.   provide access to a wide range of palliative care services.

6.   Children begin to understand both the permanence and the universality of death by the time they _____.
   a.   are in kindergarten
   b.   are in grade 2
   c.   start school
   d.   are in grade 4

7. A hypothetical life story created by an adolescent is called _____.
   a. reminiscence
   b. a personal fable
   c. an imaginary audience
   d. a personal story

8. The belief that bad things, including death, only happen to others is called
   _____.
   a. unique invulnerability
   b. a flashback
   c. denial
   d. sublimation

9. Which of the following illustrates how the prospect of death may shape one's view of time?
   a. "A stitch in time saves nine."
   b. "Time is our friend; hesitation is our enemy."
   c. "Will I have enough time to finish what I want to finish?"
   d. "I feel as if I have all the time in the world."

10. From which one of the following existential uncertainties does our fear of death stem?
    a. fear of leaving loved ones behind
    b. fear of failing to complete life work
    c. viewing death as a punishment
    d. not knowing what occurs after death

11. Regarding death, older adults _____.
    a. look forward to death
    b. fear death significantly
    c. fear the process of dying more than death itself
    d. do not contemplate death

12. Which of the following is one of the ways a person prepares for death at a practical level?
    a. inventing a personal fable
    b. becoming a nicer person
    c. reminiscing
    d. making out a will

13. Jane is beginning to say farewell to her mother who is dying. Which one of the following best describes the purpose of farewells?
    a. They may allow the dying person to disengage more readily when death comes.
    b. They indicate to the dying person that the end is coming faster then they thought.
    c. They allow the living to prolong their grieving process.
    d. They allow the living to gain autonomy in the meaning of death of a loved one.

14. Which stage, according to Kübler-Ross, may be the transition from heated emotions toward coming to terms with death?
    a. denial
    b. bargaining
    c. depression
    d. acceptance

15. Which one of the following culture views death as part of nature's cycle and is not to
be feared or fought?
    a. Japanese
    b. American Aboriginal
    c. Mexican
    d. East Indian

16. What is the study of dying called?
    a. bereavement
    b. euthanasia
    c. thanatology
    d. life transition analysis

17. Corr's task-based approach suggests that dealing with one's death is much like
    _____.
    a. coping with any other problem or dilemma
    b. realizing that all one's efforts have little meaning
    c. analyzing the themes of one's life
    d. coming to terms with how one has lived

18. Which of the following individuals fit Greer's label of stoic acceptance in response to a diagnosis of terminal cancer?
    a. a person who is devoid of hope
    b. a person who denies the diagnosis
    c. a person who responds with anxiety
    d. a person who ignores the diagnosis

19. The research linking immune system functioning and psychological responses to cancer diagnosis suggests that those who _____ tend to live longer.
    a. respond with obedience and less questioning
    b. respond with anger and express their hostility
    c. internalize their anger
    d. minimize the seriousness of their illness

20. Which of the following is a psychological function of death rituals?
    a. bringing extended family members and neighbours together
    b. helping the survivors understand the meaning of life and death
    c. showing others how much the survivors loved the person who died
    d. giving some transcendent meaning to the existential aspect of life

21. Which of the following scenarios would be most likely to cause intense grief responses?
    a. a soldier who died heroically in the line of duty
    b. a spouse whose death brought an end to his long-term suffering
    c. an elderly person who died of natural causes
    d. a person who died a sudden and violent death

22. Which of the following is *not* a suggestion for friends and family members supporting parents who have lost an infant?
    a. Don't refer to the deceased infant by name.
    b. Don't offer rationalizations that may offend the parents.
    c. Assure the grieving parents that their responses are normal.
    d. Express your own feelings of loss for the infant, if they are sincere.

23. According to research findings, which of the following describes the incidence of depression among widows and widowers?
    a. It rises substantially, but only in the first two months following bereavement.
    b. It rises substantially in the year following bereavement.
    c. It rises slightly in the year following bereavement.
    d. It rises slightly for men, but not for women.

24. Symptoms of depression brought on by death of a loved one are called _____.
    a. philosophical grief
    b. psychosomatic grief
    c. psychological grief
    d. pathological grief

25. What form of euthanasia occurs when a physician hastens a patient's death by administering a fatal dose of a drug such as morphine?
    a. active euthanasia
    b. resolved suicide
    c. palliative euthanasia
    d. assisted suicide

CASE STUDY

For several years, Mrs. Mackenzie has been the primary caregiver for her husband. Last week he died at home. The next day, Mrs. Stein, a neighbour came over to express her condolences. She found Mrs. Mackenzie enjoying watching a comedy on television. To Mrs. Stein's surprise, Mrs. Mackenzie was cheerful and invited her to come in for a cup of coffee. Now, talking to you, Mrs. Stein recalls the depression that she went through when her husband died so suddenly in a car accident. Her nightmares are slowly subsiding. She does not quite understand Mrs. Mackenzie's behaviour.

1. How can you explain to Mrs. Stein why Mrs. Mackenzie was enjoying the comedy on television the day after her husband died?

2. What accounted for Mrs. Stein's depression?

3. How can you comfort Mrs. Stein?

CHAPTER 19 ANSWER KEY

Guided Study Questions

14. In middle and late adulthood, an understanding of death goes well beyond the simple acceptance of <u>finality, inevitability, and universality</u>.

27. Kübler-Ross's model has provided <u>a common language for those who work with dying patients</u>, and her highly compassionate descriptions have, without a doubt, <u>sensitized health care workers and families to the complexities of the process of dying</u>.

44. In the year following bereavement, the incidence of depression among widows and widowers <u>rises substantially</u>, though rates of death and disease <u>rise only slightly</u>.

Practice Questions

1. b	6. c	11. c	16. c	21. d
2. c	7. b	12. d	17. a	22. a
3. a	8. a	13. a	18. d	23. b
4. b	9. c	14. d	19. b	24. d
5. d	10. b	15. b	20. c	25. a

Case Study

1. Chapter 19 (p. 596) Widows who have been caring for their spouses during a period of illness prior to death are less likely to become depressed after the death than are those whose spouses die suddenly.

2. Chapter 19 (p. 597). Sudden and violent deaths evoke more intense grief responses. Research findings indicate that almost all those whose spouses have died unnaturally and who have had PTSD symptoms are also depressed.

3. Be empathetic to Mrs. Stein and listen to her thoughts and feelings. Remind her of what you learned in Growth and Development regarding the behaviours of widows who have been caregiving for spouses who have been ill for a number of years.

POLICY QUESTION VI

DO PEOPLE HAVE A RIGHT TO DIE?

Learning Objective: Discuss the pros and cons of the issues involved in euthanasia (pp. 604–606).

1. Define the following terms:
    a. euthanasia, or mercy killing
    b. passive euthanasia
    c. active euthanasia, or assisted suicide
    d. living will

2. State two essential elements of a living will.

3. State the result of the 1997 Ipsos-Reid poll regarding the "right to die" debate. How did you react to the results?

4. List three arguments against euthanasia. Give examples of each.

5. What legislation has been passed in Canadian provinces or territories to ensure compliance with living wills? What policies have been passed in your area regarding assisted suicide? Student research could include answering the following questions:
    a. Are living wills honoured in health care facilities? Does your province/territory require health care personnel to ask all clients whether or not they have a living will? How involved does the family become is such inquiries regarding living wills?
    b. What is your understanding of quality of life?
    c. In the absence of direction from a client, how should the medical team make their decision regarding treatment?
    d. Has anyone in your province/territory been prosecuted for helping a dying person hasten death? If so, what were the circumstances and outcome of the case(s)?

6. What efforts are underway in your province/territory to legalize assisted suicide? Has there been any public debate in your area regarding such laws?

7. Have you written your own living will. How might you approach your parents or grandparents regarding their living wills?

8. A number of polls have been conducted to determine public attitudes about euthanasia and assisted suicide. What were some of the results?

9. Examine several current scholarly articles regarding the "Right to Die." What are the findings?